TEPS in TEPS

990 청해

박기혁

서울대학교 졸
(현) 메가스터디 어학센터 TEPS 강사
(현) SLA 학원 TEPS 대표 강사
(현) 중앙일보 영자 신문 중앙 데일리 교육 분야 객원 논설위원
(현) 한국 생산성 본부 영어 전임 강사
(현) PTT(Park's TEPS Teacher's Group) 대표 강사
-TEPS의 최고를 지향하는 강사들의 모임

송승룡

성균관대학교 졸업, 경희대학교 대학원 석사과정
영국 Wimbledon School of English 어학과정 이수
(현) 중앙데일리 영자 신문 객원 해설위원
(현) 민중에센스 아동영어/실용영어 연구센터 연구위원
(현) 한국생산성본부 영어 지도위원
(현) PTT(Park's TEPS Teacher's Group) 강사
-TEPS의 최고를 지향하는 강사들의 모임

TEPS in TEPS 990 청해

저자	박기혁 · 송승룡
초판 1쇄 발행	2009년 8월 14일
초판 2쇄 발행	2010년 4월 10일
발 행 인	박효상
영 업	이종선, 이태호, 이전희
기획, 진행	김상호, 강성실, 김은선, 정혜미, 조승주
출판등록	제 10-1835호
발 행 처	사람in
주 소	121-839 서울시 마포구 서교동 378-16 4F
전 화	02)338-3555(代)
팩 스	02)338-3545
E-mail	saramin@netsgo.com
Homepage	www.saramin.com

Special Staff

디자인 표지	장선숙
내지	홍수미
편 집	정선영
조 판	조지연

※ 책값은 표지 뒷면에 있습니다.
※ 파본은 교환해 드립니다.

ISBN 978-89-6049-132-8 18740
ISBN 978-89-6049-116-8 (세트)

TEPS in TEPS

990 청해

박기혁 · 송승룡

사람in
saram in.com

머리말

Preface

영어 시험을 둘러싼 여러 가지 환경 변화에 의해서 TEPS의 중요성은 나날이 강조되고 있고 그 특징 또한 뚜렷이 변화를 겪고 있다.

첫째, 갈수록 문제가 다양화되고 있고 더욱더 세련되어지고 있다.
둘째, 시험을 치루는 대상 연령층이 자꾸 낮아지고 있다.
셋째, 특목고나 외고, 로스쿨이나 의학전문대학원 진학 등 그 쓰임새가 더욱 광범위해졌다.

이러한 세 가지 변화에 발맞추어, TEPS 교재도 다양화되고 진화되어야 하는데, 현재의 교재 시장은 그러한 가시적인 변화에 능동적으로 대처하지 못하는 것이 사실이다. 이에, 이번 TEPS in TEPS 시리즈를 통해서 진화하는 TEPS에 가장 적합한 패러다임을 제시하고자 한다.

TEPS는 참으로 복잡하고 미묘한 시험이다. TOEFL처럼 학문적인 점에 초점을 맞추는 것도 아니고, TOEIC처럼 실용 언어적인 측면만을 강조하는 시험도 아니다. 어쩌면 이 둘의 장점만을 모아 놓은 시험이라 할 수 있겠다.

학문적인 내용들을 풀어가되 좀 더 현실성을 부여하여 실용적으로 쓰이는 영어들을 묻는 것이다. TEPS가 최근 시험 시장에 지각 변동을 일으키고 있는 이유는 이런 장점이 토대가 되었다고 볼 수 있다.

TEPS는 실제로 회화를 하다가 혹은 네이티브가 보는 외국 신문 등을 읽다가 느끼는 애로사항을 잘 해결해 줄 수 있는 시험이다. 어휘력의 측면에서 보아도 실생활에서 우리는 이런 어려움을 겪는다. '단어 하나하나의 해석은 되는데 왜 전체적으로는 독해가 안 되고 해석이 안 될까?', '이 상황에서 저 말은 대체 무슨 뜻으로 쓰이는 걸까?'

그것은 바로 간단한 단어라도 초보적으로 배웠던 사전적 지식 외에 실생활에서는 다양한 뜻으로 활용되기 때문이다.

이처럼 네이티브와의 가장 적절한 의사소통에 초점을 둔 TEPS는 지극히 영어수험과 영어실용의 접목이라는 공인영어시험의 목적에 가장 합당한 인증시험이라 하겠다.

TOEIC이 점수 인플레로 상위권 수험생의 변별력을 상실했다는 비판이 많다. TEPS는 TOEIC과 같은 패턴의 지속적인 반복만으로는 해결할 수 없는 시험이다. 이에 학습자들도 이런 TEPS에 대한 관심과 욕구가 더욱 늘어나고 있는 현실이다.

필자는 좀 더 실용적이고 영어 실력 향상에 도움이 되는 TEPS에 대한 관심이 높아지고 있는 것은 고무적인 일이라 생각한다. 그리고 그런 TEPS를 연구하고 학습하는데, 이 'TEPS in TEPS 시리즈'가 선구자적인 역할을 하길 진심으로 바라는 마음으로 문제 하나 설명 하나에 세심한 신경을 쓰면서 작업에 임하였다.

혼자서는 할 수 없었던 작업에 언제나 도움이 되었던 분들께 감사의 마음을 전할까 한다. 늘 미안한 마음이 드는 가족들과, 사람in 출판사의 박효상 사장님, 김상호 팀장님, 조승주 대리님 그리고 이 책의 출간에 물심양면으로 도움을 주신 류건 선생님, 신일섭 조교, 윤이랑 조교에게도 아울러 감사의 뜻을 표하고 싶다.

PTT(Park's TEPS Teacher's Group) 대표 강사

박기혁

TEPS in TEPS

학생들의 자습서와 학원 교재의 성격을 둘 다 가질 수 있게 만들었다. 그래서 학원에서의 강의는 물론 독학용으로 사용하도록 준비했다.

1. 상세한 해설을 통해 정답을 공략하는 법과 함께 오답을 피할 수 있는 Skill들을 제시하여 좀 더 높은 점수로의 도약이 가능하게 하였다.

2. TEPS의 4대 영역(독해, 어휘, 청해, 문법)과 기준 점수대별로 학습 목표와 가장 효율적인 방법들을 제시하여 좀 더 전문적이고 체계적인 학습자 맞춤형 학습이 가능하도록 하였다.

3. 애매모호한 이론이나 군더더기 설명을 최대한 배제하여 학습 시간 대비 효율성을 극대화하도록 구성하였다.

TEPS in TEPS

1. 내 실력을 미리 점검하는   Pretest

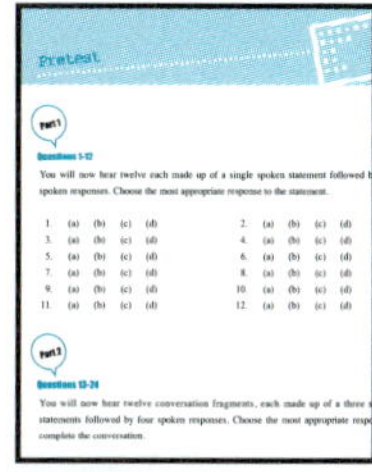

실제 시험 문제와 가장 가까운 형태의 각 Part별 Pretest를 통해 현재의 내 실력을 점검하고, 보강해야 할 부분을 스스로 점검해 본다.

2. TEPS 청해의 해결법을 제시한   Pretest Clinic

Pretest의 문제를 한글 해설과 함께 정답 포인트를 짚어봄으로써, TEPS 중요 출제 포인트를 짚는다.

3. 고득점을 위한 고난이도 문제   990 Challenge!

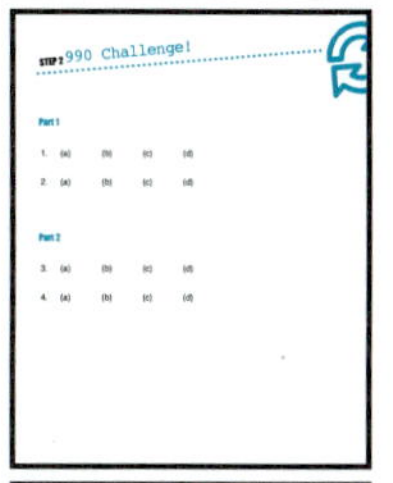

TEPS 고득점을 위해 꼭 알아야 하는 고난이도 문제 유형을 체크한다.

4. 자신만의 해결 노하우를 만들어가는   Actual Test

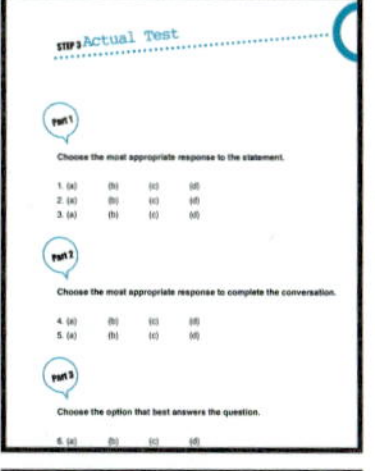

각 Part가 모두 담긴 연습 문제를 통해 실전에 대한 감각을 극대화하도록 한다. 영문 스크립트와 지문의 해석 및 해설은 정답 및 해설에서 확인하며 충분한 보충학습이 될 수 있도록 하였다.

5. 실전보다 더 실전 같은   Final Test

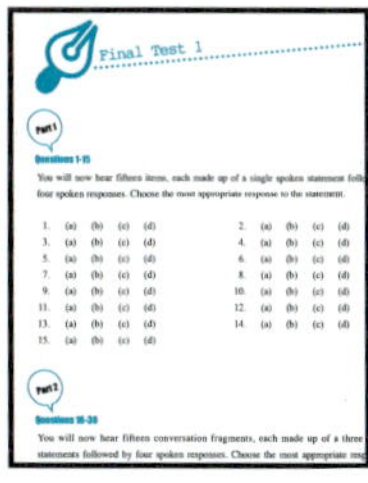

2회분의 실전 모의고사를 실었다. 난이도 있는 실전 문제를 통해 마지막 점검을 할 수 있다.

TEPS in TEPS

TEPS의 구성

TEPS는 청해, 문법, 어휘, 독해 4개 영역에 걸쳐 총 200문항으로 구성되어 있으며 시험 시간은 140분이다. 만점은 문항 반응 이론(IRT)에 따라 채점하기 때문에 전부 맞아도 990점이고 모두 틀려도 10점은 나온다.

영역	PART별 내용	문항 수	시간/배점
청 해 Listening Comprehension	Part Ⅰ : 문장 하나를 듣고 이어질 대화 고르기 Part Ⅱ : 3문장의 대화를 듣고 이어질 대화 고르기 Part Ⅲ : 6-8문장의 대화를 듣고 질문에 해당하는 답 고르기 Part Ⅳ : 단문의 내용을 듣고 질문에 해당하는 답 고르기	15 15 15 15	55분/396점
문 법 Grammar	Part Ⅰ : 대화문의 빈칸에 적절한 표현 고르기 Part Ⅱ : 문장의 빈칸에 적절한 표현 고르기 Part Ⅲ : 대화에서 어법상 틀리거나 어색한 부분 고르기 Part Ⅳ : 단문에서 어법상 틀리거나 어색한 부분 고르기	20 20 5 5	25분/99점
어 휘 Vocabulary	Part Ⅰ : 대화문의 빈칸에 적절한 단어 고르기 Part Ⅱ : 단문의 빈칸에 적절한 단어 고르기	25 25	15분/99점
독 해 Reading Comprehension	Part Ⅰ : 지문을 읽고 지문의 빈칸에 들어갈 내용 고르기 Part Ⅱ : 지문을 읽고 질문에 가장 적절한 내용 고르기 Part Ⅲ : 지문을 읽고 문맥상 어색한 내용 고르기	16 21 3	45분/396점
총계	13개 PART	200	140분/990점

청해(Listening Comprehension) 60문항

정확한 청해 능력을 측정하기 위하여 문제와 보기 문항을 문제지에 인쇄하지 않고 들려줌으로써 자연스러운 의사소통의 인지과정을 최대한 반영하였다. 다양한 의사소통 기능(Communicative Functions)의 대화와 다양한 상황(공고, 방송, 일상 업무 상황, 대학 교양 수준의 강의 등)을 이해하는 데 필요한 전반적인 청해력을 측정하기 위해 대화문(dialogue)과 담화문(monologue)의 소재를 균형 있게 다루었다.

PART 1	15문항

Listen and choose the most appropriate response.

W: How about talking over lunch on Wednesday?
M: _______________________________

(a) Sounds good She'd love it.
(b) Tell me about it.
(c) Sorry. I have an appointment. What about Friday?
(d) Fine. Thanks.

Part 1은 질의응답 문제를 다루며 한 번만 들려준다. 내용 자체는 단순하고 기본적인 수준의 생활 영어 표현으로 구성되어 있지만 교과서적인 지식보다는 재빠른 상황 판단 능력을 요구한다. 따라서 이 파트에서는 속도 적응 능력뿐만 아니라 순발력 있는 상황 판단 능력이 요구된다.

PART 2	15문항

Listen and choose the most appropriate response.

M: How come you know so much about fashion?
W: Actually, my sister is a model.
M: Wow! How long has she been in the industry?
M: _______________________________

(a) She wants to be a fashion designer.
(b) About two years.
(c) Last year she did.
(d) Modeling is a tough job.

Part 2는 짧은 대화 문제로 두 사람이 A-B-A-B 순으로 보통 속도로 대화하는 형식이며 소요 시간은 약 12초 전후로 짧게 구성되어 있다. Part 1과 마찬가지로 한 번만 들려주는 부분이다.

<table><tr><td>**PART 3**</td><td>15문항</td></tr></table>

Listen and choose the correct answer to the question.

M: Hello. I'd like to file a complaint with the city.
W: What is the complaint in regards to?
M: About the condition of Canal Street. I drove down the road this morning, and my car sustained a large amount of damage.
W: Did you run into something?
M: No, I drove through an unavoidable pothole and my car got two flat tires.
W: Okay, you're going to have to fill out this form. Someone will call you next week about compensation for the damages.
M: I have to wait one week!

Q. What can be inferred from the conversation?

(a) The man works for the city.
(b) The man is upset about the situation.
(c) Many of the city's streets are in bad condition.
(d) The man is a bad driver.

Part 3는 앞의 두 파트에 비해 다소 긴 대화를 들려 준다. 대신 대화 부분과 질문을 들려 준 뒤 다시 한 번 대화 부분을 들려 주기 때문에 길이가 긴 데 비해 많이 어렵다고는 할 수 없다.

<table>
<tr><td>**PART 4**</td><td>**15문항**</td></tr>
</table>

Listen and choose the correct answer to the question.

This year the University has enrolled 25% more foreign students than it has any year in the past. The administration hopes that this will help diversify campus life and activities, as well as participation. We would remind all students to welcome foreign students and make them feel at home on campus and in the city. As with any foreign visitors, our foreign students will be bringing with them pieces of their own cultures, and they may be unaware of certain aspects of our culture. Teach them and learn from them and then this year promises to offer many exciting opportunities for students of all ethnicities.

Q. What can be inferred from the announcement?

(a) The foreign students will not integrate well into campus life.
(b) The administration does not support campus activities.
(c) All students can grow from multicultural experiences if they work together.
(d) The administration concerns itself only with academics.

Part 4는 담화문을 다룬다. 영어권 나라에서 영어로 뉴스를 듣거나 강의를 들을 때와 비슷한 상황을 설정하여 얼마나 잘 이해하는지를 측정하는 부분이다. 이야기의 주제, 목적, 화제, 세부 사항 및 이를 근거로 한 추론 등을 다룬다. 직청 직해 실력, 즉 들으면서 곧바로 내용을 이해할 수 있는지를 잘 평가해 주는 부분이다.

Pretest

Pretest

Questions 1-12

You will now hear twelve each made up of a single spoken statement followed by four spoken responses. Choose the most appropriate response to the statement.

1.	(a)	(b)	(c)	(d)		2.	(a)	(b)	(c)	(d)
3.	(a)	(b)	(c)	(d)		4.	(a)	(b)	(c)	(d)
5.	(a)	(b)	(c)	(d)		6.	(a)	(b)	(c)	(d)
7.	(a)	(b)	(c)	(d)		8.	(a)	(b)	(c)	(d)
9.	(a)	(b)	(c)	(d)		10.	(a)	(b)	(c)	(d)
11.	(a)	(b)	(c)	(d)		12.	(a)	(b)	(c)	(d)

Questions 13-24

You will now hear twelve conversation fragments, each made up of a three spoken statements followed by four spoken responses. Choose the most appropriate response to complete the conversation.

13.	(a)	(b)	(c)	(d)		14.	(a)	(b)	(c)	(d)
15.	(a)	(b)	(c)	(d)		16.	(a)	(b)	(c)	(d)
17.	(a)	(b)	(c)	(d)		18.	(a)	(b)	(c)	(d)
19.	(a)	(b)	(c)	(d)		20.	(a)	(b)	(c)	(d)
21.	(a)	(b)	(c)	(d)		22.	(a)	(b)	(c)	(d)
23.	(a)	(b)	(c)	(d)		24.	(a)	(b)	(c)	(d)

Questions 25-30

You will now hear six complete conversations. For each item, you will hear a conversation and its corresponding question which will be read twice. Then you will hear four options which will be read only once. Choose the option that best answers the question.

25.	(a)	(b)	(c)	(d)		26.	(a)	(b)	(c)	(d)
27.	(a)	(b)	(c)	(d)		28.	(a)	(b)	(c)	(d)
29.	(a)	(b)	(c)	(d)		30.	(a)	(b)	(c)	(d)

Questions 31-36

You will now hear six spoken monologues. For each item, you will hear a monologues and its corresponding question which will be read twice. Then you will hear four options which will be read only once. Choose the option that best answers the question.

31.	(a)	(b)	(c)	(d)		32.	(a)	(b)	(c)	(d)
33.	(a)	(b)	(c)	(d)		34.	(a)	(b)	(c)	(d)
35.	(a)	(b)	(c)	(d)		36.	(a)	(b)	(c)	(d)

평서문
문제 유형

STEP 1 Pretest Clinic

평서문 문제 유형은 다양한 응답이 가능한 상황이 나오기 때문에 질문에 대한 응답을 예상하기가 쉽지 않다. 따라서 잘 듣고 질문에 가장 어울리는 선택지를 골라야 한다. 상황에 따른 응답 유형을 구체적으로 분류해 정리해 놓을 필요가 있다.

Part 1

1. W: If you're keen, you're more than welcome to go out with my friends and me tonight.

M: ___________________________________

(a) You can chime in whenever you like.
(b) Thanks, but it depends on what you guys are up to.
(c) It's a stretch.
(d) He always looks down upon me.

해설

If you're keen은 if you want와 마찬가지 의미다. 또 you're more than welcome.은 '당신은 환영 이상이다', 즉 '당신을 대환영한다'라는 뜻으로, 원한다면 함께 나가자고 제안하고 있으므로 (b)가 가장 자연스러운 응답이다.

> **어휘**
> keen 열망하는 chime in 대화에 끼어들다, 맞장구치다 stretch 억지, 과장 look down upon ~를 깔보다

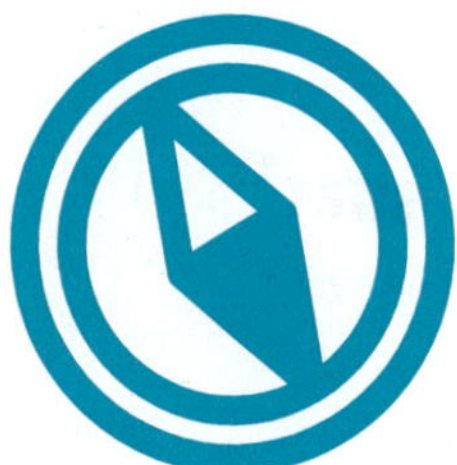

2. M: Let's start getting our thoughts geared towards taking a vacation.

W: ____

(a) No way. We're kind of pinching pennies right now.
(b) This will blow over.
(c) He's just fibbing.
(d) I took the starch out of him.

해설

휴가 가는 것에 대해 생각해 보자고 제안하고 있으므로 이에 대해 동의나 반대 의견이 담긴 선택지를 고르면 된다. 따라서 정답은 (a).

어휘

gear towards ~에 맞추다, ~에 중점을 두다 **pinch pennies** 허리띠를 졸라매다, 절약하다 **blow over** 무사히 지나가다, 흐지부지 잊혀지다 **fib** 악의 없는 거짓말을 하다 **take the starch out of** ~의 뻔뻔스러움을 약화시키다, 기를 죽이다

Part 2

13. M: How's life in the fast lane?

W: Working a lot as usual.

M: Come on. You must have more going on than just that.

W: _______________________________________

(a) I'm scared stiff.

(b) You should really toot your own horn.

(c) Seriously, I've just been working.

(d) Calm down. It's not your prom.

⬈ 해설

단지 일 말고도 다른 특별한 일이 있는 게 분명하다는 말에 진짜 일만 하고 있다고 응답한 (c)가 가장 자연스럽다. 남자의 첫 번째 대사에 나오는 How's life in the fast lane?은 직역하자면 '급행 차선에 있는 네 삶이 어때?' 정도의 뜻으로, 바쁘게 사는 사람에게 '어떻게 지냈니?' 라고 안부를 물을 때 쓸 수 있는 표현이다.

어휘

scared stiff 겁에 질려 얼어붙은 **toot one's own horn** 자화자찬을 하다 **prom** 미국 고등학교 졸업 파티

14. W: I know you're as busy as a bee, but let's do lunch together.

M: Sorry, but I just don't have the time.

W: When are you free this week?

M: ____

(a) Wednesday is fine with me.
(b) Perish the thought!
(c) Put your best foot forward.
(d) I'll knock it off in no time.

해설

이번주 언제 시간이 되는지 묻고 있으므로 요일이 언급된 (a)가 정답이다.

어휘

as busy as a bee 몹시 바쁜 Perish the thought! 집어치워!, 당치도 않아! put one's best foot forward 최선을 다하다, 좋은 인상을 주다 knock ... off ~을 후딱 해치우다 in no time 금방

Part 1

1. (a)   (b)   (c)   (d)

2. (a)   (b)   (c)   (d)

Part 2

3. (a)   (b)   (c)   (d)

4. (a)   (b)   (c)   (d)

STEP 3 Actual Test

Choose the most appropriate response to the statement.

1. (a)　　　(b)　　　(c)　　　(d)
2. (a)　　　(b)　　　(c)　　　(d)
3. (a)　　　(b)　　　(c)　　　(d)

Choose the most appropriate response to complete the conversation.

4. (a)　　　(b)　　　(c)　　　(d)
5. (a)　　　(b)　　　(c)　　　(d)

Choose the option that best answers the question.

6. (a)　　　(b)　　　(c)　　　(d)

Choose the option that best answers the question.

7. (a)　　　(b)　　　(c)　　　(d)

의문문
문제 유형

Chapter 2

의문문은 의문사 의문문과 의문사 없는 의문문으로 나눌 수 있는데, 출제 빈도가 상당히 높은 편에 속한다. 특히, 의문사 의문문은 단순 의문사보다는 복합의문사로 물어보는 경우가 많으며, 의문사 없는 의문문은 상당히 어렵게 출제되는 경우가 있으므로 시제나 인칭을 주의 깊게 잘 들어야 한다.

Part 1

3. M: What's up with you?

W: ____

(a) Congratulations! Now you can stand on your own two feet!
(b) You embarrassed me in front of our coworkers.
(c) She applied the discount on the goods.
(d) He didn't kidnap the girl.

▶ 해설

What's up with you?는 '뭐가 문제야?', '뭐가 불만이야?' 정도의 뜻을 나타내는 표현이다. 따라서 불만의 내용이 담긴 (b)가 정답이다.

> **어휘**
> **stand on one's own two feet** 자립하다   **embarrass** 부끄럽게 하다, 무안하게 하다   **kidnap** 유괴하다

4. M: How come you took a catnap during class?

W: ＿＿＿＿＿＿＿＿＿＿＿＿＿＿＿＿＿＿＿＿＿

(a) I stayed up late last night.
(b) I want to put my feet up for a while.
(c) No worries. I'll keep my eye on the clock.
(d) She's in a pickle.

해설

수업 중에 왜 졸았는지 묻고 있으므로 그 이유에 대해 언급한 (a)가 정답이다.

어휘

take a catnap 선잠을 자다 put one's feet up 누워서 쉬다 in a pickle 곤경에 빠진

Part 2

15. W: Are both of you working right now?

M: Sure, Dana and I both work at the same company.

W: Who controls the purse strings?

M: _______________________________________

(a) I will get my salary today.

(b) They are in cahoots.

(c) I look after the money.

(d) It's all smoke and mirrors.

↘ 해설

누가 경제권을 쥐고 있냐고 묻고 있으므로 자신이 돈 관리를 한다고 응답한 (c)가 정답이다.

어휘

control the purse strings 경제권을 쥐고 있다 in cahoots 한통속이 되어 smoke and mirrors 사실을 왜곡시키는 것, 진실의 은폐, 마술같이 속이는 것

16. M: I burnt the midnight oil to study for my exam.

W: Why don't you take a nap for a bit?

M: What if the teacher sees me?

W: _______________________________

(a) I don't like your talking down to me.

(b) I'll wake you up if she notices anything.

(c) I think I'll stay here for keeps.

(d) He's got big shoes to fill.

해설

자다가 들키면 어떡하냐고 묻고 있으므로 깨워 주겠다고 응답한 (b)가 적절하다. (d)는 직역하자면 '그는 채워야 할 큰 신발을 가졌다'로, 즉 '막중한 책임을 맡았다'는 뜻을 나타낸다.

어휘

burn the midnight oil 밤늦게까지 공부하다 talk down to ~에게 무시하는 투로 말하다 for keeps 언제까지나

Part 1

1. (a)   (b)   (c)   (d)

2. (a)   (b)   (c)   (d)

Part 2

3. (a)   (b)   (c)   (d)

4. (a)   (b)   (c)   (d)

5. (a)   (b)   (c)   (d)

Choose the most appropriate response to the statement.

1. (a)   (b)   (c)   (d)
2. (a)   (b)   (c)   (d)
3. (a)   (b)   (c)   (d)

Choose the most appropriate response to complete the conversation.

4. (a)   (b)   (c)   (d)
5. (a)   (b)   (c)   (d)

Choose the option that best answers the question.

6. (a)   (b)   (c)   (d)

Choose the option that best answers the question.

7. (a)   (b)   (c)   (d)

전화 관련 문제 유형

Chapter 3

전화 관련 문제는 한 문제 이상 꼭 출제된다. 일반적인 전화 통화 내용뿐만 아니라 전화와 관련된 여러 가지 용어와 상황들을 정리해 둘 필요가 있다. 특히 휴대폰과 관련한 새로운 용어나 용례도 주의 깊게 살펴봐야 할 것이다.

Part 1

5. W: I want to see your face. Let's chat in video mode.
   M: ________________________________

(a) She is on maternity leave.
(b) I'm sorry I can't. The connection is bad here.
(c) I hope I'm not calling you at a bad time.
(d) I have another call coming in.

↘ 해설

화상 통화를 하자고 제안하고 있으므로 이에 대해 긍정 또는 부정하는 내용의 선택지를 고르면 된다. 따라서 연결 상태가 좋지 않아 잘 안 보인다고 응답한 (b)가 적절하다.

어휘
maternity leave 출산 휴가

6. W: I see you are screening your calls.

M: ____

(a) This is a cutting-edge telephone.
(b) There's a lot of static on the line.
(c) Bear with me.
(d) Yes, I am.

해설

screen에는 '가려내다', '심사하다'란 뜻도 있어서 screen one's calls 하면 누군가로부터 전화가 올 때 받기 싫은 전화는 받지 않고 전화번호 뜨는 걸 보며 골라 받는 것을 의미한다. 따라서 여자의 말에 수긍하는 (d)가 정답이다. (c)의 Bear with me.는 불편하거나 지루할 때 '참아 주세요'란 뜻으로 미국인들이 자주 쓰는 표현인데, 전화 통화 중에 사용하면 '끊지 말고 기다려 주세요'란 의미가 된다.

어휘
cutting-edge 최신 기술의   static (수신기의) 잡음

Part 2

17. W: I see you have one of those newfangled portable phones.

M: Yes. It's got all the bells and whistles to go with it.

W: Wow. It has all the latest gizmos.

M: ____

(a) That's why the price was a bit on the steep side.

(b) They jacked up the price.

(c) I want to wet my whistle.

(d) These newfangled cell phones are nice.

해설

모든 최신 기능이 갖춰져 있다고 했으므로 그 때문에 가격이 비쌌다고 응답한 (a)가 가장 적절하다. 남자의 첫 번째 대사에 나오는 the bells and whistles는 보통 전자제품이나 컴퓨터 하드웨어 등에 필수적인 기능 외에도 이것저것 붙여놓은 갖가지 기능들을 나타낼 때 쓰는 표현이다. (b)의 jack up the price는 식당이나 항공사, 상점 등에서 '가격을 인상하다'라고 할 때 자주 쓰는 구어체 표현이므로 잘 기억해 두자.

어휘

newfangled 최신의, 최신 유행의 portable phone 휴대폰 gizmo 장치, 기계 steep 가파른, (요구·값 등이) 터무니 없는 wet one's whistle 목을 축이다

18. M: Can I borrow your mobile phone?

W: Why? What's wrong with yours?

M: It's out of juice and I left my charger at home.

W: ________________________________

(a) The battery is getting charged. So I have to wait.

(b) The battery is getting low, so make it short.

(c) My battery is fully charged.

(d) My battery is only half charged.

↘ 해설

휴대폰을 빌려 달라는 남자에게 배터리가 얼마 안 남았으니 짧게 하라고 말한 (b)가 정답이다. '배터리가 다돼 가고 있다'라고 할 때 The battery is getting low.라고 표현한다. 만일, 배터리가 떨어졌다면 그 경우엔 The battery is dead.라고 말한다.

어휘

out of juice 배터리가 없는   **charger** 충전기

Part 1

1.   (a)   (b)   (c)   (d)

Part 2

2.   (a)   (b)   (c)   (d)

Choose the most appropriate response to the statement.

1. (a)   (b)   (c)   (d)
2. (a)   (b)   (c)   (d)
3. (a)   (b)   (c)   (d)

Choose the most appropriate response to complete the conversation.

4. (a)   (b)   (c)   (d)
5. (a)   (b)   (c)   (d)

Choose the option that best answers the question.

6. (a)   (b)   (c)   (d)

Choose the option that best answers the question.

7. (a)   (b)   (c)   (d)

대인 관련 문제 유형

Chapter 4

대인 관련 문제에서는 인사, 초대, 제안/권유, 충고/부탁/허락, 칭찬/축하, 격려 /위로, 감사, 사과, 항의/불평에 이르기까지 다양한 상황들이 등장할 수 있다. 따라서 각각의 상황에 따른 응답 유형들을 잘 학습해 두어야 한다.

Part 1

7. W: Hi, John. How's the world been treating you?

M: ____

(a) I got a kick out of it.
(b) I just want to clear the air between you and me.
(c) So far so good.
(d) I can't let this slide.

◥ 해설

How's the world (been) treating you?는 어떻게 지내는지 안부를 묻는 표현이다. 따라서 이에 답한 (c)가 정답이다.

어휘

get a kick out of ~에 쾌감을 느끼다, 짜릿한 흥분을 맛보다 **clear the air** 오해를[의혹을] 풀다 **let ... slide** ~을 묵과하다[무시하다]

8. M: I've been offered a raise, but I'd also like a promotion.

W: ____

(a) It's all water under the bridge.
(b) You can't have your cake and eat it too.
(c) I want you to tough it out.
(d) He took a liking to me.

해설

남자가 봉급 인상과 승진 모두를 원한다고 했으므로 (b)가 가장 적절한 응답이다. 직역하자면 '케이크를 먹으면서 동시에 가지고 있을 수 없다'로, 즉 '두 마리 토끼를 동시에 잡을 수 없다'는 의미다. (a)는 이미 지나버린 과거의 일을 표현할 때 사용한다.

어휘

tough it out 어려움을 참고 견디다 **take a liking to** ~가 마음에 들다

Part 2

19. M: Can you knock off a little early and come with me?

W: Where are you going, Mr. Homebody?

M: My grandparents own a small piece of land with a garden and picnic area.

W: _______________________________________

(a) We'll take the fastest route.

(b) Sounds heavenly! Sign me up.

(c) We have come a long way.

(d) It's gonna be in limbo for a while.

↘ 해설

남자의 조부모님이 계신 곳에 정원과 소풍 장소가 있다는 말을 들었으므로 이에 대한 반응으로 가장 적절한 것은 (b)다.

어휘

knock off 일을 그만두다 homebody 집에 틀어박혀 지내는 사람 heavenly 훌륭한 sign up 참가하다, 가입하다, 등록하다 come a long way 크게 발전하다 in limbo 불확실한 상태로

20. W: I can still recall our last summer together.

M: We walked on the beach together.

W: Let's hit the beach this summer. We can both chip in for gas.

M: ________________________________

(a) Make no bones about it!

(b) I'm turning in.

(c) Don't put a bug in my ear. I'm broke.

(d) Misery loves company.

해설

해변에 가자고 제안하면서 기름 값을 나눠 낼 수 있다고 했으므로 이에 적절한 응답은 (c)가 된다. put a bug in one's ear는 직역하자면 '누군가의 귀 안에 벌레를 넣다', 즉 '그 사람에게 살짝 뭔가를 귀띔해 주다', '힌트를 주다'란 의미를 나타낸다. 또 위 대화문에서처럼 상황에 따라 '부추기다'의 뜻으로도 해석된다.

어휘

chip in for gas (여럿이서) 기름 값을 내다 make no bones about it 의심 없이 솔직히 말하다 turn in 잠자리에 들다 Misery loves company. 동병상련

Part 1

1. (a)   (b)   (c)   (d)

2. (a)   (b)   (c)   (d)

Part 2

3. (a)   (b)   (c)   (d)

4. (a)   (b)   (c)   (d)

Choose the most appropriate response to the statement.

1. (a)　　　(b)　　　(c)　　　(d)
2. (a)　　　(b)　　　(c)　　　(d)
3. (a)　　　(b)　　　(c)　　　(d)

Choose the most appropriate response to complete the conversation.

4. (a)　　　(b)　　　(c)　　　(d)
5. (a)　　　(b)　　　(c)　　　(d)

Choose the option that best answers the question.

6. (a)　　　(b)　　　(c)　　　(d)

Choose the option that best answers the question.

7. (a)　　　(b)　　　(c)　　　(d)

사회 관련 문제 유형

Chapter 5

사회 관련 문제에서는 직장이나 학교, 쇼핑, 식당 등에서 접하게 되는 여러 가지 상황들이나 (해외) 여행을 하면서 발생하는 상황들과 관련된 내용들이 등장하므로 각 상황에 자주 사용되는 표현들을 잘 익혀 두도록 하자.

Part 1

9. W: Can I use my frequent flyer points to shave off some of the cost?

M: _______________________________________

(a) I've already accumulated 100,000 miles with this airlines' frequent flyer program.
(b) They started to mow the lawn.
(c) I only want to have a shave.
(d) Sure. Let me have your frequent flyer miles card number please.

해설

항공 마일리지를 사용할 수 있는지 묻고 있으므로 이에 긍정으로 답한 (d)가 정답이다.

> **어휘**
> frequent flyer points[miles] 항공 마일리지 shave off (값을) 깎다 mow (잔디 등을) 깎다 have a shave 수염을 깎다

10. M: Our company pays us chicken feed compared to other companies.

W: _______________________________________

(a) Please keep me company.
(b) I've been stressed out.
(c) Compared to your salary, mine is low.
(d) True, but you know it's just a small company.

해설

월급이 너무 적다고 불평하는 남자의 말에 수긍하면서 회사가 작아서 그렇다고 응답한 (d)가 가장 적절하다.

어휘

keep ... company ~에게 말동무를 해주다   stress out 스트레스가 심한

Part 2

21. W: Sir, I'm afraid you'll have to turn off your cell phone before takeoff.

M: Oh, sorry. I was about to turn it off.

W: Thank you for your cooperation.

M: ____

(a) I hope that your English takes off.

(b) I have set the alarm on my cell phone.

(c) Please don't interfere in my business.

(d) No problem.

해설

휴대폰을 끄는 데 협조해 준 것에 대해 감사를 표하고 있으므로 이에 답례하는 (d)가 정답이다.

어휘

takeoff 이륙 **take off** 이륙하다, 발전하다 **interfere in** ~에 간섭하다

22. W: Would you like to pay for this with cash or plastic?

M: Plastic. Can I pay for it on installment?

W: Sure. How many months of an installment plan would you like?

M: ＿＿＿＿＿＿＿＿＿＿＿＿＿＿＿＿＿＿＿＿＿＿＿＿

(a) No, I don't. I guess I'll use my debit card.

(b) I would like a 12-month installment plan.

(c) I had to pay in full.

(d) She short-changed me 2,000won.

해설

몇 개월 할부로 할 건지 묻고 있으므로 개월 수가 언급된 (b)가 정답이다.

어휘

plastic 〈구어〉신용카드   on installment 할부로   debit card 직불카드   pay in full 일시불로 지불하다
short-change 거스름돈을 덜 주다

Part 1

1.   (a)   (b)   (c)   (d)

2.   (a)   (b)   (c)   (d)

Part 2

3.   (a)   (b)   (c)   (d)

4.   (a)   (b)   (c)   (d)

Part 1

Choose the most appropriate response to the statement.

1. (a)   (b)   (c)   (d)
2. (a)   (b)   (c)   (d)
3. (a)   (b)   (c)   (d)

Part 2

Choose the most appropriate response to complete the conversation.

4. (a)   (b)   (c)   (d)
5. (a)   (b)   (c)   (d)

Part 3

Choose the option that best answers the question.

6. (a)   (b)   (c)   (d)

Part 4

Choose the option that best answers the question.

7. (a)   (b)   (c)   (d)

공공 관련 문제 유형

Chapter 6

공공 관련 문제 유형에서는 병원이나 은행, 우체국 등에서 벌어질 수 있는 대화 내용과, 교통, 길 찾기 등과 관련된 대화 내용이 나온다. 가끔 이들 주제와 관련하여 전문 용어들이 등장하기도 하므로 잘 정리해 암기해 두도록 하자.

Part 1

11. W: What's the quickest way to get from here to Mr. Kim's office downtown?

M: _______________________________________

(a) When you are behind the wheel, you should be careful.
(b) Take your pick.
(c) I'm thinking of getting an apartment in downtown L.A.
(d) It's a jungle out there. You would be much better off taking the subway.

> **해설**
> 빨리 갈 수 있는 방법을 묻고 있으므로 이에 관해 언급한 (d)가 정답이다.

어휘
behind the wheel 운전 중인 **take one's pick** 고르다 **jungle** (대도시 등의) 번잡하고 소란한 곳

12. M: Is my cholesterol and blood pressure high?

W: _______________________________________

(a) No, I'm wracked with pain.

(b) Sure, let's check it with a thermometer.

(c) Yes. I feel so bloated.

(d) Yes, you should lay off the fatty foods.

해설

콜레스테롤과 혈압이 높은지 묻고 있으므로 이에 관한 응답과 함께 충고를 해주는 (d)가 정답이다.

어휘

be wracked with pain 통증으로 괴로워하다 thermometer 체온계 feel bloated 속이 더부룩하다 lay off 그만두다, 끊다 fatty 기름진

Part 2

23. M: I dropped by to locate my mail which I sent off last week.

W: Was it sent by registered mail?

M: Yes. But they haven't received it yet.

W: _______________________________________

(a) Let me see if I can track it down.

(b) He covered his tracks.

(c) Please put it on the scale.

(d) I'll send it by certified mail.

해설

지난주에 보낸 등기 우편물이 아직 상대방에게 도착하지 않아 어찌된 영문인지 알아보기 위해 우체국을 들른 상황이다. 따라서 확인을 해주겠다는 (a)가 이어져야 자연스럽다.

어휘

drop by 잠깐 들르다 **send off** 발송[전송]하다 **track down** 철저히 조사하다, 추적해 내다 **cover one's tracks** 행방을 감추다 **certified mail** 배달 증명 우편

24. W: Would you make a tight fist to run a blood test?

M: Ok. When can I receive the result?

W: Next Monday. Now, press down until the bleeding stops.

M: ____

(a) Can I just put a band-aid on?

(b) What blood type are you?

(c) Did you have a miscarriage?

(d) When did you have your period last?

해설

피가 멈출 때까지 누르고 있으라는 말에 이어질 응답으로, 그냥 일회용 밴드를 붙여도 되는지 묻는 (a)가 가장 적절하다.

어휘

make a fist 주먹을 쥐다 band-aid 일회용 밴드 have a miscarriage 유산하다 period 생리

Part 1

1. (a) (b) (c) (d)

Part 2

2. (a) (b) (c) (d)

3. (a) (b) (c) (d)

Choose the most appropriate response to the statement.

1. (a)　　　(b)　　　(c)　　　(d)
2. (a)　　　(b)　　　(c)　　　(d)
3. (a)　　　(b)　　　(c)　　　(d)

Choose the most appropriate response to complete the conversation.

4. (a)　　　(b)　　　(c)　　　(d)
5. (a)　　　(b)　　　(c)　　　(d)

Choose the option that best answers the question.

6. (a)　　　(b)　　　(c)　　　(d)

Choose the option that best answers the question.

7. (a)　　　(b)　　　(c)　　　(d)

주제 파악 문제 유형

Chapter 7

주제 파악하기는 Part 3, 4에서 가장 쉬운 문제 유형이다. 세부 내용은 알 필요가 없기 때문에 전체적으로 어떤 주제를 말하고자 하는지만 파악하면 된다. 주제는 보통 첫 부분이나 마지막 부분에 나와 있는 경우가 많다. 선택지 중 지문에 언급된 단어를 그대로 사용한 경우는 오답이기 쉬우며, 대개 비슷한 다른 표현으로 Paraphrasing되어서 나오는 경우가 많다.

Part 3

25. W: You seem so angry. Anything wrong?

M: My brother always uses my belongings as if they were his.

W: Oh, did he take something without your permission?

M: Yes. He went to a high school reunion in my dinner jacket that I was going to wear.

W: Well, then you can also wear his.

M: No, his clothes are not my style.

Q. What is the main topic of the conversation?

(a) Going to a high school reunion
(b) Why the man is so agitated
(c) His new dinner jacket
(d) Sharing stuff

해설

대화 첫 부분에서 여자가 남자에게 왜 화가 나 있는지 물었으며, 그 이유에 대한 얘기가 이어지므로 (b)가 정답임을 알 수 있다.

어휘
dinner jacket 약식 야회복   agitated 흥분한

26. M: I'm looking for Samuel.

W: You just missed him.

M: Oh, shoot! I really need to catch up with him.

W: Are you a friend of his?

M: Yes. We go back a long way. Can you guess where he is heading?

W: Sorry. I don't have a clue.

M: Can you call him to check where he is?

Q. What is the main focus of the conversation?

(a) The man is dying to see Samuel.

(b) The woman doesn't know where Samuel is.

(c) Samuel is the man's alumnus.

(d) The man quickened his steps to catch up with Samuel.

해설

남자가 사무엘을 어떻게든 꼭 만나려고 하고 있으므로 정답은 (a)가 된다. 남자의 세 번째 대사에 나온 We go back a long way.는 '오래 전부터 알고 지낸 친구 사이이다', '우린 오랜 친구다' 라고 말할 때 쓸 수 있는 표현이다.

어휘
catch up with ~를 따라잡다

Part 4

31. Just like humans, it is unhealthy for a dog to be overweight. Here are a few feeding rules every dog owner should keep in mind. Set regular mealtimes. An irregular eating schedule can affect your dog's digestive system and ultimately cause chronic digestive disorders. It is also important that your dog's water and food bowls are kept in the same place every day. Your dog only needs one or two meals daily, if it is fed on a regimented schedule.

Q. Which of the following best summarizes the talk?

(a) Dogs should not be fed too much at once.
(b) Dog's food and water bowl should be kept at a certain place.
(c) Dogs also have digestive disorders when fed irregularly.
(d) It's bad for both humans and dogs to be overweight.

해설
글 첫 문장이 주제문으로, 개도 인간과 마찬가지로 비만이 되면 건강에 좋지 않다는 내용을 다루고 있으므로 정답은 (d)가 된다.

어휘
unhealthy 건강에 해로운 digestive system 소화기 계통 chronic 만성의 regimented 엄격히 통제된

32. While fewer of us are now able to afford such healthy food as fresh pomegranate juice or thick fillets of wild salmon, if you're willing to cut back on convenience foods and spend more time in the kitchen, you can still fill your grocery carts with plenty of affordable, nutritious foods. The trick is planning. In order to reduce costs but keep nutritional value up, you have to plan. You have to plan your meals, plan your snacks and plan enough time for preparation.

Q. What is the main purpose of the talk?

(a) To advise people on where to shop
(b) To advise people on how to select organic foods
(c) To advise people on nutritious cooking
(d) To advise people on how to have foods which are both affordable and nutritious

해설

가격도 적당하면서 영양가 높은 음식을 먹을 수 있는 비결을 말해 주고 있으므로 정답은 (d)가 된다.

어휘

pomegranate 석류 fillet (가시를 발라낸) 생선 토막 cut back on ～을 줄이다 convenience food 인스턴트 식품 plenty of 많은 nutritious 영양가 높은 trick 비결, 요령 keep up 유지하다 nutritional value 영양가

Part 3

1. (a)   (b)   (c)   (d)

Part 4

2. (a)   (b)   (c)   (d)

Choose the most appropriate response to the statement.

1. (a)　　(b)　　(c)　　(d)
2. (a)　　(b)　　(c)　　(d)
3. (a)　　(b)　　(c)　　(d)

Choose the most appropriate response to complete the conversation.

4. (a)　　(b)　　(c)　　(d)
5. (a)　　(b)　　(c)　　(d)

Choose the option that best answers the question.

6. (a)　　(b)　　(c)　　(d)

Choose the option that best answers the question.

7. (a)　　(b)　　(c)　　(d)

내용 파악 문제 유형

Chapter 8

내용 파악하기는 다소 어려운 문제 유형이지만 고득점을 위해서는 꼭 정복해야 하는 영역이기도 하다. 세부 내용 이해에 초점을 맞춰야 하므로, 들을 때 지문에서 언급된 숫자나 장소, 그 밖의 세부적인 상황들에 대한 내용들을 메모해 두는 것이 좋다. 그리고 두 번째 들을 때는 처음 들을 때 놓친 내용들을 잘 확인해 두도록 하자.

Part 3

27. W: Front desk. May I help you?

M: This is room 302.

W: Yes, sir. Is there a problem with your room?

M: Yes, the toilet is not functioning.

W: Did you turn the handle all the way to the left?

M: Yes, I did.

W: I'll contact maintenance and send someone up immediately.

M: How long do I have to wait?

W: The engineer will be there in five minutes.

M: Okay, thank you.

Q. Which is correct according to the conversation?

(a) The faucet is not functioning.
(b) The toilet isn't working.
(c) The woman is working at the maintenance.
(d) The handle should be turned to the right.

해설

남자의 두 번째 대사를 통해 변기가 고장 났음을 알 수 있다. 따라서 정답은 (b)가 된다.

어휘

all the way to ~에 이르도록 죽, ~ 끝까지   faucet 수도꼭지

28. W: May I help you, sir?

M: I'm looking for something for my wife's birthday.

W: May I ask her age?

M: Yes, she is in her mid forties.

W: Oh, I see. How about this dress?

M: But it's solid blue. Do you have anything red with stripes?

W: Sir, solid blue is all the rage among matrons.

M: Just in case my wife doesn't like this, can I exchange it?

W: Sure, it's also refundable.

M: Thank you.

Q. Which is correct according to the conversation?

(a) Solid blue is very popular among matrons.

(b) The man does not like the color blue.

(c) The woman is convincing the man to buy the dress.

(d) The man is going to buy a red dress.

⬇ 해설

청 단색이 중년 여성들 사이에서 대유행이라고 했으므로 (a)가 정답이다.

어휘

solid blue 청 단색   be all the rage 대유행이다   matron (나이 지긋한 점잖은) 부인   refundable 환불 가능한

Part 4

33. Timber's personal life was secret, and even his close friends didn't know what he was dealing with. But what we all knew and shared was his love, his time, his generosity, and his mischief. You can check out his life story by visiting one of his exhibitions. I'm sure many celebrations will be held in his honor and the first official wake will be held on April 10, 2009 in Colorado Springs. All are welcome to join us. Exact time and location will be informed soon.

Q. According to this announcement, how can you learn about Timber's life?

(a) By reading his autobiography
(b) Through his works
(c) Through his best friends
(d) By joining his anniversary ceremony

⬊ 해설

그의 전시회를 방문함으로써 그의 일대기를 확인할 수 있다고 했으므로 정답은 (b)가 된다.

어휘

mischief 장난, 못된 짓 wake 추모식 autobiography 자서전

34. As emergency room waiting times are growing increasingly longer for urgent-care patients, a few hospitals are putting them on the Web. At Ochsner Health System, doctors say that the online based system is easing the load at four ERs in the New York area. When asked about the new system, a registration coordinator noted that people are now able to decide on whether to wait it out, or head to one of three other hospitals, which are all located within a 12 mile radius.

Q. What is the online based system?

(a) A system used to check waiting times
(b) A system used to locate hospitals
(c) An information system used by doctors
(d) A diet program being implemented in New York

해설

온라인 시스템을 통해 사람들이 기다려야 할지, 아니면 다른 병원으로 가야 할지를 바로 결정할 수 있다고 했으므로 (a)가 정답임을 알수 있다.

어휘

urgent-care patient 응급 환자   ease the load 마음의 부담을 덜다   registration coordinator 접수 코디네이터   radius 반경   implement 실행하다

Part 3

1. (a) (b) (c) (d)

Part 4

2. (a) (b) (c) (d)

Part 1

Choose the most appropriate response to the statement.

1. (a)　　(b)　　(c)　　(d)
2. (a)　　(b)　　(c)　　(d)
3. (a)　　(b)　　(c)　　(d)

Part 2

Choose the most appropriate response to complete the conversation.

4. (a)　　(b)　　(c)　　(d)
5. (a)　　(b)　　(c)　　(d)

Part 3

Choose the option that best answers the question.

6. (a)　　(b)　　(c)　　(d)

Part 4

Choose the option that best answers the question.

7. (a)　　(b)　　(c)　　(d)

추론
문제 유형

STEP 1 Pretest Clinic

추론 문제는 Part 3, 4의 마지막에 등장한다. 가장 난이도가 높은 문제 유형으로 어려운 영역에 속하지만, 900점 돌파를 위해서 꼭 넘어야 할 관문이기도 하다. 따라서 충분한 학습이 필요하며, 계속 연습하다 보면 추론 유형에 익숙해지게 될 것이다. 그리고 글의 내용을 통해 확실히 유추해 낼 수 없는 것은 결코 정답이 될 수 없음을 명심하자.

Part 3

29. M: Why are you dressed up today?

W: It's my brother's wedding day.

M: Your skirt looks perfect on you. But aren't you going with your parents?

W: They've gone ahead without me. I'm leaving in about 30 minutes.

M: Give my warmest regards to your brother for me.

W: Sure. Where are you going now?

M: I'm going to the mall. See you later, then.

Q. What can be inferred from the conversation?

(a) The man works at the mall.
(b) The woman will be late for the wedding.
(c) The man isn't going to attend the wedding.
(d) The woman bought a new skirt.

해설

(b)는 여자가 그녀의 부모보다 30분 늦게 출발한다는 것이지 결혼식장에 늦게 도착할 거란 얘기는 아니므로 맞지 않다. (a)와 (d)는 알 수 없는 내용. 따라서 남자의 마지막 대사를 통해 확실히 이끌어낼 수 있는 (c)가 정답이다.

어휘

be dressed up 정장을 차려입다

30. W: We're going to be late unless we leave right now.

M: Sorry. I'm searching for the route on the internet.

W: I know. We can hang a right at the intersection and just take freeway 66.

M: Do you know exactly where to go?

W: Of course I do. It's a shortcut.

M: Good, then let's go.

W: Don't worry. Trust me.

Q. What can be inferred from the conversation?

(a) The woman is very good with directions.

(b) The man has never taken the route before.

(c) The man and woman are going to go on a trip to somewhere.

(d) The woman will drive instead of the man.

☑ 해설

인터넷 지도를 통해 가는 길을 검색하고 있다는 것으로 보아 (b)가 정답임을 알 수 있다. (a)는 여자가 이 길을 잘 알고 있다는 것이지 길눈이 밝은지는 알 수 없으므로 정답이 될 수 없다. (c), (d) 역시 명확히 알 수 없는 내용.

어휘
hang a right 우회전하다

Part 4

35. The two astronauts, who were teachers at a middle school just five years ago, came back this Monday as heroes for what they have done during the spacewalk. Although their mission was life-risking, they finally cleared a dangerous and enormous space junk that had been a threat to the international space station and shuttle for a long time. They have done something that no one has even dreamed of trying before.

Q. What can be inferred about the two astronauts?

(a) They were threatened by something at the space station.
(b) This was their first time going to space.
(c) They had a very hard time while spacewalking.
(d) They would not go on a spacewalk anymore.

↘ 해설

그들이 맡은 일이 목숨을 건 일이었다고 했으므로 그곳에서의 임무 수행이 결코 쉽지 않았을 것임을 짐작할 수 있다. 따라서 정답은 (c)가 된다.

어휘

astronaut 우주 비행사 spacewalk 우주 유영 life-risking 목숨을 건 clear 제거하다 space junk 우주 쓰레기 shuttle 우주 왕복선

36. Spring is right around the corner. There is a tradition in our family of baking carrot cakes and sharing it every spring. This year it is my turn to make one. So, I used a recipe from the internet and made a fabulous carrot cake. It seemed perfect from the outside although I do not know the actual taste of it. My family are all really looking forward to the cake that I have made.

Q. **What can be inferred from the story?**

(a) Spring is the right season for making carrot cakes.
(b) The speaker's family take turns in making carrot cakes every year in Spring.
(c) The speaker made a carrot cake exactly the same as the picture on the internet.
(d) It is the speaker's first time in baking a carrot cake.

해설

올해는 자신이 만들 차례라고 한 것으로 보아, 매년 가족들이 번갈아가며 당근 케이크를 만들고 있음을 짐작할 수 있다. 따라서 정답은 (b)가 된다.

어휘
fabulous 아주 멋진

Part 3

1. (a)　　(b)　　(c)　　(d)

2. (a)　　(b)　　(c)　　(d)

Part 4

3. (a)　　(b)　　(c)　　(d)

Choose the most appropriate response to the statement.

1. (a)   (b)   (c)   (d)
2. (a)   (b)   (c)   (d)
3. (a)   (b)   (c)   (d)

Choose the most appropriate response to complete the conversation.

4. (a)   (b)   (c)   (d)
5. (a)   (b)   (c)   (d)

Choose the option that best answers the question.

6. (a)   (b)   (c)   (d)

Choose the option that best answers the question.

7. (a)   (b)   (c)   (d)

Final Test

Final Test 1

Part 1

Questions 1-15

You will now hear fifteen items, each made up of a single spoken statement followed by four spoken responses. Choose the most appropriate response to the statement.

1.	(a)	(b)	(c)	(d)		2.	(a)	(b)	(c)	(d)
3.	(a)	(b)	(c)	(d)		4.	(a)	(b)	(c)	(d)
5.	(a)	(b)	(c)	(d)		6.	(a)	(b)	(c)	(d)
7.	(a)	(b)	(c)	(d)		8.	(a)	(b)	(c)	(d)
9.	(a)	(b)	(c)	(d)		10.	(a)	(b)	(c)	(d)
11.	(a)	(b)	(c)	(d)		12.	(a)	(b)	(c)	(d)
13.	(a)	(b)	(c)	(d)		14.	(a)	(b)	(c)	(d)
15.	(a)	(b)	(c)	(d)						

Part 2

Questions 16-30

You will now hear fifteen conversation fragments, each made up of a three spoken statements followed by four spoken responses. Choose the most appropriate response to complete the conversation.

16.	(a)	(b)	(c)	(d)		17.	(a)	(b)	(c)	(d)
18.	(a)	(b)	(c)	(d)		19.	(a)	(b)	(c)	(d)
20.	(a)	(b)	(c)	(d)		21.	(a)	(b)	(c)	(d)
22.	(a)	(b)	(c)	(d)		23.	(a)	(b)	(c)	(d)
24.	(a)	(b)	(c)	(d)		25.	(a)	(b)	(c)	(d)
26.	(a)	(b)	(c)	(d)		27.	(a)	(b)	(c)	(d)
28.	(a)	(b)	(c)	(d)		29.	(a)	(b)	(c)	(d)
30.	(a)	(b)	(c)	(d)						

Part 3

Questions 31-45

You will now hear fifteen complete conversations. For each item, you will hear a conversation and its corresponding question which will be read twice. Then you will hear four options which will be read only once. Choose the option that best answers the question.

31. (a) (b) (c) (d)   32. (a) (b) (c) (d)
33. (a) (b) (c) (d)   34. (a) (b) (c) (d)
35. (a) (b) (c) (d)   36. (a) (b) (c) (d)
37. (a) (b) (c) (d)   38. (a) (b) (c) (d)
39. (a) (b) (c) (d)   40. (a) (b) (c) (d)
41. (a) (b) (c) (d)   42. (a) (b) (c) (d)
43. (a) (b) (c) (d)   44. (a) (b) (c) (d)
45. (a) (b) (c) (d)

Part 4

Questions 46-60

You will now hear fifteen spoken monologuess. For each item, you will hear a monologues and its corresponding question which will be read twice. Then you will hear four options which will be read only once. Choose the option that best answers the question.

46. (a) (b) (c) (d)   47. (a) (b) (c) (d)
48. (a) (b) (c) (d)   49. (a) (b) (c) (d)
50. (a) (b) (c) (d)   51. (a) (b) (c) (d)
52. (a) (b) (c) (d)   53. (a) (b) (c) (d)
54. (a) (b) (c) (d)   55. (a) (b) (c) (d)
56. (a) (b) (c) (d)   57. (a) (b) (c) (d)
58. (a) (b) (c) (d)   59. (a) (b) (c) (d)
60. (a) (b) (c) (d)

Final Test 2

Part 1

Questions 1-15

You will now hear fifteen items, each made up of a single spoken statement followed by four spoken responses. Choose the most appropriate response to the statement.

1.	(a)	(b)	(c)	(d)		2.	(a)	(b)	(c)	(d)
3.	(a)	(b)	(c)	(d)		4.	(a)	(b)	(c)	(d)
5.	(a)	(b)	(c)	(d)		6.	(a)	(b)	(c)	(d)
7.	(a)	(b)	(c)	(d)		8.	(a)	(b)	(c)	(d)
9.	(a)	(b)	(c)	(d)		10.	(a)	(b)	(c)	(d)
11.	(a)	(b)	(c)	(d)		12.	(a)	(b)	(c)	(d)
13.	(a)	(b)	(c)	(d)		14.	(a)	(b)	(c)	(d)
15.	(a)	(b)	(c)	(d)						

Part 2

Questions 16-30

You will now hear fifteen conversation fragments, each made up of a three spoken statements followed by four spoken responses. Choose the most appropriate response to complete the conversation.

16.	(a)	(b)	(c)	(d)		17.	(a)	(b)	(c)	(d)
18.	(a)	(b)	(c)	(d)		19.	(a)	(b)	(c)	(d)
20.	(a)	(b)	(c)	(d)		21.	(a)	(b)	(c)	(d)
22.	(a)	(b)	(c)	(d)		23.	(a)	(b)	(c)	(d)
24.	(a)	(b)	(c)	(d)		25.	(a)	(b)	(c)	(d)
26.	(a)	(b)	(c)	(d)		27.	(a)	(b)	(c)	(d)
28.	(a)	(b)	(c)	(d)		29.	(a)	(b)	(c)	(d)
30.	(a)	(b)	(c)	(d)						

Part 3

Questions 31-45

You will now hear fifteen complete conversations. For each item, you will hear a conversation and its corresponding question which will be read twice. Then you will hear four options which will be read only once. Choose the option that best answers the question.

31.	(a)	(b)	(c)	(d)		32.	(a)	(b)	(c)	(d)
33.	(a)	(b)	(c)	(d)		34.	(a)	(b)	(c)	(d)
35.	(a)	(b)	(c)	(d)		36.	(a)	(b)	(c)	(d)
37.	(a)	(b)	(c)	(d)		38.	(a)	(b)	(c)	(d)
39.	(a)	(b)	(c)	(d)		40.	(a)	(b)	(c)	(d)
41.	(a)	(b)	(c)	(d)		42.	(a)	(b)	(c)	(d)
43.	(a)	(b)	(c)	(d)		44.	(a)	(b)	(c)	(d)
45.	(a)	(b)	(c)	(d)						

Part 4

Questions 46-60

You will now hear fifteen spoken monologuess. For each item, you will hear a monologues and its corresponding question which will be read twice. Then you will hear four options which will be read only once. Choose the option that best answers the question.

46.	(a)	(b)	(c)	(d)		47.	(a)	(b)	(c)	(d)
48.	(a)	(b)	(c)	(d)		49.	(a)	(b)	(c)	(d)
50.	(a)	(b)	(c)	(d)		51.	(a)	(b)	(c)	(d)
52.	(a)	(b)	(c)	(d)		53.	(a)	(b)	(c)	(d)
54.	(a)	(b)	(c)	(d)		55.	(a)	(b)	(c)	(d)
56.	(a)	(b)	(c)	(d)		57.	(a)	(b)	(c)	(d)
58.	(a)	(b)	(c)	(d)		59.	(a)	(b)	(c)	(d)
60.	(a)	(b)	(c)	(d)						

정답 및 해설

STEP 1 Pretest Clinic

Part 1

1.

해석_ W: 네가 원한다면, 오늘 밤 내 친구들이랑 나랑 같이 나가는 거 대환영이야.

M: _______________________________

(a) 원할 때 언제든지 대화에 끼어들면 돼.

(b) 고마워, 근데 너희들이 뭐 할 건지 들어 보고.

(c) 그건 억지야.

(d) 그는 항상 날 깔봐.

정답_ (b)

2.

해석_ M: 휴가 가는 것에 대해 생각 좀 해보자.

W: _______________________________

(a) 안 돼. 우린 지금 허리띠를 졸라매야 한다구.

(b) 이건 흐지부지 잊혀질 거야.

(c) 그는 그냥 실없는 거짓말을 하고 있는 거야.

(d) 내가 그의 기를 죽여 놨지.

정답_ (a)

Part 2

13.

해석_ M: 어떻게 지냈니?

W: 평소처럼 일 많이 하고 지냈지.

M: 왜 이러셔. 그거 말고도 뭔가 다른 일 있잖아.

W: _______________________________

(a) 질겁을 했다니까.

(b) 넌 정말이지 자화자찬을 해야 돼.

(c) 진짜 일만 하고 있다니까.

(d) 진정해. 네 졸업 파티가 아니잖아.

정답_ (c)

14.

해석_ W: 너 무지 바쁘다는 건 알지만 같이 점심 먹자.

M: 미안한데 시간이 없어.

W: 이번주에 언제 시간 나?

M: _______________________________

(a) 수요일은 괜찮아.

(b) 집어치워!

(c) 최선을 다해 봐.

(d) 금방 후닥닥 해치울게.

정답_ (a)

STEP 2 990 Challenge!

1.

M: It's nice to finally be able to put a face to your name.

W: _______________________________

(a) Of course. I have a soft spot for you.

(b) Sure. Things have been looking up since then.

(c) Same here. Your name has popped up before.

(d) Yeah. I'm taking him on face value.

해석_ M: 이렇게 직접 만나게 되어 반가워요.

W: _______________________________

(a) 물론이죠. 전 당신이 너무 좋아요.

(b) 그럼요. 모든 일이 그때부터 잘 풀리고 있어요.

(c) 저도요. 성함은 익히 들어 알고 있어요.

(d) 네. 전 그를 액면 그대로 받아들일 거예요.

해설_ It's nice to finally be able to put a face to your name.은 말로만 전해 듣던 사람과 직접 만나게 되었을 때 쓸 수 있는 인사말이다. 두 사람이 처음 만나는 상황이므로 역시 여자의 인사말이 이어져야 자연스럽다. 따라서 정답은 (c). pop up은 '튀어오르다', '불쑥 나타나다'란 뜻인데, 머릿속에 갑자기 떠올리는 표현으로도 쓸 수 있다.

어휘_ **have a soft spot for** ~을 무척 좋아하다, ~에 약하다 **look up** 좋아지다, 향상되다 **take ... on face value** 액면 그대로 받아들이다

정답_ (c)

2.

W: Stop sticking your nose into other people's business.

M: _______________________________

(a) Bad news travels fast.

(b) My advice shouldn't fall on deaf ears.
(c) Stop ducking and covering.
(d) Surprise! Surprise! Live and learn.

해석_ W: 남의 일에 간섭 마.

M: ____________________________________

(a) 나쁜 소식은 빨리 퍼진다.

(b) 내 충고를 무시하지 마.

(c) 피하고 가리는 것 좀 그만해.

(d) 놀랍다! 놀라워! 오래 살고 볼일이야.

해설_ stick one's nose into 하면 '~에 간섭하다'란 뜻이다. 따라서 간섭하지 말라고 하고 있으므로 자신의 충고를 무시하지 말라는 (b)가 가장 적절하다. (c)에서 duck은 '오리'란 뜻이 아니라 '몸을 피하다', '도망치다'란 동사의 의미를 나타낸다.

어휘_ fall on deaf ears 무시당하다, 묵살되다   duck and cover 문제를 회피하고 진실을 가리다   live and learn 오래 살고 볼일이다, 경험으로 알다

정답_ (b)

3.

W: It's strange bumping into you here!
M: I've been coming here a lot recently.
W: I never pictured you as a moviegoer.
M: ____________________________________

(a) Well, there's more to me than meets the eye.
(b) I always like curling up with a book.
(c) My stomach is really churning.
(d) It's not rocket science.

해석_ W: 여기서 이렇게 널 만나게 될 줄이야!

M: 요즘 이곳에 자주 와.

W: 네가 영화 팬인 줄 몰랐는걸.

M: ____________________________________

(a) 음, 보기보단 다른 면이 많다구.

(b) 난 항상 웅크리고 앉아서 책 보는 걸 좋아해.

(c) 속이 정말 울렁거려.

(d) 그건 별로 어려운 일이 아니야.

해설_ 영화 팬인 줄 생각지 못했다는 여자의 반응에 이어질 응답으로 적절한 선택지는 (a)로, 직역하자면 '눈에 보이는 것보다 더 많은 것들이 내게 있다', 즉 '겉보기와는 달리 다른 내적인 면들이 많다'는 의미를 나타낸다. 여자의 첫 번째 대사에 나오는 It's

strange bumping into you here.는 안면이 있는 사람을 우연히 만났을 경우에 쓸 수 있는 표현이다.

어휘_ picture 상상하다, 마음에 그리다   moviegoer 영화 구경을 자주 가는 사람, 영화 팬   meet the eye 눈에 띄다   curl up with ~을 갖고 몸을 웅크리고 있다[눕대]   churn (속이) 메스껍다, 울렁거리다   rocket science 복잡하고 어렵고 고도의 기술/지능이 요구되는 분야를 가리키는 말

정답_ (a)

4.

M: I have taken on too many things and I don't know where to begin.
W: You have spread yourself too thin.
M: I know. And everything is beginning to pile up.
W: ____________________________________

(a) Don't pick other people's brains.
(b) Never let up.
(c) Please, remember your manners.
(d) Just get your priorities in order.

해석_ M: 너무 많은 일을 떠맡아서 어디서부터 시작해야 할지 모르겠어.

W: 넌 일을 너무 많이 벌여.

M: 나도 알아. 그리고 모든 일들이 쌓이기 시작하지.

W: ____________________________________

(a) 다른 사람들에게 조언 구하지 마.

(b) 절대 그만두지 마.

(c) 제발 예의 좀 지켜.

(d) 우선순위를 정해.

해설_ 한꺼번에 너무 많은 일을 맡아 일들이 쌓이기 시작한다는 남자의 말에 이어질 응답으로, 일의 우선순위를 정하라고 조언해 주는 (d)가 가장 적절하다. (a)의 pick other people's brains는 직역하자면 '다른 사람들의 뇌를 끄집어 내라'는 뜻으로, 즉 '다른 사람들에게 조언을 구하라'는 의미를 나타낸다.

어휘_ spread oneself too thin 일을 너무 많이 벌이다   pick one's brain ~에게 조언을 구하다   let up 그만두다   remember one's manners 예의바르게 행동하다

정답_ (d)

1.

W: I'll make a supermarket run for a few essentials. Care to tag along?

M: ________________________________

(a) He's a real hot shot.
(b) I know this inside out.
(c) I'm just getting my feet wet.
(d) Sure. I'll push a cart around the aisles.

해석_ W: 생필품 몇 가지 사러 슈퍼마켓에 갈 거야. 같이 갈래?

M: ________________________________

(a) 그는 진짜 거물이야.
(b) 난 이걸 샅샅이 알고 있어.
(c) 이제 막 시작하려고 해.
(d) 물론이지. 슈퍼마켓 안에서 내가 카트 밀어 줄게.

해설_ make a supermarket run은 go to the supermarket과 마찬가지 의미다. 또 Care to tag along?은 Want to come with me?의 뜻. 따라서 슈퍼마켓에 갈 건데 따라오겠냐고 묻고 있으므로 이에 긍정적인 응답을 한 (d)가 정답이다.

어휘_ care to ~을 바라다 tag along 따라오다 hot shot 〈속어〉 거물 inside out 구석까지 샅샅이 get one's feet wet 시작하다, 해보다

정답_ (d)

2.

M: I've been battling a persistent bug, I just can't shake it!

W: ________________________________

(a) By and large, justice wins.
(b) I'll twist some arms.
(c) We'll weather the storm together.
(d) Schedule an appointment to see the Doc.

해석_ M: 끈덕진 병과 싸우고 있는데 낫질 않네.

W: ________________________________

(a) 대체로 정의가 이기지.
(b) 내가 설득해 볼게.
(c) 함께 시련을 극복하자.
(d) 병원 예약해서 가봐.

해설_ shake는 여기서 '흔들다'가 아니라 속어로 '(근심이나 병 등을)

떨어버리다, 쫓아버리다'라는 뜻으로 사용되었다. 따라서 병이 낫지 않고 있다고 말했으므로 병원에 가보라고 충고하는 (d)가 적절하다.

어휘_ persistent 끈덕진, 계속적인 bug (병균으로 인한 가벼운) 병 by and large 대체로 twist one's arm 강요하다, 설득시키다 weather 시련을 극복하다 schedule an appointment 약속을 잡다

정답_ (d)

3.

M: Hurry up if you're going to do it anyway.

W: ________________________________

(a) Don't push me too hard. I need a break.
(b) I am in a hurry to get to the mall before noon.
(c) There was a traffic jam on my way home.
(d) I've gone too far.

해석_ M: 어차피 할 거라면 서둘러.

W: ________________________________

(a) 너무 재촉하지 마. 난 휴식이 필요해.
(b) 서둘러서 정오 전에 쇼핑몰에 가야 해.
(c) 집에 오는 길에 차가 꽉 막혔었어.
(d) 내가 심했어.

해설_ 서두르라는 충고에 부정적으로 응답한 (a)가 정답이다. 보통은 긍정적인 응답을 예상하게 되지만, 여기서처럼 부정적인 반응이 이어질 수도 있다는 점을 기억해 두자.

어휘_ go too far 지나치다, 너무하다

정답_ (a)

4.

M: Do you ever get an irrepressible craving for some munchies?
W: Yes. It usually hits me late at night.
M: Same here. I can't resist it.
W: ________________________________

(a) I'm smelling a rat.
(b) Mum's the word.
(c) Warm milk helps. It's worth a try.
(d) I'm no more a spring chicken.

해석_ M: 못 견딜 정도로 간식을 먹고 싶은 적이 있니?

W: 응. 주로 밤늦게 뭔가 먹고 싶어져.

M: 나도 그래. 참을 수가 없어.

W: ______________________________

(a) 뭔가 수상해.

(b) 입 꼭 다물고 있어.

(c) 따뜻한 우유가 도움이 될 거야. 한번 마셔 봐.

(d) 난 더 이상 영계가 아니야.

해설 간식의 유혹을 참을 수 없다는 남자의 말에 이어질 응답으로, 따뜻한 우유를 마셔 보라고 충고해 주는 (c)가 가장 적절하다.

어휘 irrepressible 견딜 수 없는 craving 갈망 munchies 간단한 식사, 스낵, 과자 smell a rat 눈치 채다, 낌새를 알아 채다 Mum's the word. 입 꼭 다물고 있어 spring chicken 젊은이, 영계, 풋내기

정답 (c)

5.

W: How do you feel about hitting the gym with me?

M: I'm not a big fan of exercising.

W: But we are both in our 30's and we could do with a workout.

M: ______________________________

(a) I'm running ragged.

(b) It's no skin off my nose.

(c) Things are looking up.

(d) You can say that again.

해석 W: 나랑 헬스 클럽에 다니는 거 어때?

M: 나 운동하는 거 별로 안 좋아해.

W: 하지만 우리 둘 다 30대야. 운동이 필요하다구.

M: ______________________________

(a) 난 녹초 상태야.

(b) 내가 알 바 아니야.

(c) 일이 잘 풀리고 있어.

(d) 네 말이 맞아.

해설 30대이므로 운동이 필요하다는 여자의 말에 동의를 나타내는 (d)가 정답이다. 여자의 첫 번째 대사에 나오는 hit the gym은 '헬스 클럽에 가다'란 뜻으로, go to the gym과 마찬가지로 자주 쓰이는 표현이다.

어휘 could do with ~을 원하다, 필요로 하다 run ragged 지치다, 녹초가 되다 be no skin off one's nose ~가 알 바 아니다, ~와 전혀 상관 없다

정답 (d)

6.

W: Which nation do you think will do better in the World Cup between Japan and Korea?

M: My money is on Japan.

W: I believe Korea might go up to the finals in the end.

M: Well, as far as I know, Japan is a cut above Korea in every degree.

W: I don't buy that. In fact, they are running neck and neck at the moment.

M: O.K. Let's wait and see what happens.

Q. What is correct according to the conversation?

(a) The woman wishes the Japanese team to lose.

(b) The man has money in Japan.

(c) The man thinks the Japanese team plays better than the Korean team.

(d) The man and woman will go to the World Cup stadium.

해석 W: 월드컵에서 일본과 한국 중 어느 나라가 더 잘할까?

M: 난 일본이 잘할 거라는 것에 걸겠어.

W: 난 한국이 결국 결승전까지 오를 거라고 생각해.

M: 글쎄, 내가 알기론 일본이 모든 면에서 한국보다 한 수 위인데.

W: 그건 아니라고 봐. 사실 현재 두 나라 실력이 막상막하야.

M: 좋아. 어떻게 될지 두고 보자구.

Q. 대화에 따르면 맞는 것은 무엇인가?

(a) 여자는 일본팀이 지길 원한다.

(b) 남자는 일본에 돈이 있다.

(c) 남자는 일본팀이 한국팀보다 실력이 더 낫다고 생각한다.

(d) 남자와 여자는 월드컵 경기장에 갈 것이다.

해설 남자는 일본이 한국보다 한 수 위라고 생각하므로 정답은 (c)가 된다. 남자의 첫 번째 대사에 나오는 My money is on ...은 '~하는 데 돈을 걸겠다'는 말로, 실제 돈을 걸겠다기보단 그만큼 확신한다는 의미를 나타낸다. 그리고 여자의 마지막 대사에 나오는 buy는 '사다'의 뜻이 아니라 '(의견을) 받아들이다, 믿다'란 뜻으로, '내 생각은 달라', '그건 못 믿겠어'라는 말을 할 때 I don't buy that.이라고 표현할 수 있다.

어휘_ go up to the finals 결승전에 오르다   a cut above ~보다 한 수 위   run neck and neck 막상막하다

정답_ (c)

7.

A new study suggests that broccoli sprouts may help to fight a common stomach bacteria associated with ulcers, cancer and gastritis. According to the report, research shows that eating 2 1/2 ounces of three-day-old broccoli sprouts every day for at least two months may offer at least some protection against the bacterium Helicobacter pylori, one of the most common bacterial infections in the world.

Q. What is the best title for the report?

(a) Types of Broccoli Sprouts
(b) Genetically Altered Broccoli
(c) The Efficacy of Broccoli Sprouts
(d) Health Benefits of Eating Broccoli Sprouts

해석_ 한 새로운 연구는 브로콜리 새싹이 궤양, 암, 그리고 위염과 연관된, 흔한 위 박테리아를 없애는 데 도움이 될 수 있음을 시사하고 있습니다. 보고서에 따르면, 3일 된 브로콜리 새싹을 매일 2와 2분의 1온스씩 최소 두 달간 먹으면 세계에서 가장 흔한 세균 감염 중 하나인 헬리코박터 파이로리 박테리아균으로부터 어느 정도 위를 보호할 수 있다는 연구 결과가 나왔습니다.

Q. 기사에 가장 적합한 제목은 무엇인가?

(a) 브로콜리 새싹의 종류
(b) 유전자 변형 브로콜리
(c) 브로콜리 새싹의 효능
(d) 브로콜리 새싹을 먹는 것의 건강상 이점

해설_ 브로콜리 새싹이 박테리아균으로부터 위를 보호해 주는 효과가 있다는 내용이므로 (c)가 가장 적절하다.

어휘_ broccoli sprouts 브로콜리 새싹   ulcers 궤양   gastritis 위염   bacterium Helicobacter pylori 헬리코박터 파이로리 박테리아균   bacterial infections 세균 감염   genetically altered 유전자 변형의   efficacy 효능

정답_ (c)

Chapter 2 의문문 문제 유형

STEP 1 Pretest Clinic

Part 1

3.

해석_ M: 뭐가 맘에 들지 않는 건데요?

W: ______________________

(a) 축하해요! 이제 자립할 수 있게 됐군요!
(b) 동료들 앞에서 날 창피 줬잖아요.
(c) 그녀는 그 상품들에 할인 가격을 적용했어요.
(d) 그는 그 소녀를 유괴하지 않았어요.

정답_ (b)

4.

해석_ M: 수업 중에 왜 졸았니?

W: ______________________

(a) 어젯밤 늦게까지 못 잤어.
(b) 잠깐이라도 누워서 쉬고 싶어.
(c) 걱정 마. 내가 시계 지켜보고 있을게.
(d) 그녀는 곤경에 빠졌어.

정답_ (a)

Part 2

15.

해석_ W: 너희 둘 다 지금 일하고 있니?

M: 네, 다나랑 전 같은 회사에 근무해요.

W: 누가 경제권을 쥐고 있니?

M: ______________________

(a) 오늘 봉급 받을 거예요.
(b) 그들은 한통속이에요.
(c) 제가 돈 관리를 해요.
(d) 그건 모두 정교한 속임수예요.

정답_ (c)

16.

해석_ M: 밤늦게까지 시험 공부했어.

W: 잠깐 자지 그래?

M: 선생님이 보시면 어떡해?

W: ______________________

(a) 네가 무시하는 투로 말하는 게 싫어.

(b) 선생님이 알아채시면 내가 깨워 줄게.

(c) 나 이곳에 계속 머무를까 봐.

(d) 그는 막중한 책임을 맡았어.

STEP 2 990 Challenge!

1.

W: Why are you running around like a headless chicken?

M: _______________________________________

(a) That's right. I am in good shape.
(b) I'm changing his signature block on his e-mail.
(c) I am a mouse potato.
(d) I can't find my wedding ring!

해석_ W: 왜 그렇게 난리법석이야?

M: _______________________________

(a) 맞아. 나 컨디션 좋아.
(b) 그의 이메일 서명란을 바꾸고 있어.
(c) 난 컴퓨터광이야.
(d) 내 결혼 반지를 찾을 수가 없어!

해설_ 정신 없이 뛰어다니는 이유에 대해 묻고 있으므로 그 내용이 언급된 (d)가 가장 적절한 응답이다.

어휘_ run around like a headless chicken 정신 없이 뛰어다니다 signature block 서명란 mouse potato 컴퓨터 광(狂)

정답_ (d)

2.

M: How come you always shake your head at everything I say?

W: _______________________________________

(a) Don't bring yourself down to his level.
(b) I think you should pick his brain about it.
(c) You don't talk very reasonably all the time.
(d) Stop being so gabby.

해석_ M: 넌 왜 항상 내가 무슨 말만 하면 다 틀리다고 하니?

W: _______________________________

(a) 그의 수준으로 네 자신을 낮추지 마.
(b) 난 네가 그것에 대해 그의 조언을 구해야 한다고 생각해.
(c) 넌 항상 사리에 맞게 말하지 않아.
(d) 수다 좀 그만 떨어.

해설_ 자신이 하는 말마다 부정적으로 반응하는 이유를 묻고 있으므로 이에 관해 언급한 (c)가 정답이다.

어휘_ shake one's head 고개를 젓다, 부정하다 bring down 끌어내리다, 낮추다 gabby 수다스러운

정답_ (c)

3.

M: What a big tummy!
W: Yeah. I've got quintuplets.
M: How are you going to you support them?
W: _______________________________________

(a) We're a double income couple.
(b) You look as if you're going to land a blow on somebody.
(c) I feel groovy because I finally got my first paycheck.
(d) I have finally become the top dog.

해석_ M: 배가 정말 많이 나왔네요!

W: 네. 다섯 쌍둥이를 가졌어요.

M: 어떻게 기르실 거예요?

W: _______________________________

(a) 우린 맞벌이 부부예요.
(b) 누군가를 때릴 것처럼 보여요.
(c) 드디어 첫 월급을 타서 기분이 무지 좋아요.
(d) 제가 마침내 승자가 됐어요.

해설_ 다섯 명의 아이를 어떻게 부양할 건지 묻고 있으므로 이에 관해 언급한 (a)가 정답이다.

어휘_ tummy 배 quintuplets 다섯 쌍둥이 land a blow 가격하다 feel groovy 기분이 아주 좋다 top dog 승자, 최고 권력을 가진 사람

정답_ (a)

4.

W: Is your pet a house cat or an outdoor cat?
M: It stays in the house at all times.
W: I see. Is it housebroken?
M: _______________________________________

(a) Not quite yet, I am still training her.
(b) Yes, it loves to eat our leftover scraps.
(c) No, I usually feed it puppy chow.
(d) Sure, my cousin is rearing a lizard.

해석_ W: 네 고양이는 실내에서 기르니, 밖에서 기르니?

M: 항상 집에만 있어.

W: 그렇구나. 용변을 잘 가리니?

M: ______________________________

(a) 아직은 아냐, 여전히 훈련시키고 있어.

(b) 응, 우리가 먹고 남긴 음식을 좋아해.

(c) 아니, 보통 퍼피 초우를 먹여.

(d) 물론이지, 내 사촌은 도마뱀을 길러.

해설_ 고양이가 용변을 잘 가리는지 묻고 있으므로 아직 훈련시키는 중이라고 응답한 (a)가 정답이다.

어휘_ housebroken 용변을 잘 가리는 leftover scraps 먹다 남은 음식 puppy chow 퍼피 초우(개 사료 이름) rear 기르다 lizard 도마뱀

정답_ (a)

5.

M: Did you get the culprit?
W: No, he smelled a rat and got away.
M: What's your Plan B?
W: ______________________________

(a) Let's just call the cops.
(b) You've got me frazzled.
(c) Don't lose your head.
(d) I like slasher movies.

해석_ M: 범인을 잡았나요?

W: 아니오, 낌새채고 도망갔어요.

M: 다음 계획은 뭔가요?

W: ______________________________

(a) 그냥 경찰을 부릅시다.

(b) 당신은 날 기진맥진하게 만들어요.

(c) 흥분하지 마세요.

(d) 난 공포 영화를 좋아해요.

해설_ 범인이 도망갔다는 말에 대안이 뭔지 묻고 있으므로 그 내용이 언급된 (a)가 정답이다.

어휘_ get the culprit 범인을 잡다 get away 도망치다 Plan B 차선책, 대안 cops 경찰 frazzled 기진맥진한 lose

one's head 흥분하다 slasher movie (부도덕 · 폭력 행위 등을 묘사한) 공포 영화

정답_ (a)

STEP 3 Actual Test

1.

W: What if I lay my heart out there and it gets stomped on?
M: ______________________________

(a) Constant erosion wears away stones.
(b) Charity begins at home.
(c) If at first you don't succeed, try, try again.
(d) If you don't make any mistakes, you will never learn.

해석_ W: 만일 마음을 열었다가 짓밟히면 어떡해?

M: ______________________________

(a) 열 번 찍어 안 넘어가는 나무 없어.

(b) 팔은 안으로 굽는 거야.

(c) 칠전팔기야.

(d) 구더기 무서워 장 못 담글까.

해설_ 마음을 열었다가 짓밟히면 어떡하냐고 걱정하는 여자에게 충고를 해주는 (d)가 가장 적절하다. 직역하자면 '어떤 실수도 하지 않으면 결코 배울 수 없다'로, 결과를 두려워 말고 마음을 열라고 충고해 주고 있다.

어휘_ lay one's heart out 마음을 열다 get stomped on 짓밟히다 erosion 부식, 침식 wear away 닳아 없애다

정답_ (d)

2.

M: So, when is your baby due?
W: ______________________________

(a) She had a hard time in labor.
(b) My water broke 30 minutes ago.
(c) At the end of April.
(d) He was born last week.

해석_ M: 그래, 출산 예정일이 언제예요?

W: ______________________________

(a) 그녀는 난산을 했어요.

(b) 30분 전에 양수가 터졌어요.

(c) 4월 말이요.

(d) 그 애는 지난주에 태어났어요.

해설_ 출산 예정일이 언제인지 묻고 있으므로 날짜가 언급된 (c)가 정답이다.

어휘_ baby due 출산 예정일 have a hard time in labor 난산하다

정답_ (c)

3.

W: What do you have against your boss?
M: _______________________________________

(a) He's always looking over my shoulder.
(b) I don't like to take a bus.
(c) You know, I like him so much.
(d) Stop going back and forth.

해석_ W: 왜 상사를 싫어하니?
M: _______________________________

(a) 그는 항상 날 감시하거든.
(b) 나 버스 타는 거 싫어해.
(c) 너도 알잖아, 나 그를 무척 좋아해.
(d) 오락가락하지 좀 마.

해설_ What do you have againt ...?는 '~에게 어떤 반감을 가지고 있니?', 즉 '왜 ~를 싫어하니?'의 의미를 나타낸다. 따라서 상사를 싫어하는 이유를 묻고 있으므로 그에 관해 언급한 (a)가 정답이다.

어휘_ look over one's shoulder 감시하다 go back and forth 오락가락하다

정답_ (a)

4.

M: How come Steve's giving you the cold shoulder?
W: We had a nasty fight yesterday.
M: What did you squabble with him about this time?
W: _________________________________

(a) It's so trivial.
(b) He is tied to his mother's apron strings.
(c) Get off the soapbox.
(d) Both teams were nip and tuck throughout the game.

해석_ M: 왜 스티브가 너한테 쌀쌀맞게 대하는 거니?
W: 어제 심하게 싸웠거든.
M: 이번엔 뭣 때문에 싸웠는데?
W: _______________________________

(a) 아주 사소한 거지.
(b) 그는 마마보이야.
(c) 그만 얘기해.
(d) 경기 내내 양쪽 팀이 막상막하였어.

해설_ 이번엔 무슨 일로 다퉜는지 묻고 있으므로 그 내용이 언급된 (a)가 정답이다. (c)의 soapbox는 나무로 만든 '비누 상자'로, 예전에 미국의 정치인들은 이 나무 비누 상자를 휴대용 연단으로 자주 사용했다고 한다. 여기서 유래하여 get on one's soapbox 하면 '연설을 늘어놓다', 반대로 get off one's soapbox 하면 '그만 얘기하다'란 의미로 쓰이게 되었다.

어휘_ give ... a cold shoulder ~에게 쌀쌀맞게 대하다 have a nasty fight 심하게 싸우다 squabble 승강이하다, 말다툼하다 be tied to one's mother's apron strings 엄마 치마폭에 싸여 있다, 마마보이다 nip and tuck 막상막하의

정답_ (a)

5.

W: Have you done those reports for me yet?
M: Not yet. How about manana?
W: Why do something today if you can put it off until tomorrow?
M: ____

(a) I'm a little bogged down.
(b) I'm so sorry. I'll make sure it's done by tomorrow morning.
(c) The copy is smudged.
(d) I was left holding the bag.

해석_ W: 내게 줄 보고서들은 다 준비된 건가요?
M: 아직요. 내일 드리면 어떨까요?
W: 내일로 미룰 수 있는 일이라면 왜 오늘 하죠?
M: _______________________________

(a) 꼼짝할 수가 없어요.
(b) 정말 죄송해요. 내일 아침까지 꼭 끝낼게요.
(c) 복사가 번졌어요.

(d) 제가 죄를 뒤집어썼어요.

해설 내일로 미룰 수 있는 일이라면 하지를 말지 왜 하냐고 나무라고 있으므로 보고서를 끝내지 못한 것에 대한 사과의 내용이 이어져야 자연스럽다. 따라서 정답은 (b).

어휘 manana 내일, 근간에 bogged down 꼼짝 못하는, 수렁에 빠진 be smudged (복사가) 번지다 be left holding the bag (죄·책임 등을) 뒤집어쓰다

정답 (b)

6.

W: May I help you?
M: I'd like to rent a car.
W: Okay. Which type of vehicle are you interested in?
M: I had my eye on that convertible.
W: That's a great car.
M: What's the rate?
W: For 12 hours, it's $28 and for 24 hours, $50.
M: Could you lower the rental fee?
W: Well... I can give you a 5% discount.
M: Great. I'll take it.

Q. Which is correct according to the conversation?

(a) The man wants to buy a convertible.
(b) The man would like to rent a car.
(c) The rental fee is $28 for 24 hours.
(d) The woman is a car dealer.

해석 W: 도와 드릴까요?
M: 차를 렌트했으면 하는데요.
W: 좋아요. 어떤 차종에 관심 있으세요?
M: 저 컨버터블이 맘에 들어요.
W: 아주 멋진 차죠.
M: 렌트비는 얼마예요?
W: 12시간에 28달러, 24시간에 50달러입니다.
M: 렌트비 좀 깎아 주세요.
W: 음… 5퍼센트 할인해 드리죠.
M: 좋군요. 그 차로 하겠어요.

Q. 대화에 따르면 맞는 것은 어느 것인가?

(a) 남자는 컨버터블을 구매하길 원한다.
(b) 남자는 차를 한 대 빌리고 싶어 한다.

(c) 렌트비는 24시간에 28달러이다.
(d) 여자는 자동차 판매원이다.

해설 남자의 첫 번째 대사를 통해 (b)가 정답임을 알 수 있다. (d)는 여자가 자동차 판매원이 아니고 차를 대여해 주는 사람이기 때문에 맞지 않다.

어휘 have one's eye on ~에 눈독을 들이다 convertible 컨버터블(지붕을 접을 수 있게 돼 있는 자동차)

정답 (b)

7.

Worms can stir an immediate fascination in kids. They wiggle and squirm, and vanish into the dirt. Worms also are incredibly useful to the backyard gardener. Worms produce compost that are used in gardening. And for a man living near Pueblo, worm farming makes for his garden-friendly business.

Q. Which of the following is NOT true according to the talk?

(a) Worms can make manure suitable for gardening.
(b) Worm farming helps with garden-friendly business.
(c) Worms are popular with children.
(d) The gardener teaches children how to farm worms.

해석 지렁이는 아이들에게 즉각적인 매력을 일으킬 수 있습니다. 지렁이는 몸을 좌우로 움직이고 꿈틀거리며 흙속으로 사라집니다. 지렁이는 또한 뒤뜰 정원사에게 굉장히 쓸모가 있습니다. 지렁이는 정원 가꾸는 데 사용되는 퇴비를 만들어 냅니다. 그리고 푸에블로 근처에 사는 한 남자에게 있어서, 지렁이 사육은 그의 친환경 정원 사업에 도움이 됩니다.

Q. 담화에 따르면 다음 중 사실이 아닌 것은 어느 것인가?

(a) 지렁이는 정원 가꾸는 데 적합한 퇴비를 만들 수 있다.
(b) 지렁이 사육은 친환경 정원 사업에 도움을 준다.
(c) 지렁이는 아이들에게 인기가 있다.
(d) 정원사는 아이들에게 지렁이 기르는 방법을 가르친다.

해설 지렁이는 아이들에게 매력적인 대상이며, 정원을 가꾸는 데 필요한 퇴비를 만드는 등 쓸모가 있다고 했으므로 정답은 글에 언급되지 않은 (d)가 된다.

어휘_ stir (감정을) 일으키다 fascination 매혹, 매료 wiggle 몸
을 (좌우로) 움직이다 squirm 꿈틀거리다 vanish 사라지
다, 없어지다 compost 퇴비 garden 정원을 가꾸다
make for ~에 도움이 되다 manure 비료, 거름, 퇴비
정답_ (d)

Chapter 3 전화 관련 문제 유형

STEP 1 Pretest Clinic

Part 1

5.

해석_ W: 네 얼굴 보고 싶어. 화상 통화하자.

M: _______________________________

(a) 그녀는 출산 휴가 중이야.

(b) 미안하지만 안 되겠어. 여기서 잘 보이지 않아.

(c) 전화 통화 가능해?

(d) 다른 전화가 왔어.

정답_ (b)

6.

해석_ W: 넌 전화를 골라서 받더라.

M: _______________________________

(a) 이건 최신 기술로 만든 전화기야.

(b) 잡음이 많이 들려.

(c) 끊지 말고 기다려 줘.

(d) 그래 맞아.

정답_ (d)

Part 2

17.

해석_ W: 너 최신 휴대폰 가지고 있더라.

M: 응. 모든 옵션기능을 갖추고 있어.

W: 와. 최신 기능이 전부 들어 있구나.

M: _______________________________

(a) 그 때문에 가격이 약간 비쌌어.

(b) 그들은 가격을 인상했어.

(c) 목을 축이고 싶어.

(d) 이 최신식 휴대폰들은 멋져.

정답_ (a)

18.

해석_ M: 네 휴대폰을 빌릴 수 있을까?

W: 왜? 네 건 어쩌고?

M: 배터리가 다 됐어. 충전기는 집에 두고 왔고.

W: _______________________________

(a) 배터리가 충전되고 있는 중이어서 기다려야 해.

(b) 배터리가 다돼 가고 있으니까 짧게 해.

(c) 배터리가 완전히 충전됐어.

(d) 배터리가 반만 충전됐어.

정답_ (b)

STEP 2 990 Challenge!

1.

W: The reception is terrible in this area.

M: _________________________________

(a) You are always avoiding my calls.

(b) You are impossible to reach by phone.

(c) Call me back when you get a better reception.

(d) You always call when I'm tied up.

해석_ W: 여기 수신 상태가 너무 안 좋아.

　　　 M: _____________________________

　　　 (a) 넌 항상 내 전화 피하더라.

　　　 (b) 전화가 안 되던데.

　　　 (c) 수신 상태가 좋을 때 다시 전화해.

　　　 (d) 넌 항상 내가 바쁠 때 전화하더라.

해설_ 수신 상태가 좋지 않다고 했으므로 상태가 좋을 때 다시 전화 달라는 (c)가 이어지는 것이 자연스럽다.

어휘_ reception 수신 상태 be tied up 바쁘다

정답_ (c)

2.

M: Mom, do you know how to text message?

W: No. It's too difficult to type on the keypad.

M: Come on. If you keep trying, you will eventually get the hang of it.

W: _________________________________

(a) They are trying to kill some time.

(b) You are swatting flies.

(c) I know, but it's such a pain.

(d) I am going to lay it on the line.

해석_ M: 엄마, 문자 메시지 어떻게 보내는지 아세요?

　　　 W: 아니. 문자 입력하는 거 너무 어렵더라.

　　　 M: 그러지 말고 해보세요. 계속 하다 보면, 결국 요령을 터득하

게 되실 거예요.

　　　 W: _____________________________

　　　 (a) 그들은 시간을 끌려고 하고 있어.

　　　 (b) 파리채로 파리를 때려잡고 있구나.

　　　 (c) 알지만 너무 힘들구나.

　　　 (d) 솔직히 말하려고 해.

해설_ 계속 하다 보면 잘하게 될 거라는 격려의 말에 힘들다며 부정적인 반응을 보이는 (c)가 적절하다.

어휘_ text message 문자 메시지를 보내다 keypad 키패드 get the hang of ~의 요령을 터득하다 swat flies 파리채로 파리를 때려잡다 lay it on the line 솔직히 털어놓다

정답_ (c)

STEP 3 Actual Test

1.

M: My phone has been ringing off the hook with job offers.

W: _________________________________

(a) Don't cop out.

(b) The phone cut out.

(c) Insults roll off him like water off a duck's back.

(d) How lucky you are!

해석_ M: 일자리를 주겠다는 전화가 계속해서 오고 있어.

　　　 W: _____________________________

　　　 (a) 발뺌하지 마.

　　　 (b) 전화가 끊겼어.

　　　 (c) 그는 모욕을 당해도 무덤덤해.

　　　 (d) 운이 정말 좋구나!

해설_ off the hook은 '전화기가 제자리에 안 놓인 상태'를 말하는 것으로, ring off the hook 하면 '전화기가 제자리에 못 놓일 만큼 벨이 계속해서 울리다'라는 뜻이 된다. 따라서 여기저기서 일자리를 주겠다는 전화가 걸려 오고 있다고 했으므로 운이 좋다고 말해 주는 (d)가 적절하다. (c)의 like water off a duck's back은 '아무 효과도 없이'의 뜻인데, 오리의 등에 물을 떨어뜨려도 등에 남아 있지 않다는 것에 비유되어 어떤 일이 전혀 효과가 없거나 누군가에게 이야기한 것이 전혀 먹혀들지 않을 경우에 쓸 수 있는 표현이다.

어휘_ cop out 책임을 회피하다, 발뺌하다 cut out (전화) 연결이

끊기다

정답_ (d)

2.

W: He sure does love his new girlfriend. Her number is the only one on his speed dial.

M: ____

(a) Are you still there?
(b) Let the answering machine get it.
(c) There's no dial tone.
(d) She has always been the apple of his eye.

해석_ W: 그는 그의 새 여자친구를 정말 사랑해. 그녀의 전화번호가 단축키에 유일하게 저장돼 있어.

M: ____

(a) 아직 내 말 듣고 있니?
(b) 자동응답기가 받게 내버려 둬.
(c) 신호가 안 떨어져.
(d) 그녀는 항상 그에게 소중한 사람이었지.

해설_ 새 여자친구를 사랑하고 그녀의 전화번호가 유일하게 단축키에 저장돼 있다는 말을 들었으므로 그에게 소중한 사람이라고 응답한 (d)가 적절하다.

어휘_ speed-dial 단축키 the apple of one's eye 소중한 사람

정답_ (d)

3.

M: I'm running out of coins, so I'll be cut off soon.

W: ____

(a) Okay. Call me back when you get home.
(b) There is no dial tone.
(c) I keep getting a busy signal.
(d) All right. We'll take care of that.

해석_ M: 동전이 떨어져가서 전화가 곧 끊길 거야.

W: ____

(a) 좋아. 집에 가서 다시 전화해.
(b) 신호가 안 떨어져.
(c) 계속 통화 중이야.
(d) 알겠습니다. 저희가 처리해 드릴게요.

해설_ 동전이 다돼 가서 전화가 곧 끊길 거라고 했으므로 (a)가 적절한

응답이다. (c)는 계속 통화 중이라고 말할 때 쓸 수 있는 표현이다.

어휘_ cut off (통화·연락 등을) 가로막다

정답_ (a)

4.

W: My friend spoke on the phone till the cows came home.

M: How long did you talk for?

W: For more than a hour and a half.

M: ____

(a) Don't have a cow, brother.
(b) Tom bought a motorcycle just for the heck of it.
(c) She talks up to old people even though she's young.
(d) That's a heck of a long time.

해석_ W: 친구랑 오랫동안 통화했어.

M: 얼마나 오래 했는데?

W: 한 시간 반 넘게.

M: ____

(a) 너무 화내지 마, 형.
(b) 톰은 이렇다 할 이유도 없이 오토바이를 샀어.
(c) 그녀는 나이도 어리면서 나이 많은 사람에게 건방지게 말해.
(d) 엄청 긴 시간이네.

해설_ 한 시간 반 넘게 통화했다는 여자의 말에 대한 남자의 반응으로 적절한 것은 (d)다. (a)의 Don't have a cow.는 상대방이 불같이 화를 낼 때 쓸 수 있는 표현이다.

어휘_ till the cows come home 언제까지나, 오랫동안 have a cow 몹시 화를 내다 for the heck of it 이렇다 할 이유도 없이 talk up to (손윗사람에게) 건방지게 말하다 a heck of 대단한, 엄청난

정답_ (d)

5.

W: I was trying to get you on the horn but you didn't answer.

M: Sorry. I dropped my phone, and broke the LCD.

W: You'd better buy a new one. There are so many new models out at the moment.

M: ____

(a) Ok, I'll buy one tomorrow.
(b) Don't play the horn at night.
(c) Let's just drop the subject.
(d) You should change the wallpaper on your cell phone.

해설_ 휴대폰을 새로 구입하는 게 낫겠다고 충고하고 있으므로 이를 받아들인 (a)가 정답이다.

어휘_ get on the horn 전화하다   LCD(= liquid crystal display) 액정 표시 장치   play the horn 호른을 불다   drop the subject 이야기를 그만두다   wallpaper 배경 화면

정답_ (a)

6.

W: How are you doing in your advanced calculus class?
M: I'm just lost most of the time.
W: That's because you skipped the beginning part of the semester.
M: I should have enrolled in an easier subject.
W: How about your other subjects?
M: They're all a piece of cake.
W: Hang in there.

Q. Which is correct according to the conversation?

(a) The woman follows the calculus class very well.
(b) The woman skipped the beginning part of the semester.
(c) The man is having difficulties with his calculus class.
(d) The man prefers calculus to other subjects.

해석_ W: 요즘 고급 미적분 수업 잘 듣고 있니?

M: 거의 헤매고 있어.

W: 네가 학기 초반 수업을 빼먹어서 그래.

M: 좀 더 쉬운 과목으로 등록했어야 했는데.

W: 다른 과목들은 어떠니?

M: 모두 누워서 떡 먹기지.

W: 잘 버텨 봐.

Q. 대화에 따르면 맞는 것은 어느 것인가?

(a) 여자는 미적분 수업을 매우 잘 이해한다.

(b) 여자는 학기 초반 수업을 빼먹었다.

(c) 남자는 미적분 수업에 어려움을 겪고 있다.

(d) 남자는 다른 과목들보다 미적분을 더 좋아한다.

해설_ 수업 때 거의 헤매고 있다고 했으므로 (c)가 정답임을 알 수 있다.

어휘_ advanced 진보한, 고급의   calculus 미적분   hang in there 곤란을 견디다, 버티다

정답_ (c)

7.

I have always been convinced that one of the biggest influences on children as they grow up is the behavior of their parents. That is, you can read all the parenting books you want and try to influence them by telling them all the right things. But, ultimately, it is difficult for most people to be consistently different in their actions from who they are. Kids spend so much of their time with their parents that they end up forming judgments about the world based on observing their behavior.

Q. What is the main point of the talk?

(a) Parent's behavior has great effect on children's growth.
(b) Children form judgments towards the world as they grow up.
(c) Parenting books are great help when raising a child.
(d) Children spend much of their time with their parents.

해석_ 저는 아이들이 자랄 때 그들에게 가장 큰 영향을 주는 것 중 하나

가 그들 부모의 행동이라고 늘 확신해 왔습니다. 즉, 당신은 원하는 모든 육아책들을 읽으면서 모든 올바른 것들을 아이들에게 말해 줌으로써 그들에게 영향을 주기 위해 노력합니다. 하지만 궁극적으로 대부분의 사람들이 그들의 행동에 있어서 그들의 참모습으로부터 끊임없이 달라지기란 어렵습니다. 아이들은 아주 많은 시간을 그들의 부모와 함께 보내기 때문에 부모의 행동을 관찰하는 것을 토대로 세상에 대한 판단력 형성을 끝마칩니다.

Q. 담화의 요점은 무엇인가?

(a) 부모의 행동은 아이의 성장에 큰 영향을 미친다.
(b) 아이들은 자라면서 세상에 대한 판단력을 형성한다.
(c) 육아책은 아이를 키우는 데 큰 도움이 된다.
(d) 아이들은 부모와 많은 시간을 함께 보낸다.

해설_ 아이들이 자라면서 부모의 행동에 의해 큰 영향을 받는다는 내용이므로 정답은 (a)가 된다.

어휘_ parenting 육아(법), 양육

정답_ (a)

Chapter 4 대인 관련 문제 유형

STEP 1 Pretest Clinic

Part 1

7.

해석_ W: 안녕, 존. 어떻게 지내니?

M: ______________________________

(a) 그것에 쾌감을 느꼈어.
(b) 너와 나 사이의 오해를 풀고 싶을 뿐이야.
(c) 그럭저럭 잘 지내.
(d) 이걸 묵과할 수는 없어.

정답_ (c)

8.

해석_ M: 봉급 인상을 제안받았는데, 승진도 했으면 좋겠어.

W: ______________________________

(a) 다 지난 일이야.
(b) 두 마리 토끼를 동시에 잡을 수는 없어.
(c) 네가 역경을 견뎌내길 바래.
(d) 그는 날 맘에 들어 했어.

정답_ (b)

Part 2

19.

해석_ M: 일 조금 일찍 끝내고 나랑 같이 갈래?

W: 집에만 틀어박혀 지내는 네가 어딜 가려구?

M: 우리 조부모님이 정원이랑 소풍 장소가 있는 작은 땅을 갖고 계셔.

W: ______________________________

(a) 최대한 빠른 길로 갈게.
(b) 멋지다! 갈게.
(c) 크게 발전했어.
(d) 그건 한동안 불확실한 상태에 있을 거야.

정답_ (b)

20.

해석_ W: 난 아직도 우리가 함께 보냈던 지난 여름을 기억해.

M: 우린 함께 해변을 걸었지.

W: 이번 여름에도 해변에 가자. 우리 둘이 기름 값을 나눠 낼 수

있잖아.

M: ______________________________

(a) 솔직히 말해!

(b) 나 잘 거야.

(c) 부추기지 마. 나 빈털터리야.

(d) 동병상련이군.

정답_ (c)

STEP 2 990 Challenge!

1.

W: Are you going to just keep sitting on the fence?

M: ______________________________

(a) Yes. It's a house name.

(b) Yes. I can't place you.

(c) No, I paid my dues.

(d) No, I'll make a decision.

해석_ W: 계속 관망만 하고 있을 거예요?

　　　M: ______________________________

　　　　(a) 네. 그 이름은 모르는 사람이 없어요.

　　　　(b) 네. 당신을 어디서 만났는지 기억이 나질 않네요.

　　　　(c) 아뇨, 난 책임을 다했어요.

　　　　(d) 아뇨, 결단을 내릴 거예요.

해설_ 팔짱 끼고 보고만 있을 거냐는 여자의 말에 부정하며 결단을 내릴 거라고 응답한 (d)가 적절하다.

어휘_ sit on the fence 형세를 관망하다 house name 가족처럼 잘 알려진 이름 place ~를 …에서 만난 기억이 나다 pay one's dues 책임을 다하다

정답_ (d)

2.

W: Sorry for barging in like this.

M: ______________________________

(a) I always watch my mouth in public.

(b) You should stay away from that siren.

(c) It's okay. I'm glad you stopped in.

(d) My boss treats me like a doormat.

해석_ W: 이렇게 불쑥 찾아와서 죄송해요.

M: ______________________________

(a) 난 항상 사람들 앞에서 입조심을 해요.

(b) 저 요부로부터 떨어져 있어야 해요.

(c) 괜찮아요. 이렇게 들러 주시니 좋은데요.

(d) 사장이 날 쓰레기 취급해요.

해설_ 연락도 없이 방문한 것에 대해 사과하고 있으므로 괜찮다고 말하며 환영하는 (c)가 적절한 응답이다.

어휘_ barge in 예고 없이 남의 집에 방문하다 watch one's mouth 입조심하다 stay away from ~에서 떨어져 있다 siren 고혹적인 미인, 요부 treat ... like a doormat ~를 굴욕적으로 대접하다, 쓰레기 취급하다

정답_ (c)

3.

W: I can't bear this chicken feed any longer!

M: It's no use complaining.

W: No, enough is enough. I'm going to give my boss a piece of my mind.

M: ______________________________

(a) How pathetic!

(b) Chill out.

(c) Live a little.

(d) Out of luck.

해석_ W: 더 이상 이 쥐꼬리만한 월급을 못 참겠어!

　　　M: 불평해 봐야 아무 소용 없어.

　　　W: 아니, 참을 만큼 참았어. 사장에게 따끔하게 한마디 해야겠어.

　　　M: ______________________________

　　　　(a) 너무 딱해!

　　　　(b) 진정해.

　　　　(c) 좀 더 즐겨.

　　　　(d) 재수가 없어.

해설_ 얼마 안 되는 월급에 대해 불평하며 사장에게 한마디 해야겠다는 여자에게 진정하라고 말해 주는 (b)가 가장 적절하다.

어휘_ chicken feed 쥐꼬리만한 월급, 푼돈 Enough is enough. 이 정도면 충분하다 give ... a piece of one's mind ~에게 따끔하게 한마디 하다 pathetic 애처로운 Chill out. 진정해, 침착해 Live a litte. 좀 더 즐겨라 Out of luck. 재수가 없어

정답_ (b)

4.

M: You look stunning in that coat.
W: You make me feel on the top of the world.
M: You look like a princess.
W: ____

(a) I know you're just putting me on, but thank you anyway.
(b) Then just renew the lease.
(c) I'm tired of reading fairy tales.
(d) I bumped heads with him on a few issues.

해석_ M: 너 그 코트 입으니까 정말 멋지다!
　　　W: 넌 날 무지 기분 좋게 만들어.
　　　M: 공주 같아.
　　　W: ________________________________

　　　(a) 놀리는 건 줄 알지만, 어쨌든 고마워.
　　　(b) 그럼 그냥 재계약해.
　　　(c) 동화 읽기도 지겹다.
　　　(d) 몇 가지 문제로 그와 티격태격했어.

해설_ 계속 이어지는 남자의 칭찬에 대한 반응으로 적절한 것은 (a)다. put on에는 여러 가지 의미가 있는데, 여기서처럼 누군가를 '놀리다'의 의미로도 쓰인다는 것을 잘 알아두자.

어휘_ stunning 놀랄 만큼 멋진, 매력적인 feel on the top of the world 기분이 매우 좋다 put ... on ~를 놀리다 lease 임대 계약 fairy tale 동화 bump heads 티격태격하다

정답_ (a)

STEP 3 Actual Test

1.

W: I'm a little upset that you were talking about me behind my back.
M: ____

(a) My car is in mint condition.
(b) I'm truly sorry about that.
(c) This exam is in the bag.
(d) Don't keep me in suspense.

해석_ W: 네가 나 없는 데서 내 얘길 해서 기분이 좀 상했어.
　　　M: ________________________________

(a) 제 차는 최상의 상태입니다.
(b) 정말 미안해.
(c) 이번 시험은 틀림없이 합격이야.
(d) 애간장 좀 태우지 마.

해설_ 기분이 상했다고 했으므로 이에 대해 사과하는 (b)가 적절하다. (a)의 in mint condition은 '최상의, 아주 완벽한 상태'란 뜻으로, 물건 등의 품질이 아주 좋거나 완벽한 상태인 경우를 나타낼 때 쓸 수 있는 표현이다. 여기서 mint는 '갓 주조된 동전'을 말한다.

어휘_ behind one's back ~의 등 뒤에서, 없는 데서 in the bag 보장된, 확실한 keep ... in suspense ~를 마음 졸이게 하다

정답_ (b)

2.

M: My bad, I missed the deadline this month.
W: ____

(a) I'm a clean freak.
(b) Better safe than sorry.
(c) He's always badmouthing the company.
(d) No sweat.

해석_ M: 미안해, 이번 달 마감일을 못 지켰어.
　　　W: ________________________________

　　　(a) 난 결벽증이 있어.
　　　(b) 후회하느니 미리 조심하는 게 나아.
　　　(c) 그 사람은 항상 회사 불평만 늘어놔.
　　　(d) 괜찮아.

해설_ 마감일을 못 지켜서 미안하다고 사과하고 있으므로 괜찮다고 응답한 (d)가 이어지는 것이 자연스럽다.

어휘_ My bad. 내 잘못이야, 미안해 clean freak 청결광 Better safe than sorry. 후회하느니 미리 조심하는 게 낫다 badmouth 헐뜯다, 욕하다 No sweat. 괜찮아, 걱정 마

정답_ (d)

3.

M: Congratulations on the great finish!
W: ____

(a) Thanks, I'll be fine.
(b) Thanks. How about painting the town red to celebrate?

(c) Cheer up, it's not that bad.

(d) I'm on top of this situation.

해석_ M: 일 잘 끝난 거 축하해!

W: _______________________

(a) 고마워, 괜찮아질 거야.

(b) 고마워. 축하하기 위해 코가 삐뚤어지게 술 마시고 놀면 어때?

(c) 기운 내, 그렇게 나쁘지 않아.

(d) 난 이 상황을 잘 처리하고 있어.

해설_ 일이 아주 잘 끝난 것에 대해 축하해 주고 있으므로 이에 답례하는 (b)가 정답이다. paint the town red는 직역하자면 '돌아다니며 빨간 페인트칠을 하다'로, 미국 영화를 보면 술 취한 애들이 스프레이 페인트를 들고 다니며 여기저기 뿌리는 장면이 나오곤 하는데, 거기서 비롯된 표현으로 '정신없이 마시고 놀다'란 뜻을 나타낸다.

어휘_ on top of the situation 상황을 잘 처리하고 있다, 감당을 잘하고 있다

정답_ (b)

4.

M: I'm starving. I didn't have time to fill the void in my belly.

W: I'm with you. Why don't we just hit the cafeteria?

M: I'm up for that. It's convenient and it won't break the bank.

W: _______________________

(a) I'm being blackballed.

(b) Let's hustle.

(c) I've been on pins and needles all day.

(d) We're not out of the woods yet.

해석_ M: 배고파 죽겠어. 허기를 채울 시간이 없었거든.

W: 나도 그래. 구내 식당에 가는 거 어때?

M: 좋아. 편리하고 비싸지도 않잖아.

W: _______________________

(a) 나 따돌림 당하고 있어.

(b) 빨리 가자.

(c) 하루 종일 마음을 졸였어.

(d) 우린 아직 위험에서 벗어난 게 아니야.

해설_ 구내 식당에 가서 먹는 데 생각을 같이하고 있으므로 (b)가 이어

지는 것이 가장 적절하다.

어휘_ fill the void in one's belly 허기를 채우다 be up for (기꺼이) ~할 준비가 돼 있다 break the bank 돈이 많이 들다 blackball (회, 클럽 따위에서) 제명하다, 배척하다 hustle 서두르다 be on pins and needles 마음을 졸이다 out of the woods 위험에서 벗어난

정답_ (b)

5.

W: My folks have been nagging me day and night.

M: Why? Did you do anything wrong?

W: They can't stand me bumming around.

M: _______________________

(a) Job-hunting would be a good solution.

(b) I'm blowing his cover.

(c) I make ends meet.

(d) It's the thought that counts.

해석_ W: 우리 부모님은 밤낮으로 나한테 잔소리하셔.

M: 왜? 뭐 잘못했어?

W: 내가 빈둥빈둥 돌아다니는 것을 못 견뎌서.

M: _______________________

(a) 구직이 좋은 해결책이 될 거야.

(b) 그 사람의 정체를 밝힐 거야.

(c) 간신히 벌어 먹고 살아.

(d) 중요한 건 생각이지.

해설_ 빈둥거리며 돌아다니는 걸 부모가 참지 못한다고 했으므로 이에 대한 조언이 담긴 (a)가 정답이다.

어휘_ one's folks 양친, 가족, 친척 nag 잔소리하다 bum around 빈둥빈둥 돌아다니다 blow one's cover 정체를 드러내게 하다, 폭로하다 make ends meet 근근이 벌어 먹고 살다 count 가치가 있다, 중요하다

정답_ (a)

6.

M: How are your preparations for the trade show going?

W: Yes, but we're having some trouble.

M: So, you mean you are falling behind schedule?

W: No, not really. But we need sample computers from this series to finish training our staff.

M: In other words, you want those computers as soon as possible.

W: That's right. We'd like to receive them by February.

M: Well, I think February is too early.

W: Then, the second week of March would be OK.

Q. Which is correct according to the conversation?

(a) Schedule of the show will be postponed.

(b) The man is not quite done with the preparation of the show.

(c) The man works at the computer company.

(d) The woman needs sample computers by the second week of March.

해석_ M: 무역 전시회 준비는 잘돼 가나요?

W: 네, 근데 문제가 좀 있어요.

M: 그럼, 예정보다 늦어질 거란 얘긴가요?

W: 아니오, 그렇진 않아요. 하지만 저희 직원들을 훈련시키는 것을 끝내기 위해 이 기종들의 샘플 컴퓨터가 필요합니다.

M: 다시 말해서, 가능한 한 빨리 그 컴퓨터들을 원하신다는 거군요.

W: 그렇습니다. 2월까지 그 컴퓨터들을 받았으면 해요.

M: 음, 2월은 너무 빠른 것 같은데요.

W: 그럼, 3월 둘째 주도 괜찮습니다.

Q. 대화에 따르면 맞는 것은 어느 것인가?

(a) 전시회 일정이 미뤄질 것이다.

(b) 남자는 아직 전시회 준비를 끝내지 못했다.

(c) 남자는 컴퓨터 회사에서 일한다.

(d) 여자는 3월 둘째 주까지 샘플 컴퓨터가 필요하다.

해설_ 3월 둘째 주까지 보내 주면 된다고 했으므로 정답은 (d)가 된다.

어휘_ fall behind schedule 예정보다 늦어지다

정답_ (d)

7.

Alaskan Wine has been produced in limited edition vintages each year since its introduction in 2003. A big beer for big winters, this brew has garnered a steady following in Alaska. Bottled for the first time in 2007, the balanced flavor collaboration between hops, malt and high alcohol showcases the barley wine style, winning first place at the 2007 Toronado Barley Wine Festival and bronze at the 2008 World Beer Cup.

Q. What is the purpose of the report?

(a) To point out both strong and weak points of Alaskan Wine

(b) To introduce Alaskan Wine

(c) To recommend the barley wine

(d) To invite people to the wine exhibition

해석_ 알래스카 와인은 2003년에 소개된 이래로 매년 한정판의 포도주를 생산해 오고 있습니다. 추운 겨울을 위한 알코올 도수가 조금 높은 이 맥주가 알래스카에서 꾸준한 인기를 얻고 있습니다. 2007년에 처음으로 유통된, 홉 열매, 엿기름, 그리고 높은 알코올 도수의 알맞게 어우러진 맛은 발리 와인 스타일을 선보였습니다. 이 와인은 2007 토론토 발리 와인 축제에서 우승하고 2008년 세계 맥주 컵에서 동메달을 차지했습니다.

Q. 기사의 목적은 무엇인가?

(a) 알래스카 와인의 장점과 단점을 지적하기 위해

(b) 알래스카 와인을 소개하기 위해

(c) 발리 와인을 추천하기 위해

(d) 사람들을 와인 박람회에 초대하기 위해

해설_ 알래스카 와인의 생산 및 판매 현황에 대한 언급이 나오고, 와인 축제와 세계 맥주 컵에서 상을 탄 얘기를 전하는 것으로 보아 알래스카 와인에 대한 소개를 하려는 것이므로 (b)가 정답이다.

어휘_ brew 양조주, 맥주 garner 획득하다, 얻다 hops 홉 열매 (맥주에 쓴맛을 내는 것) malt 엿기름 showcase (신제품 등을) 소개하다 barley wine 발리 와인(도수 높은 맥주)

정답_ (b)

Chapter 5 사회 관련 문제 유형

STEP 1 Pretest Clinic

Part 1

9.

해석_ W: 가격 할인을 받기 위해 항공 마일리지를 사용할 수 있을까요?

M: ______________________________

(a) 이 항공사 마일리지 프로그램에 벌써 십만 마일을 적립했어요.

(b) 그들은 잔디를 깎기 시작했어요.

(c) 수염만 깎아 주세요.

(d) 물론이죠. 항공 마일리지 카드 번호를 알려주세요.

정답_ (d)

10.

해석_ M: 다른 회사들에 비해 우리 회사 월급은 너무 적어.

W: ______________________________

(a) 말동무 좀 해줘.

(b) 스트레스를 많이 받았어.

(c) 네 월급에 비하면 내 월급은 적어.

(d) 사실이긴 한데, 우리 회사는 규모가 작잖아.

정답_ (d)

Part 2

21.

해석_ W: 선생님, 죄송하지만 이륙하기 전에 휴대폰을 꺼주셔야 합니다.

M: 아, 미안해요. 막 끄려고 했어요.

W: 협조해 주셔서 감사합니다.

M: ______________________________

(a) 당신의 영어가 발전하길 바래요.

(b) 저는 휴대폰으로 알람을 맞췄어요.

(c) 제발 내 일에 간섭하지 마세요.

(d) 별말씀을요.

정답_ (d)

22.

해석_ W: 현금으로 지불하시겠어요, 아님 신용카드로 지불하시겠어요?

M: 신용카드로요. 할부로 지불할 수 있을까요?

W: 물론이죠. 몇 개월 할부로 하시겠어요?

M: ______________________________

(a) 아니오. 직불카드를 사용해야 할 것 같아요.

(b) 12개월 할부로 할게요.

(c) 일시불로 지불해야 했어요.

(d) 그녀는 2,000원을 덜 거슬러 줬어요.

정답_ (b)

STEP 2 990 Challenge!

1.

W: Can the payments be spread out?

M: ______________________________

(a) Thank you for your inquiry on our product.

(b) Further delays will turn the clients away.

(c) Yes, but you'll be charged interest.

(d) Yes, I would be happy to give you our estimates.

해석_ W: 지불이 연장될 수 있을까요?

M: ______________________________

(a) 저희 제품에 대해 문의해 주셔서 감사합니다.

(b) 더 지연되면 고객들이 다른 곳으로 갈 거예요.

(c) 네, 하지만 이자를 내시게 될 거예요.

(d) 네, 당신에게 견적을 제공해 드리게 되어 기쁩니다.

해설_ 지불 연장이 가능한지 묻고 있으므로 이에 답한 (c)가 정답이다.

어휘_ spread out 연장하다 inquiry 질문, 문의 turn away 쫓아버리다 estimate 견적

정답_ (c)

2.

M: How does this cardigan grab you?

W: ______________________________

(a) You have a sticker on your pants.

(b) I have a discount coupon.

(c) Black can very easily get dusty.

(d) She wants to go in what she's wearing.

해석_ M: 이 카디건 어때?

W: ______________________________

(a) 네 바지에 스티커 붙어 있어.

(b) 나 할인 쿠폰 가지고 있어.

(c) 검정색은 먼지가 너무 잘 붙어.

(d) 그녀는 지금 입고 있는 옷을 입고 가길 원해.

해설_ 카디건이 맘에 드는지 묻고 있으므로 옷 모양이나 색상에 대한 의견이 언급된 선택지를 고르면 된다. 따라서 정답은 (c).

어휘_ cardigan 카디건 grab 마음을 사로잡다 dusty 먼지투성이의, 먼지가 많은

정답_ (c)

3.

W: You must be making a killing!
M: Actually, I burnt my fingers in the end.
W: Really? I heard you cleaned up in the real estate market.
M: ______________________________________

(a) I did in the beginning, but I eventually went bust.
(b) Yes, you must save money for a rainy day.
(c) No. The old man won ten million dollars on the lottery.
(d) No, my company will turn a profit next year.

해석_ W: 돈을 진짜 많이 버나 봐요!

M: 실은, 결국엔 손해를 많이 봤어요.

W: 정말요? 당신이 부동산 시장에서 큰돈을 벌었다고 들었는데요.

M: ______________________________

(a) 처음엔 그랬는데, 결국 파산했어요.

(b) 네, 만일의 경우에 대비해서 돈을 저축해야 해요.

(c) 아니오. 그 노인은 천만 달러짜리 복권에 당첨됐어요.

(d) 아니오, 제 회사는 내년에 흑자로 전환될 거예요.

해설_ 돈을 많이 번 것으로 들었다는 여자의 말에 처음엔 그랬지만 결국 망했다고 응답한 (a)가 정답이다. 손해를 많이 봤다는 남자의 첫 번째 대사를 통해 부정적인 내용의 응답이 이어질 것임을 짐작할 수 있다.

어휘_ make a killing 돈을 많이 벌다 burn one's fingers (사업이나 투자에서) 크게 손해를 보다 in the end 결국에는 clean up (큰돈 등을) 벌다 go bust 파산하다 for a rainy day 만일의 경우에 대비해서 turn a profit 흑자로 전환되다

정답_ (a)

4.

M: What's good here?
W: Everything is delicious. Try the pizza and pasta.
M: Okay. I'll get 2 pizzas and 3 pastas.
W: ______________________________________

(a) I think your eyes may be bigger than your stomach.
(b) I'm so stuffed. I need a doggy bag.
(c) Please, don't get your hopes up too high.
(d) I'm at the end of my rope.

해석_ M: 여기 뭐 잘해요?

W: 모두 맛있습니다. 피자랑 파스타 드셔 보세요.

M: 좋아요. 피자 두 판하고 파스타 셋 시킬게요.

W: ______________________________

(a) 주문을 너무 많이 하시는 것 같아요.

(b) 배가 너무 불러요. 남은 음식을 싸 달라고 해야겠어요.

(c) 제발 너무 기대하지 마세요.

(d) 더 이상 방법이 없어요.

해설_ 남자가 혼자 먹을 거면서 피자 두 판과 파스타 셋을 주문하고 있으므로 너무 많이 시키는 것 같다고 말해 주는 (a)가 적절하다. Your eyes may be bigger than your stomach.는 상대가 먹을 수 있는 양보다 더 많이 주문했을 때 사용할 수 있는 표현이다. 남자의 첫 번째 대사에 나오는 What's good here?는 식당에서 어떤 음식을 잘하는지 물을 때 자주 사용하는 표현으로 잘 기억해 두자.

어휘_ doggy bag (식당에서) 먹다 남은 음식을 싸주는 종이 봉투 get one's hopes up 큰 기대를 갖다 be at the end of one's rope 진퇴양난에 빠지다, 속수무책이다

정답_ (a)

STEP 3 Actual Test

1.

W: Sir, the golf clubs will cost extra to ship.
M: ______________________________________

(a) I'll try extra hard.
(b) The divers discovered the pirate's treasure in a sunken ship.
(c) At one time, clubs were considered to be

part of the baggage.
(d) I joined the golf club.

해석_ W: 손님, 골프채를 부치시려면 추가 비용을 내셔야 합니다.

　　　M: ________________________________

　　　(a) 특히 열심히 해볼게요.

　　　(b) 잠수부들은 가라앉은 배에서 해적의 보물을 발견했어요.

　　　(c) 예전엔 골프채가 수화물의 일부로 간주됐어요.

　　　(d) 골프 클럽에 가입했어요.

해설_ 추가 비용을 내야 한다는 말에 예전엔 골프채도 수화물로 취급
　　　했다며 불평하는 (c)가 적절하다.

어휘_ golf club 골프채, 골프 클럽　try extra hard 특히 열심히
　　　해보다　diver 잠수부　pirate 해적　sunken ship 난파선
　　　at one time 예전에는, 한때

정답_ (c)

2.

W: I'm Kelly Kim. I'm the new recruit here.
M: ____

(a) Hi, Ms. Kim. Welcome aboard.
(b) I want to get settled in with my job.
(c) We actively recruit new members.
(d) I'm going to really lose my temper.

해석_ W: 저는 켈리 김입니다. 이 회사 신입사원이에요.

　　　M: ________________________________

　　　(a) 안녕하세요, 김 양. 입사를 환영합니다.

　　　(b) 제 일에 적응하고 싶어요.

　　　(c) 우리는 적극적으로 새 회원을 모집해요.

　　　(d) 저 정말 화낼 거예요.

해설_ 신입사원이 인사를 하고 있으므로 환영의 인사가 이어져야 자연
　　　스럽다. 따라서 정답은 (a). welcome aboard는 원래 기장이나
　　　선장 등이 승객에게 하는 환영 인사인데, 여기서처럼 신입사원
　　　을 환영할 때도 쓸 수 있다.

어휘_ get settled in ~에 정착하다, 자리잡다　lose one's
　　　temper 화내다

정답_ (a)

3.

M: Are you sure your business will survive in
　　China?
W: ____

(a) I'm up to my ears in work.
(b) We are trying to target the niche market.
(c) Well, I'm dying to live in China.
(d) I'm sorry, but I have to work on my project.

해석_ M: 당신 사업이 중국에서 살아남을 거라고 확신해요?

　　　W: ________________________________

　　　(a) 일 때문에 꼼짝 못하겠어요.

　　　(b) 틈새 시장을 공략해 보려구요.

　　　(c) 글쎄요, 중국에서 살고 싶어 죽겠어요.

　　　(d) 죄송하지만, 제 프로젝트 일을 해야 해요.

해설_ 사업이 살아남을 수 있겠냐는 질문에 틈새 시장을 공략할 거라
　　　고 응답한 (b)가 정답이 된다. 이런 문제 유형의 경우, 긍정이나
　　　부정의 응답이 나오는 것이 보통이지만 이처럼 간접적으로 응답
　　　하는 경우도 있다는 걸 명심해 두자.

어휘_ be up to one's ears in work 일이 밀려 있다　niche
　　　market 틈새 시장　be dying to ~하고 싶어 죽겠다

정답_ (b)

4.

M: Where do we pick up our luggage?
W: I should have a gander at the information
　　map.
M: Ok, but get a move on because the taxi is
　　waiting.
W: ____

(a) I went to the department store to window
　　shop.
(b) Clue in.
(c) Don't worry. I'll be back in a jiffy.
(d) Let's get a move on.

해석_ M: 우리 짐을 어디서 찾지?

　　　W: 내가 안내도를 한번 보고 올게.

　　　M: 좋아, 근데 택시가 기다리고 있으니까 서둘러.

　　　W: ________________________________

　　　(a) 윈도쇼핑하러 백화점에 갔어요.

　　　(b) 주의해.

　　　(c) 걱정 마. 금방 올게.

　　　(d) 서두르자.

해설_ 서둘러 보고 오라고 했으므로 금방 오겠다는 (c)가 이어지는 것
　　　이 적절하다.

5.

W: I've worked so hard, and I want a raise.
M: So, how do you plan on doing that?
W: I'll hit up my boss for it.
M: ___________________________________

(a) I've been on edge lately with my job.
(b) Don't boss me around.
(c) They have two thoughts on the subject.
(d) Break a leg.

해석_ W: 난 아주 열심히 일해 왔으니 월급 인상을 원해.

M: 그래서 어쩌려구?

W: 사장에게 월급 인상을 부탁할 거야.

M: ___________________________

(a) 요새 일 때문에 신경이 곤두서 있어.

(b) 나한테 이래라저래라 하지 마.

(c) 그들은 그 문제에 관해 두 가지 견해를 가지고 있어.

(d) 행운을 빌게.

해설_ 여자가 사장에게 월급 인상을 부탁할 거라고 했으므로 행운을
빌어 주는 (d)가 가장 적절하다. 유럽인들은 요정이나 귀신들이
사람들의 행복을 시기하여 해코지한다고 믿었기에 공연이나 경
기를 앞두고 있는 배우나 선수에게 반어적으로 Break a leg.이
라고 말하면서 행운을 빌어 주었다고 한다. 여기서 비롯되어 '행
운을 빌어', '잘 해'라고 할 때 이 표현을 사용한다.

어휘_ hit up ... ~에게 부탁하다 be on edge 안절부절못하다,
신경이 곤두서 있다 boss ... around ~에게 이래라저래라
하다

정답_ (d)

6.

M: You know what?
W: What?
M: I played pool with Eddie yesterday.
W: Who was the winner?
M: Me. I put him in his place.
W: Good job. It was just the other day he was
   bragging about his pool skills.
M: Well, he is no match for me.

Q. What is the main focus of the conversation?

(a) The man beat Eddie in a pool match
    yesterday.
(b) The man bragged about his pool skills.
(c) The woman dislikes Eddie.
(d) The woman had a match with the man.

해석_ M: 너 그거 알아?

W: 뭘?

M: 어제 에디랑 포켓볼 쳤어.

W: 누가 이겼는데?

M: 나. 그 녀석 콧대를 꺾어놨지.

W: 잘했다. 며칠 전에 자기 포켓볼 실력에 대해 자랑을 늘어 놨
   었는데.

M: 음, 걘 나한테 상대가 안 돼.

Q. 대화의 주된 내용은 무엇인가?

(a) 남자는 어제 포켓볼 시합에서 에디를 이겼다.

(b) 남자는 그의 포켓볼 실력에 대해 자랑했다.

(c) 여자는 에디를 싫어한다.

(d) 여자는 남자와 시합을 했다.

해설_ 남자가 포켓볼 시합에서 이긴 얘기를 하고 있으므로 정답은 (a)
다. 남자의 세 번째 대사에 나오는 I put him in his place.는 직
역하자면 '그를 그의 자리에 돌려놨다', 즉 '분수를 알게 해줬
다', '콧대를 꺾어놨다'란 뜻을 나타낸다.

어휘_ play pool 포켓볼 치다 brag about ~에 대해 자랑하다,
허풍을 떨다 be no match for ~에게 적수가 되지 못하다

정답_ (a)

7.

Hispanics made up nearly half of the more than
1 million people who became U.S. citizens last
year. The number of Latinos who became
Americans in fiscal year 2008 more than
doubled over the previous year, to 461,317.
That's nearly half of 1,046,539 new citizens
overall in 2008, a 58 percent increase from
2007. Others arrived from places such as
Cuba, El Salvador, Nicaragua, and Guatemala,
just to name a few.

Q. What is the main idea the speaker is trying
   to make?

(a) Lots of illegal immigrants in America

(b) Increasing Latin immigrants in the U.S.

(c) Hispanics acquiring citizenship

(d) The unwillingness of the U.S. government to accept immigrants

해석_ 작년에 미국 시민이 된 100만 명 이상의 사람들 중 거의 절반이 라틴 아메리카인이었습니다. 2008 회계 연도에 미국인이 된 라틴 아메리카인의 수는 461,317명이었던 작년보다 두 배 이상 많았습니다. 그것은 2007년부터 58퍼센트 증가하여, 2008년 총 1,046, 539명의 새로운 시민들 중 거의 절반에 해당합니다. 나머지 사람들은, 몇몇 예를 들면, 쿠바, 엘살바도르, 나카라과, 그리고 과테말라와 같은 나라에서 왔습니다.

Q. 화자가 이야기하려고 하는 요지는 무엇인가?

(a) 미국의 많은 불법 이민자들

(b) 증가하고 있는 미국의 라틴계 이민자

(c) 시민권을 획득한 라틴 아메리카인

(d) 이민자들을 더 이상 받고 싶지 않은 미국 정부

해설_ 라틴 아메리카 이민자 수가 증가하고 있다는 내용이므로 정답은 (b)가 된다.

어휘_ fiscal year 회계 연도 just to name a few 몇 가지 예를 들면

정답_ (b)

Chapter 6 공공 관련 문제 유형

STEP 1 Pretest Clinic

Part 1

11.

해석_ W: 여기서 시내에 있는 김 씨 사무실에 가는 데 가장 빠른 방법이 뭔가요?

M: ＿＿＿＿＿＿＿＿＿＿＿＿＿＿＿＿

(a) 운전 중일 땐 조심하세요.

(b) 고르세요.

(c) 로스엔젤레스 시내에서 아파트를 구할까 생각 중이에요.

(d) 바깥 교통이 혼잡해요. 지하철을 타는 게 훨씬 나을 거예요.

정답_ (d)

12.

해석_ M: 콜레스테롤과 혈압이 높나요?

W: ＿＿＿＿＿＿＿＿＿＿＿＿＿＿＿＿

(a) 아니오, 아파 죽겠어요.

(b) 네, 체온계로 한번 재 봅시다.

(c) 네. 속이 아주 더부룩해요.

(d) 네, 기름진 음식을 먹지 말아야 해요.

정답_ (d)

Part 2

23.

해석_ M: 지난주에 전송한 제 우편물이 어디쯤에 있는지 알아보려고 들렸어요.

W: 등기 우편으로 보내셨나요?

M: 네. 근데 아직 못 받았대요.

W: ＿＿＿＿＿＿＿＿＿＿＿＿＿＿＿＿

(a) 어디 위치 추적을 할 수 있는지 한번 볼게요.

(b) 그는 행방을 감췄어요.

(c) 저울에 올려 놓으세요.

(d) 배달 증명 우편으로 보낼게요.

정답_ (a)

24.

해석_ W: 혈액 검사하게 주먹을 꽉 쥐어 주시겠어요?

M: 네. 검사 결과는 언제 받을 수 있나요?

W: 다음주 월요일이에요. 이제 피가 멈출 때까지 누르고 계세요.

M: ______________________________

(a) 그냥 일회용 밴드를 붙여도 되나요?

(b) 혈액형이 뭐예요?

(c) 유산했었나요?

(d) 마지막으로 생리한 게 언제였죠?

정답_ (a)

STEP 2 990 Challenge!

1.

W: Please take off your shoes and put them on the scanner.

M: ______________________________

(a) It's sort of pricey.
(b) Ok, just a sec.
(c) It's a flophouse.
(d) Give the go-by.

해석_ W: 신발을 벗어서 스캐너 위에 놓아 주세요.

M: ______________________________

(a) 그건 좀 비싼 거예요.

(b) 알겠어요, 잠깐만요.

(c) 거긴 값싼 여인숙이에요.

(d) 무시하세요.

해설_ 공항 검색대에서 접할 수 있는 대화 내용으로, 스캐너 위에 신발을 올려 놓으라고 했으므로 이에 응하는 (b)가 정답이다.

어휘_ flophouse 값싼 여인숙 give the go-by 무시하다

정답_ (b)

2.

W: You shouldn't violate the traffic laws.

M: But there is no crosswalk here.

W: Look. There is a pedestrian overpass just over there.

M: ______________________________

(a) Sorry, officer. I will be more careful next time.
(b) I don't want to walk all the way there.
(c) You shouldn't run the light.
(d) The road was congested.

해석_ W: 교통 법규를 위반해서는 안 돼.

M: 하지만 여긴 횡단보도가 없잖아.

W: 봐. 저쪽에 육교가 있어.

M: ______________________________

(a) 죄송해요, 경관님. 다음엔 더 조심할게요.

(b) 거기까지 걸어가기 싫어.

(c) 신호를 무시하고 건너면 안 돼.

(d) 도로가 혼잡했어.

해설_ 저쪽에 육교가 있다는 말에, 거기까지 걸어가기 싫다고 응답한 (b)가 가장 적절하다.

어휘_ violate 위반하다 pedestrian overpass 육교 run the light 신호를 무시하고 가다 congested 혼잡한

정답_ (b)

3.

W: You are always sawing wood.

M: Am I? No, I don't.

W: Trust me. Every time you pig out, you snore.

M: ______________________________

(a) You had better face the music now.
(b) That was a half-baked scheme.
(c) Oh, I'm never going to pig out again.
(d) Hicks are mentally more laid-back.

해석_ W: 넌 항상 코를 골아.

M: 내가? 아니야, 나 코 안 골아.

W: 날 믿어. 넌 과식할 때마다 코를 골아.

M: ______________________________

(a) 지금 잘못을 인정하는 게 나아.

(b) 그건 현실성 없는 계획이었어.

(c) 이런, 다신 과식하지 않을 거야.

(d) 촌사람들은 정신적으로 더 느긋해.

해설_ 과식할 때마다 코를 곤다는 말을 들었으므로 다신 많이 먹지 않겠다는 (c)가 이어지는 것이 적절하다.

어휘_ saw wood(= snore) 코를 골다 pig out 과식하다 face the music 당당히 벌을 받다, 잘못을 인정하다 half-baked 현실성 없는, 불충분한 hick 시골뜨기 laid-back 느긋한, 한가로운

정답_ (c)

1.

M: If you just shoot me the correct address, I'll log it into a navigation device.

W: _______________________________________

(a) Don't shoot a look at me.
(b) Great. I'll send you the address by text.
(c) You can shoot me.
(d) He was a navigator.

해석_ M: 정확한 주소를 알려주시면, 네비게이션에 입력할게요.

W: _______________________________

(a) 절 힐끗 보지 마세요.
(b) 잘됐군요. 문자로 주소 보내 드릴게요.
(c) 당신은 날 쏠 수 있어요.
(d) 그는 항해자였어요.

해설_ 주소를 알려 달라고 했으므로 문자로 보내 주겠다고 응답한 (b)가 정답이다.

어휘_ shoot 보내 주다, ~을 건네주다   log 기록하다   shoot a look at ~을 힐끗 보다   navigator 항해자

정답_ (b)

2.

W: Do I have to fill anything out to mail this by overnight delivery?

M: _______________________________________

(a) I have a bun in the oven.
(b) I feel bummed out.
(c) Yes. Let me get the form for you.
(d) It was a nightmare.

해석_ W: 이것을 익일 배송으로 보내기 위해 작성해야 할 게 있나요?

M: _______________________________

(a) 나 임신했어요.
(b) 기분이 꿀꿀해요.
(c) 네. 신청 용지를 드릴게요.
(d) 그건 악몽이었어요.

해설_ 작성해야 할 것이 있는지 묻고 있으므로 이에 답한 (c)가 정답이다.

어휘_ fill out 작성하다   mail ~을 우송하다, 우편에 부치다

overnight delivery 익일 배송   have a bun in the oven 임신 중이다   bummed out 우울한, 낙담한   nightmare 악몽

정답_ (c)

3.

M: Do I need an appointment?

W: _______________________________________

(a) You need to see a doctor.
(b) Yes, you're supposed to meet Dr. Jang at 2 p.m.
(c) I suggest you brush regularly.
(d) No. It's on a first come, first served basis.

해석_ M: 예약을 해야 하나요?

W: _______________________________

(a) 당신은 병원에 가야 해요.
(b) 네, 당신은 오후 2시에 장 선생님을 뵙기로 돼 있어요.
(c) 규칙적으로 이를 닦을 것을 권합니다.
(d) 아뇨. 선착순이에요.

해설_ 예약이 필요한지 묻고 있으므로 선착순이라고 응답한 (d)가 정답이다.

어휘_ first come, first served 선착순

정답_ (d)

4.

W: You are really starting to gain weight.

M: I know. I'm going to start doing weight training and weightlifting for 3 hours per day.

W: That's a pretty heavy load to carry!

M: _______________________________________

(a) He's become a real gym rat.
(b) Then I'll run on a treadmill for a half hour every day instead.
(c) It looks like he's run out of steam.
(d) I have lungs like a horse.

해석_ W: 너 정말 살 찌기 시작했어.

M: 나도 알아. 하루 3시간씩 웨이트 트레이닝과 역도 운동을 하기 시작할 거야.

W: 그건 너무 과한 것 같다!

M: ________________________________

(a) 그는 완전히 체육관에서 살더라구.

(b) 그럼 대신 매일 30분 동안 러닝머신 위에서 뛸 거야.

(c) 그는 지쳐 보여.

(d) 난 폐활량이 아주 좋아.

해설_ 운동 분량이 너무 과한 것 같다는 여자의 의견을 받아들여 대신 러닝머신을 30분씩 하겠다고 응답한 (b)가 정답이다.

어휘_ weightlifting 역도 heavy load to carry 한번에 하기에 너무 많은 분량 gym rat 체육관에서 운동만 열심히 하는 사람 treadmill 러닝머신 run out of steam 힘이 빠지다, 지치다 have lungs like a horse 폐활량이 아주 좋다

정답_ (b)

5.

M: Are you feeling okay?

W: No, I'm feeling under the weather.

M: Let me feel your forehead. It's really hot.

W: ________________________________

(a) I should take a remedy for my fever.

(b) Your gums are bleeding.

(c) I had a nosebleed this afternoon.

(d) I feel like there is a rock in my stomach.

해석_ M: 괜찮니?

W: 아니, 몸이 좀 안 좋아.

M: 이마를 짚어 볼게. 진짜 뜨겁다.

W: ________________________________

(a) 해열제를 먹어야겠어.

(b) 네 잇몸에서 피가 나.

(c) 오늘 오후에 코피가 났어.

(d) 소화가 전혀 안 되는 것 같아.

해설_ 남자가 이마가 뜨겁다고 했으므로 해열제를 먹어야겠다는 (a)가 가장 적절하다.

어휘_ feel under the weather 몸 상태가 좋지 않다 feel one's forehead 이마를 짚어 보다 remedy 치료약 gum 잇몸 have a nosebleed 코피가 나다

정답_ (a)

6.

M: Hey, Susan. I'd like to have a word with you.

W: Sure. What's up?

M: Why do you take it out on me whenever anything goes wrong these days?

W: Please don't get me wrong. I've just been stressed lately. It's nothing personal.

M: Still, it's starting to become a real problem.

W: Well, actually, I broke up with my boyfriend just a couple of weeks ago.

Q. Which is correct according to the conversation?

(a) The man just didn't see eye to eye with the woman on a lot of things.

(b) The woman wants to know why the man takes it out on her.

(c) The woman parted ways with her boyfriend.

(d) The man is very stressed out these days.

해석_ M: 야, 수잔. 너랑 잠깐 얘기를 나눴으면 하는데.

W: 그래. 무슨 일인데?

M: 요즘 뭐가 잘못 될 때마다 왜 나한테 화풀이하는 거니?

W: 제발 오해하지 마. 요즘 그냥 스트레스를 받아서 그래. 개인적인 감정이 있어서 그런 건 아니야.

M: 그래도 정말 거슬리기 시작하고 있어.

W: 저어, 실은 남자 친구랑 불과 몇 주 전에 헤어졌어.

Q. 대화에 따르면 맞는 것은 어느 것인가?

(a) 남자는 여자와 많은 것에 관해 의견이 맞지 않았다.

(b) 여자는 남자가 왜 그녀에게 화풀이하는지 알기를 원한다.

(c) 여자는 그녀의 남자 친구와 헤어졌다.

(d) 남자는 요즘 스트레스를 많이 받고 있다.

해설_ 여자의 마지막 대사를 통해 (c)가 정답임을 알 수 있다.

어휘_ take it out on ~에게 화풀이하다 get ... wrong ~를 오해하다 see eye to eye with ~와 의견이 일치하다 part ways with ~와 헤어지다

정답_ (c)

7.

Imagine $23 billion in quarters, nickels and dimes. That's how much money Americans drop into vending machines each year. The most popular snack sold on Earth in a vending machine is a Snickers bar. The average vending price for this chocolate bar is 70 cents. At a typical supermarket or discount store, the price is about 55 cents per bar, a difference of 15 cents. Why do you think people drop lots of money into vending machines? Office worker Chris knows why "Because I'm lazy."

Q. What is the main point the speaker is trying to make?

(a) Vending machines are more useful than stores.
(b) Many people drop coins under vending machines.
(c) Various vending machines have come out since last year.
(d) It's not economical buying goods from vending machines.

해석_ 230억 달러를 25센트, 5센트, 그리고 10센트 동전으로 상상해 보세요. 그것은 미국인들이 매년 자판기에 넣는 돈의 액수입니다. 자판기에서 팔린 가장 인기 있는 스낵은 스니커즈 바입니다. 이 초콜릿 바의 평균 자판기 가격은 70센트입니다. 일반 슈퍼마켓이나 할인점에서는 그 가격이 15센트 차이가 나는 약 55센트입니다. 여러분은 왜 사람들이 많은 돈을 자판기에 넣는다고 생각하십니까? 회사원 크리스는 자신이 게으르기 때문이라고 생각합니다.

Q. 화자가 이야기하려고 하는 요점은 무엇인가?

(a) 자판기는 상점보다 더 유용하다.
(b) 많은 사람들이 자판기 밑에 동전을 떨어뜨린다.
(c) 작년부터 다양한 자판기가 출시되었다.
(d) 자판기에서 상품을 사는 것은 경제적이지 않다.

해설_ 자판기에서 파는 초콜릿 바의 가격이 일반 상점에서 파는 것보다 더 비싸다는 얘기를 통해 결국 자판기에서 상품을 사는 것이 돈 낭비임을 시사하고 있다. 따라서 정답은 (d)가 된다.

어휘_ **quarter** 25센트 **nickel** 5센트 **dime** 10센트 **come out** (상품을) 출시하다

정답_ (d)

Chapter 7 주제 파악 문제 유형

STEP 1 Pretest Clinic

Part 3

25.

해석_ W: 너 많이 화난 것 같다. 무슨 일이니?
　　M: 우리 형은 늘 내 물건을 마치 자기 것처럼 써.
　　W: 아, 그가 네 허락 없이 뭔가 가져갔니?
　　M: 응. 내가 입으려고 했던 약식 야회복을 입고 고등학교 동창회에 갔어.
　　W: 음, 그럼 너도 형 거 입으면 되잖아.
　　M: 싫어. 형 옷은 내 스타일이 아니야.

　　Q. 대화의 주제는 무엇인가?

　　(a) 고등학교 동창회에 가기
　　(b) 남자가 매우 흥분한 이유
　　(c) 그의 새 약식 야회복
　　(d) 물건 나눠 쓰기

정답_ (b)

26.

해석_ M: 사무엘을 찾고 있어요.
　　W: 방금 나가셨어요.
　　M: 이런! 그를 꼭 만나야 하는데요.
　　W: 그의 친구분이세요?
　　M: 네. 우린 오랜 친구예요. 그가 어디를 가는 중인지 짐작이 가세요?
　　W: 죄송해요. 전혀 모르겠는데요.
　　M: 그에게 전화를 걸어 어디에 있는지 확인해 주실 수 있나요?

　　Q. 대화의 주된 내용은 무엇인가?

　　(a) 남자는 사무엘을 몹시 보고 싶어 한다.
　　(b) 여자는 사무엘이 어디 있는지 모른다.
　　(c) 사무엘은 남자의 대학 동창생이다.
　　(d) 남자는 사무엘을 따라잡기 위해 발걸음을 서둘렀다.

정답_ (a)

Part 4

31.

해석_ 인간과 마찬가지로 개도 비만이 되면 건강에 해롭습니다. 여기에 모든 개 주인이 먹이를 줄 때 명심해야 할 몇 가지 규칙이 있습니다. 규칙적인 식사 시간을 정하세요. 불규칙적인 식사 시간

은 개의 소화 계통에 영향을 줄 수 있고 결국에는 만성적인 소화 불량의 원인이 됩니다. 개의 물과 음식 그릇을 매일 같은 장소에 놓아두는 것 또한 중요합니다. 만약 엄격히 통제된 시간에 먹이를 주게 되면 당신의 개는 단지 매일 한 끼나 두 끼의 식사만을 필요로 하게 됩니다.

Q. 담화를 가장 잘 요약한 것은?

(a) 개는 한번에 너무 많은 먹이를 먹어서는 안 된다.
(b) 개의 음식과 물 그릇은 일정한 장소에 두어야 한다.
(c) 개들도 불규칙적으로 먹이를 먹으면 소화 불량에 걸린다.
(d) 인간과 개 모두 살이 찌는 것은 안 좋다.

정답_ (d)

32.

해석_ 우리들 중 몇 안 되는 사람들만이 지금 신선한 석류 주스나 자연산 연어의 두툼한 토막과 같은 건강 식품을 고를 여유가 있습니다만, 만약 인스턴트 식품을 줄이고 주방에서 더 많은 시간을 보내는 것을 마다하지 않는다면 여러분은 여전히 여러분의 식료품 카트를 적당한 가격의, 영양가 높은 음식들로 가득 채울 수 있습니다. 비결은 계획을 세우는 것입니다. 비용을 줄이면서 영양가를 유지하기 위해서는 계획을 세워야 합니다. 여러분은 식사를 계획하고, 간식을 계획하고, 요리 준비 시간을 잘 계획해야 합니다.

Q. 담화의 주된 목적은 무엇인가?

(a) 사람들에게 쇼핑할 곳을 알려주기 위해서
(b) 사람들에게 유기농 식품을 고르는 방법에 관해 알려주기 위해서
(c) 사람들에게 영양가 높은 요리에 관해 알려주기 위해서
(d) 가격도 적당하면서 영양가 있는 음식을 먹는 방법에 관해 알려주기 위해서

정답_ (d)

STEP 2 990 Challenge!

1.

M: It's unbelievable how much winter brings me down.
W: Yeah. I sometimes feel depressed during winter.
M: What should I do to lift my spirit?
W: How about going on a trip?
M: Any suggestions on where I can go?
W: Hawaii. You'll feel rejuvenated.

M: That's not a bad idea.

Q. What are the speakers talking about?

(a) Planning their trip to Hawaii
(b) Taking a trip for refreshment
(c) Why the woman is depressed
(d) Why they dislike winter

해석_ M: 겨울이 되니까 우울해 죽겠어.
W: 그래. 나도 겨울엔 이따금씩 우울하더라.
M: 어떻게 하면 기분이 좋아질까?
W 여행을 가면 어때?
M: 추천해 줄 만한 곳 있어?
W 하와이. 네게 활기를 되찾게 해줄 거야.
M: 그거 괜찮은 생각이다.

Q. 화자들은 무엇에 관해 이야기하고 있는가?

(a) 그들의 하와이 여행 계획
(b) 기분 전환을 위한 여행 가기
(c) 여자가 우울한 이유
(d) 그들이 겨울을 싫어하는 이유

해설_ 우울해하는 남자에게 여행을 제안하고 있으므로 정답은 (b)가 된다.

어휘_ **bring down** 우울하게 하다, 축 처지게 하다   **lift one's spirit** 원기를 북돋다, 기분을 고조시키다   **feel rejuvenated** 활기를 되찾다

정답_ (b)

2.

General Motors Corp. is planning to temporarily close most of its U.S. factories for up to nine weeks this summer because of slumping sales and growing inventories of unsold vehicles, a GM spokesman announced today. The exact dates of the closures are not yet known, but he said they will occur around the normal two-week shutdown period in July whereby GM changes from one model year to the next. He further suggested that a few plants which make more popular models could remain open for part of the shutdown period, but at reduced assembly line speeds.

Q. Which of the following is the best title for the

report?

(a) GM Workers Being Laid-off
(b) GM's Decision on 9-Week Shutdown
(c) GM Closing Plants as Part of Reconstruction
(d) Unsold Vehicles Due to Stronger Competition

해석_ GM은 판매 부진과 안 팔린 자동차 재고의 증가로 인해 올 여름 최장 9주 동안 미국 내 대부분 공장의 문을 임시 닫을 계획이라고 GM 대변인이 오늘 발표했습니다. 정확한 폐업 일자는 아직 알려지지 않았지만, 대변인은 GM이 차 모델을 바꾸는 시점인 7월의 정상적인 2주간의 조업 중지 기간 즈음이 될 것이라고 말했습니다. 또한 그는 보다 인기 있는 모델들을 제조하는 몇몇 공장들은 조업 중지 기간 중에도 얼마 동안 계속 가동시킬 수 있지만 조립공정 속도는 늦춰질 것이라고 밝혔습니다.

Q. 기사의 제목으로 가장 적절한 것은?

(a) 일시 해고되는 GM 근로자들
(b) 9주간 임시 폐업을 결정한 GM
(c) 구조 조정의 일환으로서 공장 문을 닫는 GM
(d) 더 치열해진 경쟁으로 인해 안 팔린 자동차

해설_ GM이 판매 부진과 재고 누적으로 인해 공장을 임시 폐쇄할 것이라는 내용을 전하고 있으므로 정답은 (b)가 된다.

어휘_ inventory 재고품 (목록) closure 폐쇄, 폐업 shutdown 일시 휴업, 조업 중지 laid-off 일시 해고된 reconstruction 구조 조정

정답_ (b)

STEP 3 Actual Test

1.

W: I received an invitation for a housewarming, but I can't figure out what to take.

M: _______________________________________

(a) The gift was such a surprise.
(b) My housewarming party was such a big hassle.
(c) I'm working my tail off to prepare for a housewarming.
(d) You'd better give them something useful for their new pad.

해석_ W: 집들이 파티에 초대를 받았는데 뭘 가져가야 할지 모르겠어.

M: _______________________________________

(a) 그 선물은 놀랄 만한 것이었어.
(b) 우리 집들이는 정말 대단히 성가신 일이었어.
(c) 집들이 준비를 위해 죽어라 일하고 있어 .
(d) 새집에 유용한 걸 주는 게 좋아.

해설_ 집들이 선물로 뭘 사야 할지 고민하고 있으므로 이에 관한 해결책을 제시해 주는 (d)가 이어지는 것이 가장 적절하다.

어휘_ figure out 해결하다 hassle 성가신 일 work one's tail off (꼬리가 빠지도록) 아주 열심히 일하다 pad 〈속어〉 아파트, 집

정답_ (d)

2.

M: Hey, babe, how about getting hitched?
W: _______________________________________

(a) It's okay. You don't owe me an explanation.
(b) Let's do it!
(c) You should consider a career change.
(d) You're dragging your feet!

해석_ M: 자기야, 우리 결혼할까?

W: _______________________________________

(a) 괜찮아. 해명 안 해도 돼.
(b) 그렇게 하자!
(c) 직업 바꾸는 걸 고려해 봐.
(d) 꾸물거리고 있네!

해설_ 여자에게 결혼하자고 제안하고 있으므로 이를 받아들이는 (b)가 정답이다.

어휘_ get hitched 결혼하다 owe ... an explanation ~에게 해명해야 하다 drag one's feet 꾸물거리다

정답_ (b)

3.

M: This is the seventh reject we've had in an hour!

W: _______________________________________

(a) The machine is probably out of whack.
(b) So you're not available at the moment?
(c) The meeting was cancelled yesterday.
(d) It's your turn to decide now.

해석_ M: 한 시간에 7번째 불량품이 나왔어!

W: ________________________________

(a) 기계가 아마도 고장인가 봐.

(b) 그래서 지금 시간이 없어?

(c) 회의는 어제 취소됐어.

(d) 지금은 네가 결정할 차례야.

해설_ 한 시간 동안 불량품이 7번째 나오고 있다고 했으므로 기계가 고장 난 것 같다고 응답한 (a)가 가장 적절하다.

어휘_ reject 불량품 out of whack 고장 난

정답_ (a)

4.

M: Holy cow! I can't get a dial tone.

W: Do you want to make an outgoing phone call?

M: Yeah. Can you tell me how to do it?

W: ________________________________

(a) I'll pass it on to him.

(b) The line is busy.

(c) Dial 9 and you'll get a dial tone.

(d) This is a call for you.

해석_ M: 이런! 신호음이 안 들리네요.

W: 외부 전화 하시길 원하세요?

M: 네. 어떻게 하면 되죠?

W: ________________________________

(a) 그에게 전해 줄게요.

(b) 지금 통화 중입니다.

(c) 9번을 누르시면 신호음이 들릴 거예요.

(d) 전화 받으세요.

해설_ 외부 전화 사용법을 묻고 있으므로 이에 관해 설명해 주는 (c)가 정답이다.

어휘_ outgoing phone call 외부 전화 pass on 전달하다

정답_ (c)

5.

W: What's your take on Schubert?

M: He was a prodigy. His music makes my heart flutter.

W: Really? Why's that?

M: ________________________________

(a) My heart flutters whenever I see her.

(b) Because his music is so beautiful and

surreal.

(c) It's still cold. So I have goose bumps.

(d) I can play Schubert.

해석_ W: 슈베르트에 대해서 어떻게 생각해?

M: 그는 천재였어. 그의 음악을 들으면 가슴이 두근거려.

W: 정말? 그건 왜?

M: ________________________________

(a) 그녀를 만날 때마다 가슴이 두근거려.

(b) 그의 음악은 너무 아름답고 환상적이거든.

(c) 아직 추워. 그래서 닭살이 돋았어.

(d) 난 슈베르트 곡을 연주할 수 있어.

해설_ 슈베르트 음악을 들으면 왜 가슴이 두근거리는지 묻고 있으므로 그 이유가 언급된 (b)가 정답이다.

어휘_ take 〈구어〉 견해 prodigy 천재 flutter 마음이 설레다, 두근거리다 surreal 환상적인 have goose bumps 닭살이 돋다, 소름이 끼치다

정답_ (b)

6.

M: Mom, I need a new computer.

W: Why? You have a laptop computer.

M: It takes ages to download anything from the net.

W: Didn't you say you wouldn't need another computer for a while.

M: But mom, please! It's way too slow.

W: Cut it out! We are in financial difficulty.

Q. What is the main focus of the conversation?

(a) The man's computer is broken out.

(b) The man wants to buy a new computer.

(c) The woman can't afford to buy her son a computer.

(d) The woman's computer is too slow.

해석_ M: 엄마, 저 새 컴퓨터가 필요해요.

W: 왜? 너 노트북 있잖아.

M: 인터넷에서 다운받는 데 시간이 너무 오래 걸려요.

W: 한동안 다른 컴퓨터는 필요 없다고 하지 않았니?

M: 하지만 엄마, 제발요! 너무 느리다구요.

W: 그만둬! 우리집은 경제적인 어려움에 처해 있어.

Q. 대화의 주된 내용은 무엇인가?

(a) 남자의 컴퓨터가 고장 났다.

(b) 남자는 새 컴퓨터를 사고 싶어 한다.

(c) 여자는 그녀의 아들에게 컴퓨터를 사 줄 형편이 안 된다.

(d) 여자의 컴퓨터는 속도가 너무 느리다.

해설_ 컴퓨터 속도가 너무 느려 새 컴퓨터를 사 달라고 조르는 상황이므로 정답은 (b)가 된다. 남자의 마지막 대사에 나오는 **way too** 는 무엇인가가 너무 지나치거나, 혹은 너무 심해서 좋지 않다는 것을 나타내고자 할 때 쓸 수 있는 강조 표현으로, 여기서는 컴퓨터 속도가 너무 느리다는 것을 강조하고 있다.

어휘_ take ages 오래 걸리다 Cut it out! 그만둬!, 입 닥쳐!

정답_ (b)

7.

My issue with this almost theatrical bike show is the disregard for traffic safety. If you are going to promote safe biking, why are you disregarding all traffic rules? Is not a bicycle like a car when using it for transportation on a busy street? I would happily support your cause if you were obeying both traffic and pedestrian lights. I have traveled to cities like Amsterdam where the bike is the most popular form of transportation.

Q. Which is correct according to the talk?

(a) Riding a bicycle on a busy street is recommendable.
(b) Most people like cycling on busy streets.
(c) The speaker is advertising a bike.
(d) Traffic rules must be kept even when riding a bicycle.

해석_ 이런 거의 과장된 자전거 쇼에 대한 나의 논점은 교통 안전에 대한 무시입니다. 만약 당신이 안전한 자전거 타기를 장려하고자 한다면, 왜 당신은 모든 교통 규칙을 무시합니까? 번화가에서 교통 수단으로 이용할 때 자전거는 자동차와 같지 않나요? 만약 당신이 교통 신호와 보행자 신호를 준수한다면 저는 당신의 주장을 기꺼이 지지하는 바입니다. 저는 자전거가 가장 대중적인 교통 수단인 암스테르담과 같은 도시들을 여행했습니다.

Q. 담화에 따르면 맞는 것은 어느 것인가?

(a) 번화가에서는 자전거를 이용하는 것이 좋다.

(b) 대부분의 사람들은 번화가에서 자전거 타기를 좋아한다.

(c) 화자는 자전거를 홍보하고 있다.

(d) 자전거를 탈 때에도 교통 규칙을 지켜야 한다.

해설_ 자전거를 탈 때에도 교통 규칙을 준수해야 한다는 내용이므로 정답은 (d)가 된다.

어휘_ theatrical 과장된   disregard 무시, 경시   pedestrian light 보행자 신호

정답_ (d)

Chapter 8 내용 파악 문제 유형

STEP 1 Pretest Clinic

Part 3

27.

해석 W: 프런트입니다. 뭘 도와 드릴까요?

M: 302호인데요.

W: 네, 손님. 방에 무슨 문제가 있으신가요?

M: 네, 변기가 작동을 않는군요.

W: 손잡이를 왼쪽 끝까지 돌리셨나요?

M: 네, 그랬어요.

W: 관리실에 전화해서 즉시 사람을 보내도록 하겠습니다.

M: 얼마나 기다려야 하나요?

W: 기술자가 5분 후면 도착할 겁니다.

M: 알겠어요, 고마워요.

Q. 대화에 따르면 맞는 것은 어느 것인가?

(a) 수도꼭지가 작동을 안 한다.

(b) 변기가 고장 났다.

(c) 여자는 관리실에서 일하고 있다.

(d) 손잡이를 오른쪽으로 돌려야 한다.

정답 (b)

28.

해석 W: 뭘 도와 드릴까요, 손님?

M: 아내에게 줄 생일 선물을 찾고 있어요.

W: 아내 분의 나이를 여쭤봐도 될까요?

M: 네, 40대 중반입니다.

W: 아, 그러시군요. 이 드레스 어떠세요?

M: 하지만 그건 청 단색이네요. 줄무늬가 있는 빨간색 옷은 없나요?

W: 손님, 청 단색이 중년 여성들 사이에서 유행입니다.

M: 혹시 아내가 이 옷을 싫어하면 교환할 수 있을까요?

W: 물론이죠. 환불도 가능합니다.

M: 고마워요.

Q. 대화에 따르면 맞는 것은 어느 것인가?

(a) 청 단색은 중년 여성들 사이에서 매우 인기 있다.

(b) 남자는 파란색을 좋아하지 않는다.

(c) 여자는 남자가 드레스를 사도록 설득하고 있다.

(d) 남자는 빨간 드레스를 살 것이다.

정답 (a)

Part 4

33.

해석 팀버의 개인적인 삶은 비밀이었고, 심지어 그의 가까운 친구들 조차도 그가 무슨 일을 겪고 있는지 알지 못했습니다. 그러나 우리 모두가 알고 공유했던 것은 그의 사랑, 그의 시간, 그의 아량, 그리고 그의 장난이었습니다. 여러분은 그의 전시회들 중 한 곳을 방문하심으로써 그의 일대기를 확인하실 수 있습니다. 저는 그의 명예를 기리기 위해 많은 기념식이 열릴 것이라 확신하며, 첫 공식 추모식은 2009년 4월 10일에 콜로라도 스프링스에서 열릴 것입니다. 참석하시는 모든 분들을 환영합니다. 정확한 시간과 장소는 곧 알려 드리겠습니다.

Q. 이 안내문에 따르면, 팀버의 삶에 대해 어떻게 알 수 있는가?

(a) 그의 자서전을 읽음으로써

(b) 그의 작품을 통해서

(c) 그의 가장 절친한 친구들을 통해서

(d) 그의 기념식에 참석함으로써

정답 (b)

34.

해석 응급 환자들의 응급실 대기 시간이 점점 더 길어짐에 따라, 몇몇 병원은 홈페이지에 대기 시간을 올리고 있습니다. 옥스너 헬스 시스템의 의사들은 그 온라인 시스템이 뉴욕 지역에 위치한 네 곳 응급실의 부담을 덜어 주고 있다고 말합니다. 그 새로운 시스템에 대해, 접수 코디네이터는 사람들이 기다려야 할지, 아니면 12마일 반경 이내에 모두 위치해 있는 다른 세 개의 병원 중 한 곳으로 가야 할지를 바로 결정할 수 있다고 말했습니다.

Q. 온라인 시스템은 무엇인가?

(a) 대기 시간을 확인하는 데 사용되는 시스템

(b) 병원의 위치를 알아내는 데 사용되는 시스템

(c) 의사들에 의해 사용되는 정보 시스템

(d) 뉴욕에서 실행되고 있는 식이요법 프로그램

정답 (a)

STEP 2 990 Challenge!

1.

M: I heard you are heading off to Florida this week. What's the occasion?

W: I have been obsessed with Florida since the age of 11. I went to Disney World and the beach with my family for the first time ever there.

M: How long are you planning on staying there for?

W: Just until the end of spring break. So I will be back on the 24th.

M: I hope you have a blast. I have a test right after the break, so I need to spend my time studying.

W: That's too bad.

Q. What is correct according to the conversation?

(a) The woman used to like Florida when she was young.

(b) The woman is going to Disney World in Florida.

(c) The man has never been to Florida.

(d) The man will spend the most of the spring studying.

해석_ M: 이번주에 플로리다 간다면서? 무슨 일로 가는 거야?

W: 11살 때부터 플로리다를 정말 좋아했어. 거기서 처음으로 가족과 함께 디즈니 월드랑 해변에 갔었지.

M: 거기서 얼마나 오래 머무를 계획이니?

W: 봄 방학 끝날 때까지만. 그러니까 24일에 돌아올 거야.

M: 즐거운 시간 보내길 바랄게. 난 방학 끝나자마자 시험이 있어서 공부하면서 보내야 해.

W: 그거 안됐구나.

Q. 대화에 따르면 맞는 것은 무엇인가?

(a) 여자는 어렸을 때 플로리다를 좋아했었다.

(b) 여자는 플로리다의 디즈니 월드에 갈 것이다.

(c) 남자는 플로리다에 가본 적이 없다.

(d) 남자는 봄 방학 대부분을 공부하면서 보낼 것이다.

해설_ 봄 방학이 끝나자마자 시험이 있어서 공부하면서 지낼 거라고 했으므로 (d)가 정답임을 알 수 있다. (a)는 어릴 때만 좋아했던 게 아니라 지금도 좋아하기 때문에 틀리며, (c)는 알 수 없는 내용이다.

어휘_ be obsessed with ~에 사로잡히다 have a blast 즐거운 시간을 보내다

정답_ (d)

2.

Jack Cardiff, the British filming director who won an Academy Award for his stunning color work on the 1947 drama "Black Narcissus" and who later became an Oscar-nominated director, has died. He was 94. Cardiff, who as a filming director was known as a pioneer of Technicolor and a "master of light," died on Wednesday of age-related causes at his home in Ely, England. Cardiff began as a child actor in silent movies and continued to remain professionally active until about three years ago.

Q. Which of the following is NOT mentioned in this report?

(a) He started his career as an actor.

(b) He participated in the development of a Technicolor film.

(c) He didn't win the award for Best Director.

(d) He continued to work until the age of 91.

해석_ 1947년 드라마 〈검은 수선화〉에서 놀랄 만큼 멋진 컬러 작업으로 아카데미 상을 받았고, 후에 오스카 감독상 후보에도 오른 영국의 영화 촬영 감독 잭 카디프가 사망했다. 그의 나이 94세였다. 테크니컬러의 개척자, 그리고 '빛의 거장'으로 알려진 카디프는 수요일 영국 엘리에 있는 그의 자택에서 노환으로 사망했다. 카디프는 무성 영화에서 아역 배우로 시작하여 약 3년 전까지 전문적으로 활동을 계속했었다.

Q. 이 기사에서 언급되지 않은 것은 어느 것인가?

(a) 그는 배우로서 그의 일을 시작했다.

(b) 그는 테크니컬러 영화의 개발에 참여했다.

(c) 그는 최우수 감독상을 받지 못했다.

(d) 그는 91세까지 일을 계속했다.

해설_ 테크니컬러의 개척자라고 했지 테크니컬러 영화의 개발에 참여했다는 언급은 없으므로 (b)가 정답이다.

어휘_ filming director 영화 촬영 감독 stunning 놀랄 만큼 멋진, 탁월한 pioneer 개척자, 선구자 Technicolor 테크니컬러 silent movie 무성 영화

정답_ (b)

1.

W: Do a favor for me and have a taste of this stew I'm making.

M: ________________________________

(a) It's up in the air.
(b) You're a godsend.
(c) Way to go!
(d) Oh, I like this.

해석_ W: 내가 만들고 있는 이 스튜 맛 좀 봐 줄래?

M: ________________________

(a) 아직 결정되지 않았어.
(b) 넌 하느님이 보낸 선물이야.
(c) 잘했어!
(d) 아, 맛있는데.

해설_ 스튜 맛을 봐 달라고 했으므로 이에 대한 평가가 언급된 (d)가 정답이다.

어휘_ do a favor for (= do ... a favor) ~의 부탁을 들어주다 up in the air 아직 결정되지 않은, 미정인 godsend 하느님이 주신 선물, 뜻하지 않은 행운 Way to go! 잘했어!, 훌륭히 해냈어!

정답_ (d)

2.

M: I swear you look better every time I see you. You're a poster child for good looks.

W: ________________________________

(a) It was nothing but a pipe dream.
(b) Mark my word!
(c) Flattery will get you everywhere.
(d) He's a tough nut to crack.

해석_ M: 넌 볼 때마다 진짜 좋아 보인다. 미모의 광고모델 같아.

W: ________________________

(a) 그건 단지 허황된 생각이었어.
(b) 내 말 잘 들어!
(c) 듣기 좋은 소리를 하는구나.
(d) 그는 처치 곤란한 사람이야.

해설_ 미모의 광고모델 같다고 칭찬하고 있으므로 (c)가 적절하다. Flattery will get you everywhere.는 칭찬을 들었을 때 장난스

럽게 되받는 말로, '아부는 어디서나 통하는 법이지', '듣기 좋은 소리를 하는구나' 정도로 해석된다. 참고로, '아부해도 소용 없어'라고 할 땐 Flattery will get you nowhere.라고 표현한다.

어휘_ poster child (선전용 포스터에 등장하는) 이미지 캐릭터 good looks 미모 pipe dream 허황된 생각[계획, 희망] mark ~에 주의를 기울이다 flattery 아첨 a tough nut to crack 처치 곤란한 사람[일]

정답_ (c)

3.

M: We hope you'll be able to make it.

W: ________________________________

(a) I'll be happy to.
(b) I bet.
(c) Guess what.
(d) Have a good time.

해석_ M: 우리는 당신이 와 주길 바래요.

W: ________________________

(a) 기꺼이 그러겠습니다.
(b) 틀림없어요.
(c) 알아맞춰 보세요.
(d) 좋은 시간 보내세요.

해설_ 초대를 하고 있으므로 이에 기꺼이 응한 (a)가 정답이다.

어휘_ make it 오다, 출석하다

정답_ (a)

4.

W: Did you watch the soccer match last Friday night?

M: No, I didn't. What did I miss?

W: The World Cup semifinals. I guess you don't follow soccer.

M: ________________________________

(a) I'm afraid it's not my cup of tea.
(b) You're right. I am a soccer fan.
(c) I'm not a jazz fan.
(d) I'll follow him.

해석_ W: 지난 금요일 밤 축구 경기 봤어?

M: 아니, 안 봤어. 무슨 경기였는데?

W: 월드컵 준결승전. 넌 축구에 관심이 없나 보구나.

M: ________________________________

(a) 유감이지만 내 취향이 아니야.

(b) 맞아. 난 축구 팬이야.

(c) 난 재즈 팬이 아니야.

(d) 난 그를 따라갈 거야.

해설_ 축구에 관심이 없는 것 같다는 말을 들었으므로 축구를 좋아하
지 않는다는 (a)가 이어지는 것이 적절하다.

어휘_ semifinals 준결승 follow 관심을 가지다 one's cup of
tea 기호에 맞는 물건[사람]

정답_ (a)

5.

M: Do you have any time to discuss business
this Friday?

W: Sorry. I have my hands full until the end of
next week.

M: It's urgent. Find a way to slip me into your
schedule.

W: ________________________________

(a) Don't brush me off.

(b) Alright, I'll reschedule.

(c) It's not going to be a kangaroo court.

(d) We will keep plugging away.

해석_ M: 이번주 금요일에 일에 대해 의논할 시간 있어?

W: 미안. 다음주 말까지 무지 바빠.

M: 급한 일이야. 어떻게든 시간 좀 내.

W: ________________________________

(a) 나 무시하지 마.

(b) 좋아, 스케줄 조정할게.

(c) 엉터리 재판이 되진 않을 거야.

(d) 우리는 계속해서 열심히 할 거야.

해설_ 바빠서 만나기 어렵다는 여자에게 급한 일이니 시간을 내보라고
하고 있으므로 스케줄을 조정하겠다는 (b)가 정답이다. (c)의
kangaroo court는 정식 절차를 밟지 않은 불법적인 엉터리 재
판을 뜻하는 표현으로, 서부의 금광을 캐러 몰려들었던 Gold
Rush 시기에 호주 사람들이 남이 찾은 금광을 자기 금이라고
우겼던 일화를 두고 사람들이 손가락질하며 힐난한 데서 생겨난
표현이라고 한다.

어휘_ have one's hands full 매우 바쁘다 slip into ~에 살짝
넣다 brush ... off ~를 무시하다 plug away (공부·일
을) 열심히 하다

정답_ (b)

6.

M: What is this for?

W: It's Native American style necklace.

M: Oh, I see. What is it made of?

W: It's made of jade.

M: How about this one?

W: It's a Canoe made by an Eskimo.

M: Oh, it's very unique. What is it made of?

W: It's made of animal skin and bones.

M: I like it. Let me have it.

W: Very good choice.

M: Do you accept plastic?

W: Sure.

Q. Where is this conversation most likely taking
place?

(a) At a cocktail lounge

(b) At a barbershop

(c) At a butcher's shop

(d) At a souvenir shop

해석_ M: 이건 용도가 뭐죠?

W: 아메리카 인디언 스타일의 목걸이입니다.

M: 아, 그렇군요. 뭐로 만들어진 거죠?

W: 비취로 만들어졌습니다.

M: 이건 뭐예요?

W: 에스키모인이 만든 카누입니다.

M: 아, 매우 독특하군요. 뭐로 만들어진 거죠?

W: 동물 가죽과 뼈로 만들어졌습니다.

M: 맘에 드네요. 그걸로 주세요.

W: 아주 잘 선택하셨습니다.

M: 신용카드 받나요?

W: 물론이죠.

Q. 이 대화가 이루어지고 있는 장소가 어디일 것 같은가?

(a) 휴게실에서

(b) 이발소에서

(c) 정육점에서

(d) 기념품점에서

해설_ 아메리카 인디언 스타일의 목걸이, 에스키모인이 만든 카누가
나오는 것으로 보아 기념품점에서 이루어지는 대화임을 짐작할

수 있다. 따라서 정답은 (d).

어휘_ jade 비취, 옥 cocktail lounge (호텔·공항 등의) 바, 휴게실 butcher's shop 정육점 souvenir shop 기념품점

정답_ (d)

7.

If you're super religious, perhaps you should skip this as it may cause a rift between you and the entire theatre. This is a great movie, full of the same questions from Bill Maher, but no straight answers from the people he encounters. Check this movie out if you have a sense of humor about religion and don't practice anything.

Q. What is the purpose of this advertisement?

(a) To advertise that the movie is very well-made
(b) To convince people to watch the movie
(c) To introduce the film director
(d) To introduce the summary of the movie

해석_ 만약 당신이 신앙심이 매우 깊다면, 당신과 극장 안의 모든 사람들 간에 분열을 일으킬 수 있기 때문에 그냥 보지 않는 것이 좋을 것입니다. 이것은 빌 마허가 마주치는 사람마다 똑같은 질문을 던지지만, 솔직한 답변은 얻지 못하는 내용의 훌륭한 영화입니다. 만약 당신이 종교에 대해 웃어 넘길 수 있는 사람이고, 어떤 종교적인 활동도 하고 있지 않다면 이 영화를 한번 보세요.

Q. 이 광고의 목적은 무엇인가?

(a) 영화가 매우 잘 만들어졌다는 것을 홍보하기 위해
(b) 사람들로 하여금 영화를 보게 하기 위해
(c) 영화 감독을 소개하기 위해
(d) 영화 줄거리를 소개하기 위해

해설_ 영화에 대한 얘기를 하면서 글 마지막 부분에 한번 보라고 했으므로 정답은 (b)가 된다.

어휘_ super 극도의 religious 신앙의, 신앙심이 깊은 rift 금, 균열, 불화 straight 솔직한 encounter (우연히) 만나다, 마주치다

정답_ (b)

Chapter 9 추론 문제 유형

STEP 1 Pretest Clinic

Part 3

29.

해석_ M: 오늘 왜 정장을 차려입었니?

W: 우리 오빠 결혼식날이야.

M: 네가 입은 스커트가 너랑 너무 잘 어울린다. 근데 부모님이랑 같이 안 가니?

W: 부모님은 먼저 가셨어. 난 약 30분 후에 출발할 거야.

M: 네 오빠한테 축하한다고 전해 줘.

W: 그래. 넌 지금 어디 가는 길이니?

M: 쇼핑 센터에 가는 길이야. 그럼 나중에 보자.

Q. 대화를 통해 추론할 수 있는 것은?

(a) 남자는 쇼핑 센터에서 일한다.
(b) 여자는 결혼식에 늦을 것이다.
(c) 남자는 결혼식에 참석하지 않을 것이다.
(d) 여자는 스커트를 새로 샀다.

정답_ (c)

30.

해석_ W: 지금 바로 출발하지 않으면 늦을 거야.

M: 미안. 인터넷에서 가는 길을 검색하고 있어.

W: 나 알아. 교차로에서 우회전해서 66번 고속도로를 타면 돼.

M: 가는 길 확실히 아는 거야?

W: 물론이지. 그건 지름길이야.

M: 좋아, 그럼 가자.

W: 걱정 마. 날 믿어.

Q. 대화를 통해 추론할 수 있는 것은?

(a) 여자는 길눈이 매우 밝다.
(b) 남자는 전에 이 길을 가본 적이 없다.
(c) 남자와 여자는 어디론가 여행을 떠나려고 한다.
(d) 남자 대신 여자가 운전을 할 것이다.

정답_ (b)

Part 4

35.

해석_ 불과 5년 전 중학교 선생님이었던 그 두 우주 비행사는 우주 유영 동안 그들이 한 일로 영웅이 되어 이번주 월요일에 돌아왔습니다. 그들의 임무는 목숨을 건 일이었지만, 그들은 마침내 오랫

동안 국제 우주 정거장과 우주 왕복선을 위협해 온 위험하면서
도 거대한 우주 쓰레기를 제거했습니다. 이전에 아무도 시도할
생각조차 못했던 일을 그들이 해낸 것입니다.

Q. 그 두 우주 비행사에 대해 추론할 수 있는 것은?

(a) 그들은 우주 정거장에서 어떤 물체에 의해 위협을 당했다.

(b) 그들이 우주에 간 것은 이번이 처음이었다.

(c) 그들은 우주 유영을 하는 동안 매우 힘든 시간을 보냈다.

(d) 그들은 더 이상 우주 유영을 하지 않을 것이다.

정답_ (c)

36.

해석_ 바야흐로 봄입니다. 저희 집은 매년 봄마다 당근 케이크를 만들
어 함께 나눠 먹는 전통을 가지고 있습니다. 올해는 제가 만들 차
례죠. 그래서 인터넷에 나와 있는 요리법을 사용하여 아주 근사
한 당근 케이크를 만들었습니다. 실제 맛은 어떨지 몰라도 겉보
기엔 완벽해 보였습니다. 저희 가족 모두 제가 만든 케이크의 맛
을 무척 기대하고 있습니다.

Q. 이야기를 통해 추론할 수 있는 것은?

(a) 봄은 당근 케이크를 만들기에 알맞은 계절이다.

(b) 화자의 가족은 매년 봄마다 한 사람씩 번갈아가며 당근 케이
크를 만든다.

(c) 화자는 인터넷에 나온 당근 케이크와 완전히 똑같이 만들었
다.

(d) 화자가 당근 케이크를 만드는 것은 이번이 처음이다.

정답_ (b)

STEP 2 990 Challenge!

1.

W: Why did you beat up my younger brother?

M: I'm sorry and I really want to apologize. But
even with a silver tongue, I still wouldn't
know what to say to him.

W: You should be sorry and must let him know.

M: I will. Could you tell me where he is?

W: He is in his room.

M: Thanks. I really feel bad.

Q. What can be inferred from the conversation?

(a) The man is violent.

(b) The man will meet the woman's brother.

(c) The woman got beat up by the man.

(d) The woman's brother will not forgive the
man.

해석_ W: 너 왜 내 동생을 마구 때렸어?

M: 미안해. 정말 사과하고 싶어. 하지만 입이 열 개라도 할 말이
없어.

W: 걔한테 미안하다고 말해야 해.

M: 그럴게. 걔 어딨는지 말해 줄 수 있니?

W: 자기 방에 있어.

M: 고마워. 정말 미안해.

Q. 대화를 통해 추론할 수 있는 것은?

(a) 남자는 폭력적이다.

(b) 남자는 여자의 동생을 만날 것이다.

(c) 여자는 남자한테 마구 맞았다.

(d) 여자의 동생은 남자를 용서하지 않을 것이다.

해설_ 여자의 동생이 어디 있는지 물었으므로 그를 만나러 갈 것임을
알 수 있다. 따라서 정답은 (b). (a)와 (d)는 대화 내용으로부터
알 수 없는 사항이므로 정답이 될 수 없다.

어휘_ even with a silver tongue 입이 열 개라도

정답_ (b)

2.

M: I am not sure what I'm supposed to do
here.

W: No worries. The manager has asked me to
show you the ropes.

M: You know your way around. How long have
you been here for?

W: About three years. Look, this is the storage
room.

M: What do I have to do here?

W: Mostly you have to check stuff against the
invoice.

M: What else?

Q. What can be inferred from the conversation?

(a) The boss has high reliability on the woman.

(b) The woman is jumping rope.

(c) The man is a new employee of the

company.

(d) The man is having difficulty in performing his duties.

해석_ M: 여기서 무슨 일을 해야 하는지 잘 모르겠어요.

W: 걱정 마세요. 부장님이 당신한테 업무를 알려주라고 했어요.

M: 당신은 훤히 잘 아는군요. 여기서 얼마나 오랫동안 일했어요?

W: 약 3년이요. 보세요, 여기가 저장실이에요.

M: 여기서 뭘 해야 하죠?

W: 대부분 송장과 대조하여 물품을 확인해야 해요.

M: 그 밖에 또 할 일은요?

Q. 대화를 통해 추론할 수 있는 것은?

(a) 상사는 여자를 매우 신임하고 있다.

(b) 여자는 줄넘기를 하고 있다.

(c) 남자는 이 회사에 새로 온 직원이다.

(d) 남자는 그의 업무 수행에 어려움을 겪고 있다.

해설_ 여자에게 앞으로 해야 할 업무에 대해 배우고 있는 것으로 보아 남자가 이 회사에 새로 온 직원임을 알 수 있다. 따라서 정답은 (c). (a)는 알 수 없으며, (b)는 ropes를 이용한 함정이다. 또 (d)는 남자가 해야 할 업무에 대해 알지 못했기 때문에 역시 정답이 아니다.

어휘_ show ... the ropes ~에게 뭔가 하는 방법을 설명하다, 요령을 가르쳐 주다 know one's way around ~에 정통하다 storage room 저장실 invoice 송장 jump rope 줄넘기하다

정답_ (c)

3.

Friends ask me from time to time what I find most difficult about adjusting to life in Korea after so many years abroad. That's a question that can elicit many answers, but I generally find myself bringing up three general categories of issues: The pollution, both of the air and of the waterways; the traffic, in which I include congestion as well as drivers who violate the law; and public rudeness on both the streets and on the public transportation system.

Q. What can be inferred about the speaker?

(a) He prefers living abroad.

(b) He dislikes people violating traffic laws.

(c) He thinks that pollution and public rudeness are the problem.

(d) It has not been long since he came back to Korea.

해석_ 친구들은 때때로 내게 오랜 기간 외국에서 보낸 후 한국에서의 생활에 적응하는 데 어떤 어려움이 있는지 물어본다. 많은 대답을 이끌어낼 수 있는 질문이지만, 일반적으로 내가 말하는 것은 다음의 세 가지 범주의 논점, 즉 대기오염과 하천오염, 그리고 교통이다. 교통에는 법규를 위반하는 운전자들뿐 아니라 교통 혼잡, 그리고 거리와 대중 교통에서의 공중 질서를 무시하는 것도 포함된다.

Q. 화자에 대해 추론할 수 있는 것은?

(a) 그는 외국에서 사는 걸 더 좋아한다.

(b) 그는 교통 질서를 위반하는 사람들을 싫어한다.

(c) 그는 오염과 공중 질서 무시가 문제라고 생각한다.

(d) 그는 한국에 돌아온 지 얼마 안 됐다.

해설_ 오랜 외국 생활 후 돌아온 한국에서의 생활에 대한 어려움에 대해 대기오염과 하천오염, 그리고 교통 질서에 대한 무시를 언급했으므로 이런 것들을 문제로 생각하고 있음을 알 수 있다. 따라서 정답은 (c). 나머지 선택지들은 주어진 내용만으론 명확히 알 수 없으므로 정답이 될 수 없다.

어휘_ elicit 이끌어내다 bring up (논거·화제 등을) 내놓다 waterway 수로, 배수로

정답_ (c)

STEP 3 Actual Test

1.

M: It's very hard to swallow that you're 35 years old. You've got such a baby face.

W: ___________________________________

(a) I don't want to play second fiddle.

(b) That's kind of you to say, thanks.

(c) As you sow, so shall you reap.

(d) Everything is in apple pie order.

해석_ M: 네가 서른 다섯이라는 건 말도 안 돼. 완전 동안이잖아.

W: ___________________________

(a) 남의 밑에서 일하고 싶지 않아.

(b) 그렇게 말해 줘서 고마워.

(c) 뿌린 대로 거두는 법이야.

(d) 모든 게 질서 정연해.

해설_ 남자가 동안이라고 칭찬하고 있으므로 이에 답례하는 (b)가 이어져야 적절하다.

어휘_ swallow (남의 이야기 등을) 곧이곧대로 듣다, 무턱대고 받아들이다   play second fiddle 남의 밑에서 일하다, 보조역을 맡다   As you sow, so shall you reap. 뿌린 대로 거둔다.   be in apple pie order 질서 정연하다, 깨끗이 정돈돼 있다

정답_ (b)

2.

M: I'm sure you're up in arms about things not going as well as you expected.

W: _______________________________________

(a) That's not the half of it! I just want to throw in the towel.
(b) Forget it. I think you're squeaky clean.
(c) Cheer up! You are such a sourpuss.
(d) Meet me halfway.

해석_ M: 일이 생각대로 잘 안 풀려서 화났구나.

　　　 W: _______________________________

　　　 (a) 그건 약과야. 아예 포기하고 싶어.

　　　 (b) 잊어버려. 난 네가 결백하다고 생각해.

　　　 (c) 힘내! 넌 참 우거지상이야.

　　　 (d) 나랑 타협하자.

해설_ 일이 잘 안 돼서 화난 게 분명하다는 남자의 말에 포기하고 싶을 정도라고 응답한 (a)가 가장 적절하다.

어휘_ up in arms (~에) 격분하여   throw in the towel 포기하다   squeaky clean 청결한, 결백한   sourpuss 시무룩한 사람, 늘 인상을 찌푸리고 있는 사람   meet ... halfway ~와 타협하다

정답_ (a)

3.

M: Do you know how often the subway runs?
W: _______________________________________

(a) You must transfer at the next station.
(b) Every 3 minutes, I believe.

(c) By all means.
(d) First come, first served.

해석_ M: 지하철이 몇 분마다 오는지 아세요?

　　　 W: _______________________________

　　　 (a) 다음 역에서 갈아타셔야 해요.

　　　 (b) 3분마다 올걸요.

　　　 (c) 좋고 말고요.

　　　 (d) 선착순입니다.

해설_ 지하철 배차 간격에 대해 알고 있는지 묻고 있으므로 이에 답한 (b)가 정답이다.

어휘_ By all means. (승낙의 뜻을 강조하여) 좋고 말고요, 물론이죠

정답_ (b)

4.

W: Dad, you've got to let me buy a car.
M: Over my dead body!
W: But dad, all the other kids have their own cars.
M: _______________________________________

(a) He might pressure me.
(b) She always finds faults with me.
(c) You should paddle your own canoe.
(d) The movie was so sappy.

해석_ W: 아빠, 차 한 대 사 주세요.

　　　 M: 절대 안 돼!

　　　 W: 하지만 아빠, 다른 애들은 다 자기 차를 가지고 있단 말이에요.

　　　 M: _______________________________

　　　 (a) 그는 내게 압력을 가할지도 몰라.

　　　 (b) 그녀는 항상 내 흠을 잡아.

　　　 (c) 네 힘으로 사.

　　　 (d) 그 영화는 너무나 감상적이었어.

해설_ 차를 사 달라고 조르고 있으므로 혼자 힘으로 해결하라는 (c)가 적절하다.

어휘_ find faults with ~의 흠을 잡다   paddle one's own canoe 혼자 힘으로 살아가다, 자립하다   sappy 매우 감상적인

정답_ (c)

5.

W: It's such a beautiful morning. Are you interested in a tour?

M: Yes, I'm indeed. Do you have any package tours to Sri Lanka.

W: Sure. We have flights to Sri Lanka which leave as regular as clockwork.

M: ________________________________

(a) I feel like a fish out of water.

(b) Great. Can you quote me some prices?

(c) You'll catch on in no time flat.

(d) The tour will last an hour.

해석_ W: 너무 아름다운 아침이네요. 관광하는 것에 관심 있으세요?

M: 네, 그래요. 스리랑카로 가는 패키지 투어가 있나요?

W: 물론이죠. 스리랑카 정기 항공편이 있습니다.

M: ____________________________

(a) 어색하네요.

(b) 좋군요. 가격이 얼마죠?

(c) 금방 이해할 거예요.

(d) 관광은 1시간 동안 이어질 겁니다.

해설_ 정기적으로 스리랑카로 떠나는 항공편이 있다고 했으므로 그 가격을 묻는 (b)가 이어지는 것이 자연스럽다.

어휘_ as regular as clockwork 매우 규칙적인 feel like a fish out of water 어색하다, 소외감을 느끼다 quote a price 가격 견적을 내보다 catch on 이해하다, 알다 in no time flat 금방

정답_ (b)

6.

M: What has brought your daughter here?

W: She has a slight fever and has broken out in a rash over her body.

M: Do you have a pet at home?

W: Yes. I have a young Syberian husky.

M: She needs to be tested for flea allergies.

W: Is it quite serious?

M: Not at all. Once testing has been completed, I can prescribe an effective remedy.

Q. What can be inferred from the conversation?

(a) The woman's daughter is allergic to dogs.

(b) The woman is very ill.

(c) The woman's daughter needs medical treatment.

(d) The woman will not keep a pet anymore for her daughter.

해석_ M: 무슨 일로 따님이 여기 왔죠?

W: 미열이 있고 온몸에 두드러기가 났어요.

M: 집에 애완동물이 있나요?

W: 네. 어린 시베리안 허스키를 기르고 있어요.

M: 벼룩 알레르기 검사를 해야겠어요.

W: 많이 심각한가요?

M: 그렇진 않아요. 일단 검사가 끝나야 효과적인 치료약을 처방할 수 있어요.

Q. 대화를 통해 추론할 수 있는 것은?

(a) 여자의 딸은 강아지 알레르기가 있다.

(b) 여자는 많이 아프다.

(c) 여자의 딸은 약물 치료가 필요하다.

(d) 여자는 그녀의 딸을 위해 더 이상 애완동물을 기르지 않을 것이다.

해설_ 알레르기 검사 후 약 처방을 내리겠다고 했으므로 (c)가 정답임을 알 수 있다. (a)와 (b)는 내용에 어긋나며, (d)는 알 수 없는 사항이므로 정답이 될 수 없다.

어휘_ break out in a rash 두드러기가 나다 flea 벼룩 remedy 치료약

정답_ (c)

7.

On the morning of her birthday, he woke her up early and took her to a local theme park. They went on every ride until they had no more energy left. Five hours later they staggered out of the theme park, their head reeling and their stomach feeling like it was upside down. However, after a short break, they went to a movie with hot dogs, and popcorn.

Q. What is true according to the story?

(a) The man and woman enjoyed all the rides in the theme park.

(b) The man and woman went to a local park.

(c) The man and woman had an upset stomach.

(d) The man and woman went to the movies right after coming out of the theme park.

해석_ 그녀의 생일 아침에 그는 그녀를 일찍 깨워 근처의 놀이 공원으로 데려갔습니다. 그들은 힘이 다 빠질 때까지 모든 놀이 기구를 탔습니다. 5시간 후 그들은 머리가 어질어질하고 속이 뒤집힌 듯한 상태로 비틀거리면서 놀이 공원을 나왔습니다. 하지만 잠깐 휴식을 취하고 그들은 핫도그와 팝콘을 사 가지고 영화를 보러 갔습니다.

Q. 이야기에 따르면 사실인 것은 무엇인가?

(a) 남자와 여자는 놀이 공원에 있는 모든 놀이 기구를 즐겼다.

(b) 남자와 여자는 동네 공원에 갔다.

(c) 남자와 여자는 배탈이 났다.

(d) 남자와 여자는 놀이 공원에서 나오자마자 영화를 보러 갔다.

해설_ 놀이 공원에 있는 놀이 기구를 모두 탔다고 했으므로 (a)가 정답이다.

어휘_ go on a ride 놀이 기구를 타다 stagger out of 비틀거리면서 ~에서 나오다 reel 현기증을 일으키다

정답_ (a)

Final Test 1

Part 1

1.

M: Who's footing the bill for that?

W: ________________________________

(a) Tom is a marked man.

(b) He had an edge over me.

(c) My mom'll open her purse.

(d) Susan always talks big.

해석_ M: 돈은 누가 낼 거야?

W: ________________________________

(a) 톰은 요주의 인물이야.

(b) 그가 나보다 유리한 입장에 있어.

(c) 엄마가 내실 거야.

(d) 수잔은 늘 큰소리만 쳐.

해설_ 누가 비용을 부담할 것인지 묻고 있으므로 엄마가 낼 거라고 응답한 (c)가 정답이다.

어휘_ foot the bill 비용을 부담하다 a marked man 요주의 인물 have an edge over ~보다 유리한 입장에 있다 open one's purse 돈을 내놓다 talk big 큰소리 치다, 허풍 치다

정답_ (c)

2.

W: Where'd you get your intel from?

M: ________________________________

(a) A little bird told me.

(b) I'm working on this dinosaur computer.

(c) My dad is such a hard nut to crack.

(d) You're under the gun at work.

해석_ W: 누가 너한테 그런 말을 한 거니?

M: ________________________________

(a) 누가 그러더라.

(b) 난 이 구식 컴퓨터로 일하고 있어.

(c) 우리 아빠는 아주 까다로운 분이셔.

(d) 넌 당장 해야 할 일이 있잖아.

해설_ 어디서 정보를 얻었는지 묻고 있으므로 누군가에게서 들었다고 응답한 (a)가 정답이다. A little bird told me.는 누군가에게 들

었거나 소문으로 알게 된 이야기를 꺼낼 때, 특히 이야기의 출처
를 밝히기 곤란한 상황에서 주로 쓰이는 표현이다.

어휘_ intel 정보   dinosaur 거대하여 다루기 힘든 것, 시대에 뒤떨
어진 것(사람)   a hard nut to crack 다루기 힘든 사람[일]
under the gun (어떤 일에) 큰 부담을 받는

정답_ (a)

3.

M: You sound like you're miles away.

W: ____

(a) Then, I'll hang up and call again.
(b) I'm up to my ears in work.
(c) I'll make a video phone call.
(d) He's just stepped out.

해석_ M: 네 목소리가 잘 안 들려.

　　 W: ________________________________

　　 (a) 그럼, 내가 끊고 다시 전화할게.
　　 (b) 나 무지 바빠.
　　 (c) 내가 화상 전화 걸게.
　　 (d) 그는 잠깐 나갔어.

해설_ 목소리가 잘 안 들린다고 했으므로 끊고 다시 전화하겠다는 (a)
가 이어지는 것이 적절하다. (b)의 be up to one's ears in
work은 직역하자면 '해야 할 일이 몸의 귀 부분까지 꽉 차 있다'
로, 즉 '할 일이 무척 많다', '정신없이 바쁘다'는 뜻을 나타낸다.

어휘_ miles away 몇 마일이나 떨어져   hang up 전화를 끊다
step out 잠시 자리를 비우다

정답_ (a)

4.

W: My daughter just got accepted into a
prestigious university with a full scholarship.

M: ____

(a) The clock is ticking.
(b) I'm out of favor with him.
(c) Can you put this on the cuff?
(d) That's fantastic! What a remarkable
achievement!

해석_ W: 우리 딸이 전액 장학금을 받고 일류 대학에 들어갔어요.

　　 M: ________________________________

　　 (a) 시간이 가고 있어요.
　　 (b) 그 사람 눈밖에 났어요.
　　 (c) 이거 외상으로 주실래요?
　　 (d) 그거 굉장하군요! 놀랄 만한 일을 해냈어요!

해설_ 전액 장학금을 받고 일류 대학에 들어갔다는 말을 들었으므로
축하의 의미가 담긴 (d)가 이어지는 것이 적절하다. (a)는 '시간
이 가고 있다', '시간이 없다'란 뜻으로 상황의 위급함을 나타낼
때 쓸 수 있는 표현이다.

어휘_ prestigious 일류의, 이름이 난   be out of favor with
~의 눈밖에 나다   on the cuff 외상으로

정답_ (d)

5.

M: I have to pull up stakes.

W: ____

(a) All the luck in the world to you.
(b) Money is the root of all evil.
(c) They really whooped it up at the party.
(d) They are nickel-and-dimers.

해석_ M: 직장을 옮겨야 해.

　　 W: ________________________________

　　 (a) 행운을 빌게.
　　 (b) 돈은 모든 악의 근본이야.
　　 (c) 그들은 파티에서 진짜 마구 떠들고 놀았어.
　　 (d) 걔네들은 시시한 애들이야.

해설_ 남자가 직장을 옮겨야 한다고 말하고 있으므로 행운을 빌어 주
는 (a)가 적절하다. pull up stakes는 직역하자면 '말뚝을 뽑아
가다'란 뜻으로, 직장을 옮기거나, 또는 이사 간다고 말할 때 쓸
수 있는 구어 표현이다. (d)의 nick-and-dimer는 '하찮은', '시
시한'이란 뜻의 nick-and-dime이 의인화된 표현으로, '시시한
사람'을 의미한다.

어휘_ whoop it up 마구 떠들고 놀다

정답_ (a)

6.

W: I can't find the words to tell you how
grateful I am.

M: ____

(a) Thrilled to meet you.
(b) It's not necessary.
(c) I'm not feeling up to par today.
(d) You are such a sucker.

해석_ W: 얼마나 감사한지 말로 표현할 수가 없군요.

M: _______________________________

(a) 만나서 너무 반가워요.
(b) 별말씀을요.
(c) 오늘 몸 컨디션이 좋지 않아요.
(d) 당신은 정말 잘 속는군요.

해설_ 감사를 표하고 있으므로 이에 답례하는 (b)가 이어져야 자연스럽다.

어휘_ up to par 몸의 컨디션이 좋은   sucker 잘 속는 사람, 어리석은 사람

정답_ (b)

7.

W: It really irks me when I'm waiting in line and then somebody jumps in front of me.

M: _______________________________

(a) I hate that too.
(b) He is not worth his salt.
(c) It's no laughing matter.
(d) You should keep a low profile till your dad calms down.

해석_ W: 줄 서서 기다리고 있는데 누군가 새치기하면 정말 짜증 나.

M: _______________________________

(a) 나도 그건 너무 싫더라.
(b) 그는 자기 밥값도 못해.
(c) 웃을 일이 아니야.
(d) 네 아빠의 노여움이 가라앉을 때까지 쥐 죽은 듯이 있어.

해설_ 새치기하는 사람이 너무 싫다는 여자의 말에 동조하는 (a)가 적절한 응답이다.

어휘_ irk 짜증나게 하다   wait in line 줄 서서 기다리다   be worth one's salt 제 몫을 하다, 제 밥값을 하다   laughing matter 웃을 일   keep a low profile 저자세를 취하다, 쥐 죽은 듯이 있다

정답_ (a)

8.

M: What's your pastime?

W: _______________________________

(a) Reading was her favorite pastime.
(b) Many people get the jitters at examination time.
(c) I really like playing computer games.
(d) Don't try to do a snow job on me.

해석_ M: 취미가 뭐예요?

W: _______________________________

(a) 독서는 그녀가 가장 즐기는 취미였어요.
(b) 많은 사람들이 시험 시간에 초조해져요.
(c) 컴퓨터 게임하는 걸 정말 좋아해요.
(d) 날 속이려 들지 마세요.

해설_ 취미를 묻고 있으므로 이에 관해 언급한 (c)가 정답이다. (d)의 do a snow job은 '그럴 듯한 말로 눈가림하다', '속이다'란 뜻이다. 눈이 내리면 온 세상이 아름답고 깨끗하게 보이지만, 눈이 녹으면서 그 속에 감춰져 있던 지저분한 길바닥 등이 드러나게 된다. 이렇게 눈은 일시적으로 더러움이나 불결함을 감추는 역할을 하는데, 여기서 유래된 말이 snow job이라고 한다.

어휘_ pastime 취미, 오락, 심심풀이   get the jitters 초조해지다

정답_ (c)

9.

M: How do I set up an Internet banking account?

W: _______________________________

(a) You can open a virtual account.
(b) You just go to our site on the Internet and open an account.
(c) I'm computer illiterate.
(d) I log on to the internet once a day.

해석_ M: 인터넷 뱅킹 계좌를 개설하려면 어떻게 해야 하죠?

W: _______________________________

(a) 가상 계좌를 개설하시면 돼요.
(b) 저희 은행 인터넷 사이트에 가서서 계좌를 개설하세요.
(c) 전 컴맹이에요.
(d) 전 하루에 한 번 인터넷에 접속해요.

해설_ 인터넷 뱅킹 계좌의 개설 방법을 묻고 있으므로 이에 관해 알려주는 (b)가 정답이다.

어휘_ set up[open] an account 계좌를 개설하다   virtual account 가상 계좌   computer illiterate 컴맹의

정답_ (b)

10.

M: I actually popped in to make a reservation.

W: ___________________________________

(a) Ok, sir. Please give me your information then.
(b) I can recommend Mr. Kim without any reservation.
(c) He popped the question.
(d) Welcome to the hotel California.

해석 M: 실은 예약하려고 들렀어요.
W: ___________________________________
(a) 알겠습니다, 손님. 그럼 인적 사항을 말씀해 주세요.
(b) 난 무조건 김 씨를 추천해요.
(c) 그가 청혼했어요.
(d) 캘리포니아 호텔에 오신 걸 환영합니다.

해설 예약하기 위해 들렀다고 했으므로 인적 사항을 묻는 (a)가 이어지는 것이 적절하다.

어휘 pop in 잠깐 들르다 without any reservation 주저하지 않고, 무조건적으로 pop the question 청혼하다

정답 (a)

11.

W: That new teacher! He frightens the pants off me.
M: ___________________________________

(a) She wishes he'd lighten up.
(b) She scares me.
(c) He acts tough to get the students working harder.
(d) He likes to wear short pants.

해석 W: 그 새로 오신 선생님 말이야! 날 너무 무섭게 해.
M: ___________________________________
(a) 그녀는 그가 느긋해지길 바래.
(b) 그녀가 날 겁줘.
(c) 학생들이 더 열심히 공부하게 하려고 엄하게 하시는 거야.
(d) 그는 짧은 바지 입는 것을 좋아해.

해설 새로 온 선생님이 무섭다는 여자의 말에 이어질 응답으로, 학생들에게 공부를 시키려고 엄하게 하시는 것이라고 말해 주는 (c)가 가장 잘 어울린다.

어휘 frighten[scare] the pants off ~를 너무 무섭게 하다 lighten up 덜 심각해지다, 느긋해지다

정답 (c)

12.

W: Excuse me, but where can I find laundry detergent?
M: ___________________________________

(a) I'll help you carry it to your car.
(b) I go to the laundromat every Sunday.
(c) It's at the end of this aisle.
(d) I don't need any dishwashing liquid.

해석 W: 실례지만, 세탁용 세제가 어디 있죠?
M: ___________________________________
(a) 차까지 운반하는 것을 도와 드릴게요.
(b) 일요일마다 빨래방에 가요.
(c) 이 줄 끝에 있어요.
(d) 식기 세척제는 필요 없어요.

해설 세탁용 세제가 어디 있는지 묻고 있으므로 위치를 알려주는 (c)가 적절하다.

어휘 laundry detergent 세탁용 세제 laundromat 빨래방 dishwashing liquid 식기 세척제

정답 (c)

13.

M: Could you ring this up for me?
W: ___________________________________

(a) I would like this gift-wrapped.
(b) Sure. The total comes to $50.63.
(c) You can't make monthly payments.
(d) You can get a refund.

해석 M: 이것 좀 계산해 주실래요?
W: ___________________________________
(a) 이거 선물 포장해 주세요.
(b) 네. 총 50달러 63센트입니다.
(c) 할부는 안 됩니다.
(d) 환불받으실 수 있어요.

해설 계산을 해 달라고 했으므로 금액을 언급한 (b)가 정답이다. (a)는 선물 포장을 요청할 때 사용하는 표현인데, Can I get this gift-wrapped?도 마찬가지 의미로 자주 쓰인다.

어휘 ring up 계산해 주다 come to 합계 ~이 되다 make monthly payment 할부로 계산하다

정답 (b)

14.

W: It would be smarter to go bulk, wouldn't it?

M: _______________________________________

(a) Geniuses think alike!

(b) Let's hit the bricks.

(c) You've twisted my arm.

(d) The biggest culprit is greed.

해석_ W: 무더기로 사는 게 좋지 않을까?

　　　　M: _______________________________

　　　　(a) 나도 같은 생각이야!

　　　　(b) 여기저기 돌아다니자.

　　　　(c) 네가 먼저 하자고 한 거다.

　　　　(d) 가장 큰 죄인은 탐욕이야.

해설_ 무더기로 사는 게 좋지 않겠냐는 의견에 동의를 표하는 (a)가 정
답이다. Geniuses think alike.는 직역하자면 '천재들은 생각이
잘 맞아'로, 즉 '나도 같은 생각이야'라고 상대방의 말에 맞장구
칠 때 쓸 수 있는 표현이다.

어휘_ go bulk 무더기로 사다, 대량으로 사다　hit the bricks 여
기저기 돌아다니다　culprit 범죄자, 죄인　greed 탐욕

정답_ (a)

15.

W: I think I perm and dye my hair too often.

M: _______________________________________

(a) And I want it blow-dried and styled.

(b) That's why your hair is unmanageable.

(c) A chin length cut would go well with your
face.

(d) I'd like to get my hair bobbed.

해석_ W: 제가 파마랑 염색을 너무 자주하는 것 같아요.

　　　　M: _______________________________

　　　　(a) 드라이하고 스타일링도 해주세요.

　　　　(b) 그래서 머리가 말을 잘 안 듣는군요.

　　　　(c) 턱까지 오는 단발머리가 손님 얼굴과 잘 어울릴 것 같네요.

　　　　(d) 단발로 자르고 싶어요.

해설_ 파마와 염색을 자주 하는 것 같다고 했으므로 머리가 말을 안 듣
는 이유를 알겠다는 (b)가 이어지는 것이 적절하다.

어휘_ blow-dry 드라이하다　unmanageable 관리[제어]하기 힘
든　bob 단발로 하다

정답_ (b)

Part 2

16.

W: You have many acquaintances and you
seem to get along well with everybody.

M: I'm a people person.

W: I hope there are more people like you.

M: _______________________________________

(a) He's been walking on air ever since he
bought a house.

(b) I'm licking my lips just thinking about it.

(c) Your compliment is making me blush.

(d) You took a sideswipe at the management.

해석_ W: 당신은 인맥도 넓고 모든 사람들과 잘 지내는 것 같아요.

　　　　M: 전 사교적인 사람이거든요.

　　　　W: 당신 같은 사람들이 좀 더 많았으면 좋겠어요.

　　　　M: _______________________________

　　　　(a) 그는 집을 산 후부터 잔뜩 들떠 있어요.

　　　　(b) 그것에 대해 생각만 해도 입에 군침이 돌아요.

　　　　(c) 당신 칭찬을 들으니 쑥스러운데요.

　　　　(d) 당신은 경영진을 간접적으로 비난했어요.

해설_ 칭찬을 받았으므로 이에 쑥스럽다는 (c)가 적절한 응답이다.

어휘_ people person 사교적인 사람　walk on air 잔뜩 들떠 있
다, 좋아 어쩔 줄 모르다　lick one's lips 군침을 삼키다, 입맛
을 다시다　compliment 칭찬　make ... blush ~를 부끄
럽게 만들다　take a sideswipe at 간접적으로 비난하는
견해를 취하다

정답_ (c)

17.

M: What are you doing to keep yourself so fit
and trim?

W: I keep an early morning exercise ritual.

M: So that's it, huh? You look like a million
bucks!

W: _______________________________________

(a) Spare my blushes.

(b) Things went like clockwork.

(c) That's a knee slapper.

(d) Don't fly off the handle over such trivial
matters.

해석_ M: 넌 어떻게 몸매 관리를 하니?

W: 이른 아침 운동을 꾸준히 하고 있어.

M: 그게 비결이야? 정말 멋져 보인다!

W: _______________________________

(a) 치켜세우지 마.

(b) 모든 일이 순조로웠어.

(c) 그거 진짜 웃긴다.

(d) 그런 사소한 거에 열 받지 마.

해설_ You look like a million bucks.는 '정말 멋져 보인다.', '아주 좋아 보인다'라는 뜻의 표현이다. 따라서 칭찬의 말에 이어질 적절한 응답은 부끄럽게 치켜세우지 말라는 (a)가 된다.

어휘_ fit 좋은 건강 상태인 trim (몸매가) 균형 잡힌 ritual (의식처럼) 반드시 지키는 일 spare one's blushes 부끄러워지게 하지 않다 go like clockwork 순조롭게 진행되다 knee slapper (무릎을 치고 웃을 만큼) 기막힌 농담 fly off the handle 자제심을 잃다, 발끈하다

정답_ (a)

18.

W: Congrats on moving up the ladder! You're the Head Honcho now.

M: The news made my day.

W: How does it feel to be in charge?

M: _______________________________

(a) It's no picnic, you know.

(b) We are standing our ground.

(c) I'll touch base with him later today.

(d) You are the bomb.

해석_ W: 승진 축하해! 이제 사장님이구나.

M: 그 소식 덕분에 오늘 기분이 아주 좋았어.

W: 책임자가 된 기분이 어때?

M: _______________________________

(a) 쉬운 일이 아냐, 너도 알걸.

(b) 우린 물러서지 않을 거야.

(c) 오늘 늦게 그와 연락을 취할게.

(d) 넌 정말 매력적이야.

해설_ 책임자가 된 기분이 어떤지 묻고 있으므로 쉬운 일이 아니라고 응답한 (a)가 적절하다. 여자의 첫 번째 대사에 나오는 congrats는 congratulations를 줄여 쓴 표현이다. (d)의 You are the bomb.은 '넌 폭탄이야'라는 말이 아니라, '넌 짱이야', '넌 정말 매력적이야'라는 뜻을 나타낸다.

어휘_ move up the ladder 승진하다 Head Honcho 사장, 지도자 make one's day ~를 즐겁게 하다 no picnic 쉬운 일이 아닌 stand one's ground 자기 주장을 굽히지 않다, 버티다 touch base with ~와 연락을 취하다

정답_ (a)

19.

M: After a long engagement, my youngest son is finally tying the knot.

W: Congratulations! How do you feel?

M: Well, I have mixed emotions about it.

W: _______________________________

(a) You get the picture?

(b) I'm certain they'll live a life of bliss.

(c) He is just kvetching.

(d) They lambasted each other.

해석_ M: 오랜 약혼 끝에 막내 아들이 마침내 결혼해요.

W: 축하해요! 기분이 어때요?

M: 글쎄요, 착잡하네요.

W: _______________________________

(a) 감 잡았니?

(b) 그들은 분명 멋진 삶을 살게 될 거예요.

(c) 그는 불평만 하고 있어요.

(d) 그들은 서로 호되게 비난했어요.

해설_ 기분이 착잡하다는 남자의 말에 결혼해서 잘 살 거라고 위로해 주는 (b)가 이어지는 것이 적절하다. I have mixed emotions.는 직역하자면 '혼합된 감정을 가지고 있다'는 말로, '시원섭섭하다', '착잡하다'란 뜻을 나타낸다.

어휘_ live a life of bliss 축복의 삶을 살다 kvetch 늘 불평만 하다, 투덜거리다 lambast 호되게 비난하다, 꾸짖다

정답_ (b)

20.

W: Have you noticed anything different about the way I look?

M: You had your hair done. Why did you cut it so short?

W: I just wanted to try something different.

M: _______________________________

(a) She's playing hard to get.

(b) I don't want you to lower your sights.

(c) It was fair to middling.
(d) Keep on taking care of yourself.

해석_ W: 나 뭔가 달라 보이지 않아?

M: 머리했구나. 왜 그렇게 머리를 짧게 잘랐니?

W: 그냥 뭔가 변화를 주고 싶었어.

M: ______________________________

(a) 걔 일부러 관심 없는 척하는 거야.

(b) 네 목표를 낮추지 않았으면 해.

(c) 그런대로 괜찮았어.

(d) 계속 잘 가꿔라.

해설_ 뭔가 변화를 주고 싶었다는 여자의 말에 앞으로도 계속 잘 가꾸
라고 격려해 주는 (d)가 가장 적절하다.

어휘_ play hard to get 일부러 관심 없는 척하다 lower one's
sights 자신의 목표를 낮추다 fair to middling (용모 등이)
그저 그만한, 어지간한

정답_ (d)

21.

W: I really appreciate what you've done for me.

M: If you were in my shoes, you would have
done the same.

W: At any rate, please know that my gratitude
is heartfelt.

M: ______________________________

(a) I read your mind.
(b) Money doesn't grow on trees!
(c) That's the last straw.
(d) I've been racking my brain.

해석_ W: 제게 베풀어 주신 것에 대해 정말 감사드립니다.

M: 당신이 내 입장이었다면 당신도 그렇게 했을 거예요.

W: 어쨌든 진심으로 감사드린다는 거 알아 주세요.

M: ______________________________

(a) 당신 마음 알아요.

(b) 돈이 하늘에서 떨어지는 줄 알아요?

(c) 더 이상 못 참겠어요.

(d) 궁리하는 중이었어요.

해설_ 진심으로 감사하고 있다고 했으므로 그 마음을 알고 있다는 (a)
가 가장 적절하다. (b)는 직역하자면 '돈은 나무에서 열리지 않
는다'로, 우리말의 '땅 파면 돈이 나오는 줄 알아?', '돈이 하늘
에서 떨어지는 줄 알아?'에 해당하는 표현이다. (c)의 the last

straw는 It is the last straw that breaks the camel's back.
이라는 속담에서 유래된 것인데, 이미 많은 짐을 실은 후엔 아무
리 가벼운 지푸라기(straw)라도 낙타의 등이 부러질 수 있다는
뜻에서 비롯, '더 이상 참을 수 없는 상태'를 말한다.

어휘_ at any rate 어쨌든, 아무튼 heartfelt 진심에서 우러난
read one's mind ~의 마음을 알다, ~의 생각을 알아채다
rack one's brain 머리를 짜다, 궁리하다

정답_ (a)

22.

M: I'm sick of surfing these channels. There is
just nothing good on.

W: I know. Not even one decent program.

M: That's what I was saying.

W: ______________________________

(a) They have been stabbed in the back.
(b) I am such a procrastinator.
(c) They have really gone downhill over the
years.
(d) You are such a copy cat!

해석_ M: 이 채널들 돌려보는 데 넌더리가 난다. 볼 만한 게 하나도 없
어.

W: 나도 알아. 괜찮은 프로그램이 한 개도 없지.

M: 내 말이 그 말이야.

W: ______________________________

(a) 그들은 믿는 도끼에 발등 찍혔어.

(b) 난 아주 늑장꾸러기야.

(c) 채널들이 여러 해 동안 정말 질이 떨어졌어.

(d) 넌 정말 따라쟁이야!

해설_ 볼 만한 프로가 나오는 채널이 하나도 없다며 불평을 하는 상황
이므로 채널들의 질이 떨어졌다고 말한 (c)가 이어지는 것이 적
절하다.

어휘_ surf the channel 채널을 이리저리 돌려보다 decent 괜
찮은, 그럴 듯한 be stabbed in the back 배신당하다, 믿
는 도끼에 발등 찍히다 procrastinator 항상 어떤 일을 미루
는 사람, 늑장 부리는 사람 go downhill 질이 떨어지다
copy cat 모방자

정답_ (c)

23.

W: What kind of place is this? This place is just
totally repulsive.

M: I like this Western bar.

W: I want to blow this joint and go dancing instead.

M: _________________________________

(a) My boss gave me the green light.

(b) My ears are really burning.

(c) I am green with envy!

(d) All right. Be my guest.

해석_ W: 여기 뭐 이래? 여기 정말 별로다.

M: 난 이 웨스턴 바가 맘에 드는데.

W: 이 싸구려 술집에서 빨리 나가서 춤추러 가고 싶어.

M: _________________________

(a) 사장이 허락해 줬어.

(b) 귀가 간질간질해.

(c) 부러워 죽겠다!

(d) 좋아. 네 맘대로 해.

해설_ 술집이 마음에 들지 않아 나가고 싶다고 했으므로 이에 응한 (d)가 정답이다. (b)는 '귀가 간질간질하다'의 뜻으로, 우리가 흔히 '누가 내 얘기 하나 봐. 귀가 간지러워'라고 말하는 것을 영어에서는 '귀가 불에 타는 것처럼 화끈거린다'라는 표현으로 My ears are burning.이라고 말한다. (d)의 Be my guest.는 '네 맘대로 해', '좋을 대로 해', '물론이지'의 뜻으로, 상대방의 부탁을 흔쾌히 수락하거나 허락할 때 자주 쓰이는 표현이다.

어휘_ repulsive 불쾌한, 혐오감을 일으키는 blow ~에서 급히 나가다 joint 무허가[싸구려] 술집 give ... the green light ~에게 허가를 내주다 green with envy 몹시 부러워하는

정답_ (d)

24.

W: Why are you always picking on your brother?

M: You're always telling me off. I think you must have it in for me.

W: No excuses! Go to your room for thirty minutes!

M: _________________________________

(a) This is too harsh!

(b) The London Bridge became a white elephant.

(c) I caught a cold and I have a frog in my throat.

(d) This is our turf now.

해석_ W: 넌 왜 항상 동생을 못살게 구니?

M: 엄만 늘 저만 나무라세요. 제가 미우신가 봐요.

W: 변명은 안 돼! 30분 동안 방에 가 있어!

M: _________________________________

(a) 이건 너무 심해요!

(b) 런던 브릿지는 무용지물이 되었어요.

(c) 감기가 걸려서 목이 쉬었어요.

(d) 이제 여긴 우리 구역이에요.

해설_ 자기만 꾸중하는 엄마에게 불만을 가지고 있는 터에 30분 동안 방에 가 있으라는 말까지 들었으므로 이어질 응답으로는 심하다고 항의하는 (a)가 적절하다. (b)의 white elephant는, 그 어원을 살펴보면, 옛날 샴(타일랜드의 옛 이름)에서는 흰 코끼리를 신성시해서 모든 흰 코끼리는 왕의 소유물이 되었고, 그의 허락 없이는 처분할 수 없었다. 왕은 자기가 싫어하는 신하에게 흰 코끼리를 선물로 하사하곤 했는데, 받은 사람은 엄청난 돈을 써 가며 코끼리를 돌봐야 했기 때문에 매우 곤란했다는 것. 여기서 유래하여 white elephant 하면 유지비가 상당히 많이 들지만 그렇다고 처분할 수도 없는 쓸모없는 물건을 뜻하게 되었다.

어휘_ pick on 괴롭히다, 못살게 굴다 tell off 야단치다, 잔소리하다 have it in for ... ~를 싫어하다 harsh 가혹한, 무자비한 have a frog in one's throat 목이 쉬다 turf 세력권, 영역, 구역

정답_ (a)

25.

M: I'm sorry but I'm not going to be able to fix this heap up.

W: But you told me that you could fix it.

M: Yes, but you need three thousand dollars more.

W: _________________________________

(a) Don't try to butter me up.

(b) This room looks like a pigsty.

(c) I'd better just buy a brand-new car instead.

(d) I'm peachy keen.

해석_ M: 죄송하지만, 이 고물 자동차 못 고칠 것 같아요.

W: 하지만 고칠 수 있다고 했잖아요.

M: 네, 하지만 3,000달러를 더 내셔야 해요.

W: _________________________

(a) 나한테 아첨하려고 하지 마세요.

(b) 이 방은 돼지우리 같아요.

(c) 차라리 그냥 새 차를 사는 게 낫겠어요.

(d) 난 잘 지내.

해설_ 3,000달러를 더 내야 수리를 할 수 있다고 했으므로 차라리 새로 사는 게 낫겠다고 응답한 (c)가 적절하다.

어휘_ fix up 수리하다, 손질하다 heap 고물 자동차[오토바이, 비행기] butter ... up ~에게 아첨하다 pigsty 돼지우리 peachy keen 아주 좋은

정답_ (c)

26.

M: How is your new job going?

W: It was hard going at first, but now I'm making a go of it.

M: Good! If there's anything else you need, let me know.

W: _______________________________________

(a) It goes in one ear and out the other.

(b) Thanks a million.

(c) We must keep an eye on him.

(d) I'm fine. Just leave me alone.

해석_ M: 새 일은 잘돼 가요?

W: 처음엔 힘들었는데, 지금은 잘해 나가고 있어요.

M: 잘됐네요! 뭐 필요한 거 있으면 말해 주세요.

W: _______________________________________

(a) 한 귀로 듣고 한 귀로 흘려버려요.

(b) 정말 고마워요.

(c) 우리는 그를 지켜봐야만 해요.

(d) 괜찮아요. 그냥 저 혼자 있게 내버려 두세요.

해설_ 뭐 필요한 게 있으면 말하라고 했으므로 이에 대해 감사를 표하는 (b)가 이어지는 것이 적절하다. Thanks a million.은 격의 없이 고맙다는 말을 강조하고 싶을 때 쓸 수 있다. (a)는 우리말 속담의 '한 귀로 듣고 한 귀로 흘리다'에 해당하는 영어 표현이다.

어휘_ make a go of it 성공하다, 잘해 나가다 keep an eye on ~를 지켜보다

정답_ (b)

27.

W: Which course would you like to take?

M: I'd like to sign up for Microbiology.

W: I'm sorry, but that course is closed.

M: _______________________________________

(a) I don't need a course description booklet.

(b) I want to drop the course.

(c) Then, I'd like to register for Geology.

(d) Sign me up.

해석_ W: 어떤 과목을 수강하고 싶으세요?

M: 미생물학을 수강하고 싶은데요.

W: 죄송하지만 그 과목은 마감됐습니다.

M: _______________________________________

(a) 저는 수강과목 편람이 필요 없어요.

(b) 그 과목을 취소하고 싶어요.

(c) 그럼 지질학을 수강하고 싶어요.

(d) 나도 끼워 줘.

해설_ 미생물학을 수강하고 싶은데 이미 마감되었다고 했으므로 대신 지질학을 듣겠다고 응답한 (c)가 적절하다.

어휘_ microbiology 미생물학 course description booklet 수강과목 편람 drop 취소하다, 그만두다 geology 지질학

정답_ (c)

28.

M: How do you like the French exchange student?

W: He's nice, but I'm in over my head with my school work at the moment.

M: Why is that?

W: _______________________________________

(a) Try to keep a stiff upper lip.

(b) I want to stay low-key for a while.

(c) I don't always talk shop.

(d) My French is not top-notch.

해석_ M: 그 프랑스 교환 학생 어때?

W: 멋져, 근데 난 지금 학교 공부로 벅차.

M: 왜 그러는데?

W: _______________________________________

(a) 참고 견뎌 봐.

(b) 잠시 조용히 있고 싶어.

(c) 내가 늘 일 얘기만 하는 건 아니야.

(d) 내 프랑스어 실력이 뛰어나질 않아.

해설_ 학교 공부가 벅찬 이유를 묻고 있으므로 이에 관해 언급한 (d)가

정답이다.

어휘_ be in over one's head 능력이 미치지 못하다 keep a stiff upper lip 참고 견디다 low-key (감정·태도 등을) 억제한, 삼가는 talk shop (때와 장소를 가리지 않고) 전문적인 이야기만 하다, 일 얘기만 하다 top-notch 최고의, 일류의

정답_ (d)

29.

M: Hi. You don't look familiar to me.
W: I'm a newbie here. I've just transferred from another school.
M: Well, let's hang out sometime.
W: ____

(a) I will cherish my school days forever.
(b) I rest my case.
(c) You took the words right out of my mouth.
(d) Let's get down to the nitty-gritty.

해석_ M: 안녕. 넌 본 적이 없는 것 같은데.

W: 여기 새로 왔어. 다른 학교에서 막 전학왔어.

M: 음, 언제 한번 같이 놀자.

W: ________________________________

(a) 학창시절의 추억을 영원히 고이 간직할 거야.

(b) 더 이상 할 말이 없어.

(c) 내가 먼저 말하려고 했는데.

(d) 본론으로 들어가자.

해설_ 친하게 지내자는 말에 자신이 먼저 하고 싶었던 말이었다고 응답한 (c)가 가장 적절하다. 상대방이 내가 말하려는 것을 먼저 말했을 때 사용할 수 있는 표현으로, '그게 바로 내가 하려던 말이었어', '내가 먼저 말하려고 했는데'의 뜻을 나타낸다.

어휘_ look familiar to ~에게 낯익다 newbie 신참, 미숙자 hang out 어울리다, 가까이 지내다 cherish 소중히 하다, (추억을) 고이 간직하다 rest one's case 더 이상 할 말이 없다 get down to the nitty-gritty 본론으로 들어가다

정답_ (c)

30.

W: I have my heart set on this laptop.
M: How about a desktop computer?
W: No way. A laptop is much handier than a desktop computer.
M: ____

(a) It's maybe just a bit beyond my means.
(b) I got them at a real steal.
(c) You're using windows 98 which is outdated.
(d) Well. Whichever works for you.

해석_ W: 이 노트북 정말 갖고 싶어요.

M: 데스크탑 컴퓨터는 어때?

W: 싫어요. 데스크탑 컴퓨터보다 노트북이 훨씬 더 편리해요.

M: ________________________________

(a) 내가 사기엔 좀 비싼 것 같아.

(b) 정말 싸게 샀어.

(c) 넌 구식 윈도우 98을 사용하고 있잖아.

(d) 음. 뭐든 본인한테 좋은 걸로 해야지.

해설_ 데스크탑 컴퓨터를 권하는 남자의 말에 노트북이 더 편하다고 말했으므로 본인한테 좋은 걸로 하라는 (d)가 적절하다.

어휘_ have one's heart set on ~을 간절히 바라다, ~하려고 마음먹다 beyond one's means 분에 넘치는, 감당할 수 없는 at a steal 싼값에 outdated 구식의

정답_ (d)

Part 3

31.

M: What do you think of our new boss?
W: Well, he seems a bit unfriendly.
M: Unfriendly? I have had it with him.
W: Why, what's the problem?
M: He's always using four-letter words.
W: Really? He never speaks like that around me.

Q. What are the speakers mainly talking about?

(a) Their new friend
(b) Their problems
(c) Their first day at work
(d) Their new boss

해석_ M: 새로 온 상사에 대해 어떻게 생각하니?

W: 음, 약간 불친절한 것 같은데.

M: 불친절해? 난 더 이상 못 참겠어.

W: 왜, 뭐가 문제야?

M: 그는 항상 욕을 해.

W: 정말? 나한텐 욕설한 적 없는데.

Q. 화자들은 주로 무엇에 관해 이야기하고 있는가?

(a) 그들의 새 친구

(b) 그들의 문제

(c) 그들의 직장에서의 첫날

(d) 그들의 새 상사

해설_ 새로 온 상사에 대해 얘기를 나누고 있으므로 정답은 (d)가 된다. 남자의 마지막 대사에 나오는 four-letter words는 '욕'을 지칭하는 말로, Shit, Fuck, Damn 등 대부분의 영어로 된 욕이 네 글자인데서 비롯된 표현이다.

어휘_ have had it 더 이상 못 참겠다

정답_ (d)

32.

W: I heard you have a new intern in your department.

M: That's right. He is handsome but...

W: But what?

M: We really don't like his attitude.

W: Why? What is he like?

M: Well, he doesn't mix with other people.

Q. What is the main purpose of the conversation?

(a) To talk about a new intern

(b) To talk about the appearance of the new intern

(c) To freeze a new intern out

(d) To gossip about the new intern

해석_ W: 당신 부서에 새 인턴이 들어왔다고 들었어요.

M: 맞아요. 그는 잘생겼지만…

W: 근데 뭐요?

M: 그의 태도가 맘에 안 들어요.

W: 왜요? 어떤 사람이길래요?

M: 음, 다른 사람들이랑 잘 어울리지 못해요.

Q. 대화의 주된 목적은 무엇인가?

(a) 새 인턴에 대해 이야기하기 위해

(b) 새 인턴의 용모에 대해 이야기하기 위해

(c) 새 인턴을 내쫓기 위해

(d) 새 인턴의 험담을 하기 위해

해설_ 남자의 부서에 새로 온 인턴에 관한 얘기를 하고 있으므로 정답

은 (a)가 된다.

어휘_ freeze out 내쫓다, 몰아내다

정답_ (a)

33.

M: What's your favorite sport?

W: I don't like any type of sports.

M: Oh dear. How can you live without sport?

W: Don't be that way! Do you play any instruments then?

M: No! I don't have a talent for it.

W: Then let's just call it even.

Q. Which is correct according to the conversation?

(a) The woman has no interest in sports.

(b) The man is a sports freak.

(c) The woman made the man mad.

(d) The man is not in favor of music.

해석_ M: 어떤 운동을 좋아하세요?

W: 전 운동을 좋아하지 않아요.

M: 세상에. 운동 없이 어떻게 사세요?

W: 그렇게 말씀하지 마세요! 그러는 당신은 연주할 수 있는 악기가 있나요?

M: 아뇨! 재능이 없어요.

W: 그럼 피장파장이네요.

Q. 대화에 따르면 맞는 것은 어느 것인가?

(a) 여자는 운동에 관심이 없다.

(b) 남자는 스포츠광이다.

(c) 여자가 남자를 화나게 했다.

(d) 남자는 음악을 싫어한다.

해설_ 스포츠를 좋아하지 않는다고 했으므로 (a)가 정답이다. (b)는 대화 내용만으로 알 수 없으며, (d) 역시 악기 연주에 재능이 없다고 했지 음악을 싫어하는지는 명확히 알 수 없으므로 정답이 될 수 없다.

어휘_ have a talent for ~에 재능이 있다 Let's call it even. 피장파장이다 in favor of ~을 선호하여

정답_ (a)

34.

W: Did you get the document I asked for?

M: What the hell are you talking about?

W: It must have slipped your mind.

M: What was it about? Oh, that's right. The financial report!

W: I told you a million times.

M: Sorry, I had my mind on something else. I'll go and get it straight away.

Q. What did the man forget?

(a) A financial report

(b) An appointment with the woman

(c) Writing a report

(d) His brief case

해석_ W: 내가 부탁한 서류 가져왔니?

　　 M: 도대체 무슨 말 하는 거야?

　　 W: 깜박했구나.

　　 M: 뭐였더라? 아, 맞다. 재정보고서!

　　 W: 내가 수없이 말했잖아.

　　 M: 미안. 다른 일로 정신이 없었어. 곧장 가서 가져올게.

　　 Q. 남자는 무엇을 깜박 잊었는가?

　　 (a) 재정보고서

　　 (b) 여자와의 약속

　　 (c) 보고서 작성

　　 (d) 서류 가방

해설_ 여자가 부탁한 재정보고서를 깜박 잊었으므로 정답은 (a)다.

어휘_ slip one's mind 깜박 잊다　straight away 곧바로

정답_ (a)

35.

W: Sorry. I lost track of time.

M: Don't tell me you found another sale.

W: I did. These handbags were on sale at 50% off.

M: They're lovely!

W: And I bought these silk scarves.

M: That must have cost a pretty penny.

W: Yeah, I guess I overdid it.

Q. Which is correct according to the conversation?

(a) The woman does not have a watch.

(b) The man is not interested in shopping.

(c) The woman purchased a purse at a low price.

(d) The woman is shopaholic.

해석_ W: 미안. 시간 가는 줄 몰랐어.

　　 M: 너 또 세일하는 데 찾았구나?

　　 W: 응, 그래. 이 핸드백들은 50% 세일하고 있었어.

　　 M: 멋지다!

　　 W: 이 실크 스카프들도 샀어.

　　 M: 꽤 비쌌겠네.

　　 W: 응, 내가 너무 무리한 것 같아.

　　 Q. 대화에 따르면 맞는 것은 어느 것인가?

　　 (a) 여자는 시계가 없다.

　　 (b) 남자는 쇼핑에 관심이 없다.

　　 (c) 여자는 핸드백을 싼값에 샀다.

　　 (d) 여자는 쇼핑 중독자다.

해설_ 핸드백은 50% 세일을 했다고 했으므로 (c)가 정답임을 알 수 있다.

어휘_ lose track of ~을 잊어버리다　cost a pretty penny 돈이 꽤 들다　overdo 무리하다, 지나치게 사용하다　shopaholic 쇼핑 중독자

정답_ (c)

36.

W: Do you know when Joe's going to be in?

M: Oh, didn't you hear? He got sacked yesterday.

W: Really? But I thought he was doing really well.

M: No, he just fudged the sales outcome.

W: Oh, I see. I guess he thought he could pull the wool over everyone's eyes.

M: Well, he thought wrong.

Q. What is correct about Joe?

(a) He will not show up at work anymore.

(b) He got good actual results.

(c) He successfully carried out his work.

(d) He is not very thoughtful.

해석_ W: 조가 언제 들어오는지 아세요?

M: 아, 못 들었어요? 그는 어제 해고됐어요.

W: 정말요? 근데, 전 그가 일을 잘 하고 있다고 생각했어요.

M: 아니에요, 그는 판매 실적을 조작했어요.

W: 아, 그렇군요. 그는 모든 사람들을 속일 수 있을 거라고 생각했나 봐요.

M: 음, 그가 잘못 생각했죠.

Q. 조에 관해 맞는 것은 무엇인가?

(a) 그는 더 이상 회사에 나오지 않는다.

(b) 그는 좋은 실적을 올렸다.

(c) 그는 일을 성공적으로 해냈다.

(d) 그는 사려 깊지 못하다.

해설_ 남자의 첫 번째 대사에서 해고됐다는 내용이 나오므로 (a)가 정답임을 알 수 있다.

어휘_ get sacked 해고되다 fudge 조작하다, 속이다 pull the wool over one's eyes ~의 눈을 속이다

정답_ (a)

37.

M: Did you ever get a chance to go to that new tavern I told you about?

W: No. By the time I finish work, I'm too tired to go out drinking.

M: Too bad. I hate to hear that someone is working so hard that they can't enjoy life.

W: I wouldn't say that. I enjoy my work and the extra money is really going to come in handy.

M: What are you planning to do with the money?

W: I'm getting a new car.

M: Knowing you, I bet it will be more economical and practical rather than sporty.

Q. What is correct about the woman?

(a) She will earn money to buy a new car.

(b) She can't drink much alcohol.

(c) She is in a bad financial state.

(d) She works just to earn money.

해석_ M: 혹시 내가 말했던 그 새로 생긴 술집에 가봤니?

W: 아니. 일을 끝낼 쯤엔 너무 피곤해서 술 마시러 못 가겠어.

M: 정말 유감이다. 누군가 너무 열심히 일만 해서 자기 인생을

즐길 수 없다는 소리를 듣는 게 싫어.

W: 그렇지 않아. 난 내 일이 즐겁고, 또 여윳돈이 생기면 정말 유용하니까.

M: 그 돈 가지고 뭐 하려고?

W: 새 자동차를 살 거야.

M: 너를 잘 아니까, 그 자동차가 사치스러운 게 아니라 경제적이고 실용적일 거라 확신해.

Q. 여자에 대해 맞는 것은 무엇인가?

(a) 그녀는 돈 벌어서 새 차를 구입할 것이다.

(b) 그녀는 술을 잘 못 마신다.

(c) 그녀는 재정적인 어려움에 처해 있다.

(d) 그녀는 단지 돈을 벌기 위해 일한다.

해설_ 여자의 마지막 대사에서 차를 살 거라고 말했으므로 (a)가 정답이다.

어휘_ tavern (선)술집 come in handy 여러모로 편하다, 유용하다 sporty 사치한, 화려한

정답_ (a)

38.

M: You've been hot air ballooning, haven't you?

W: Just once in New Zealand.

M: How was it?

W: It was so amazing. It's one of the best places in the world for hot air ballooning.

M: What makes it so amazing?

W: I guess it's the large area of countryside and the wind currents in that area. Plus it's very affordable.

M: How much was it?

W: I don't remember exactly, but it cost a lot less compared to most other places.

M: But I think the New Zealand dollar has gotten stronger, so it'll cost more now.

Q. Why does the woman think that New Zealand is the best place for hot air ballooning?

(a) Because she likes New Zealand

(b) Because of the variety of hot air ballooning

(c) Because of the large area of countryside and the wind currents

(d) Because she can ride it for free

해석_ M: 너 열기구 타본 적 있지 않아?

W: 뉴질랜드에서 딱 한 번.

M: 어땠어?

W: 아주 놀라웠지. 뉴질랜드는 열기구 타기에 세계에서 가장 좋은 곳 중 하나야.

M: 뭐가 그렇게 놀라운데?

W: 넓은 전원과 그 지역의 바람기류 때문인 것 같아. 게다가 값도 아주 저렴해.

M: 얼마였는데?

W: 정확히 기억은 안 나는데, 대부분 다른 곳에 비해 훨씬 쌌어.

M: 하지만 뉴질랜드 달러가 강세를 띠고 있어서 지금 더 비싸졌을 거야.

Q. 여자는 왜 뉴질랜드가 열기구 타기에 가장 좋은 장소라고 생각하는가?

(a) 그녀가 뉴질랜드를 좋아하기 때문에

(b) 열기구의 종류가 다양하기 때문에

(c) 넓은 전원과 바람기류 때문에

(d) 공짜로 탈 수 있기 때문에

해설_ 여자의 세 번째 대사에서 넓은 전원과 바람기류에 관한 언급을 했으므로 (c)가 정답이다.

어휘_ hot air balloon 열기구에 타다 current 기류

정답_ (c)

39.

W: What's the hang-up?

M: We might be staging a mass walk-out.

W: Did the wage negotiation go to naught?

M: We're looking for a 10% bump on wages, but they won't budge an inch.

W: I hope you don't get burned.

M: Thanks. But it's a little ominous.

Q. What is the man concerned about?

(a) A walk-out at work

(b) His ominous dream

(c) His hangover

(d) The woman's wages

해석_ W: 뭐 고민 있니?

M: 집단 파업을 할지도 몰라.

W: 임금 협상이 실패로 끝났어?

M: 우린 10% 인상을 원하고 있는데 그들은 한 치의 양보도 없어.

W: 네가 피해받게 되지 않길 바란다.

M: 고마워. 하지만 약간 불길해.

Q. 남자는 무엇을 걱정하고 있는가?

(a) 직장에서의 파업

(b) 그의 불길한 꿈

(c) 그의 숙취

(d) 여자의 임금

해설_ 고민 있느냐는 여자의 질문에 파업을 할지도 모른다고 했으므로 남자가 이에 대해 걱정하고 있음을 알 수 있다. 따라서 정답은 (a)가 된다.

어휘_ hang-up 고민거리 stage a mass walk-out 집단 파업을 벌이다 go to naught 실패로 끝나다 bump 인상, 승급, 격상 not budge an inch 조금도 양보하지 않다 ominous 불길한

정답_ (a)

40.

W: So how was your date last night?

M: Amazing! Wow, she was smoking.

W: Is it real this time or just another crush?

M: I think that she might be the one.

W: What is it about her that's caught your eye?

M: She's got an air about her.

Q. What caught the man's eye about her?

(a) Attractive body

(b) Her smoking

(c) Beautiful face

(d) Something special about her

해석_ W: 그래서 어젯밤 데이트는 어땠어?

M: 굉장했지! 와, 그 여자 정말 멋지더라.

W: 이번엔 진짜야, 아님 그냥 또 한순간 끌림이야?

M: 내 생각엔 그녀가 진짜 내 짝인 것 같아.

W: 그녀의 어떤 점이 네 눈을 사로잡았는데?

M: 그녀는 뭔가 특별해.

Q. 그녀의 어떤 점이 그의 눈을 사로잡았는가?

(a) 매력적인 몸매

(b) 담배 피우는 모습

(c) 아름다운 얼굴

(d) 뭔가 특별한 매력

해설_ 남자의 마지막 대사에서 그녀에겐 뭔가 특별한 것이 있다고 했으므로 (d)가 정답임을 알 수 있다.

어휘_ smoking 아주 멋진, 굉장한 crush 홀딱 반함, 일시적 끌림 the one 내 짝, 나한테 딱 맞는 사람

정답_ (d)

41.

W: How's your back feeling?

M: Not good. I've got to make some time to see a back-cracker.

W: It's very likely that you threw your back out of line when you were carrying those heavy boxes.

M: It's probably that, and the fact that I pushed myself too hard playing tennis this morning.

W: You can't say enough about stretching out and warming up before you do something physical.

M: Yeah. I'll be more careful next time.

Q. What is the man's problem?

(a) He hurt his back.

(b) He was too harsh on himself while playing tennis.

(c) He does not like working out.

(d) He can not move the boxes by himself.

해석_ W: 허리 좀 어때?

M: 좋지 않아. 시간 좀 내서 척추 치료사한테 가봐야겠어.

W: 그 무거운 상자들 옮길 때 등을 다친 게 분명해.

M: 아마도 그런 것 같아. 그리고 오늘 아침에 테니스를 심하게 쳐서 그랬을 거야.

W: 뭔가 몸을 쓰는 일을 하기 전에 스트레칭과 몸 풀기 운동은 중요한 거야.

M: 그래. 다음번엔 좀 더 주의할게.

Q. 남자의 문제는 무엇인가?

(a) 그는 등을 다쳤다.

(b) 그는 테니스를 심하게 쳤다.

(c) 그는 운동하는 걸 싫어한다.

(d) 그는 혼자 상자들을 옮길 수 없다.

해설_ 척추 치료사에게 가봐야겠다는 것으로 보아 (a)가 정답임을 알 수 있다.

어휘_ back-cracker 척추 치료사

정답_ (a)

42.

W: I heard your sister is in a difficult financial state.

M: She's working two jobs at the moment but still can't pay the debt.

W: Can't you give her a hand?

M: I'm in debt up to my ears so I can't.

W: Well, I would have to update my bankbook and see if I can lend her some money.

M: That's so kind of you.

Q. What will the woman likely do after the conversation?

(a) She will lend some money to the man.

(b) She will help the man's sister get employed.

(c) She will go to the bank.

(d) She will pay the debt for the man's sister.

해석_ W: 네 동생이 경제적인 어려움에 처해 있다고 하던데.

M: 일을 두 개나 하고 있는데도 아직 빚을 못 갚고 있어.

W: 네가 도와줄 수 없니?

M: 나도 빚이 많아서 그럴 수가 없어.

W: 그녀에게 돈을 빌려 줄 수 있는지 통장 정리를 해봐야겠다.

M: 넌 정말 친절해.

Q. 대화 이후에 여자는 무엇을 할 것 같은가?

(a) 남자에게 돈을 빌려 줄 것이다.

(b) 남자의 여동생이 일자리 얻는 것을 도와줄 것이다.

(c) 은행에 갈 것이다.

(d) 남자의 여동생의 빚을 대신 갚아 줄 것이다.

해설_ 통장 정리를 해봐야겠다고 했으므로 은행에 갈 것임을 알 수 있다. 따라서 정답은 (c).

어휘_ give ... a hand ~를 돕다 be in debt up to one's ears 상당한 빚을 지고 있다

정답_ (c)

43.

W: Do you know if there is a flight on Friday night to Korea?

M: I'm not sure, but you can ask Jake. He works at the airport.

W: Do you know where he is at the moment?

M: He might be at home. Why don't you give him a call?

W: Ok. By the way, how about that croissant?

M: Well, they all look good. I can't decide.

Q. Where are they having the conversation?

(a) At a bakery

(b) At an airport

(c) At Jake's office

(d) At the man's house

해석_ W: 너 금요일 밤에 한국행 비행편이 있는지 아니?

M: 확실히 몰라, 근데 제이크에게 물어봐. 걔 공항에서 일하거든.

W: 지금 어디 있는지 알아?

M: 집에 있을걸. 전화해 보지 그래?

W: 알았어. 그건 그렇고, 저 크로아상 빵은 어때?

M: 글쎄, 빵들이 모두 맛있어 보인다. 결정할 수가 없네.

Q. 그들은 어디에서 대화를 나누고 있는가?

(a) 제과점에서

(b) 공항에서

(c) 제이크의 사무실에서

(d) 남자의 집에서

해설_ 대화 마지막 부분을 통해 빵을 고르고 있음을 알 수 있으므로 정답은 (a)가 된다.

어휘_ croissant 크로아상

정답_ (a)

44.

W: Do you realize how important Tom's role is in our project?

M: Sure I do. He is a core part of our team.

W: But he wants to quit.

M: Don't worry. Just let me talk with him. I can handle it.

W: What are you talking about?

M: I have him wrapped around my finger.

Q. What can be inferred from the conversation?

(a) The man will wrap his finger with a bandage.

(b) The man is confident about convincing Tom.

(c) The woman will ask Tom to continue working with them.

(d) The man and woman will fight with Tom.

해석_ W: 너 톰이 우리 프로젝트에 얼마나 중요한 역할을 하는지 알고 있니?

M: 물론. 그는 우리 팀의 핵이지.

W: 근데 그는 그만두길 원해.

M: 걱정 마. 내가 그와 얘기해 볼게. 내가 처리할 수 있어.

W: 무슨 말 하고 있는 거야?

M: 그는 내 말이면 꼼짝 못하거든.

Q. 대화를 통해 추론할 수 있는 것은?

(a) 남자는 그의 손가락을 붕대로 감았다.

(b) 남자는 톰을 설득할 자신이 있다.

(c) 여자는 톰에게 계속 함께 일해 줄 것을 부탁할 것이다.

(d) 남자와 여자는 톰과 싸울 것이다.

해설_ 톰을 꽉 잡고 있다는 남자의 마지막 대사를 통해 (b)가 정답임을 알 수 있다.

어휘_ have ... wrapped around one's finger ~를 완전 통제하다, 꽉 잡고 있다

정답_ (b)

45.

W: Can I see your notes for the end of semester test?

M: If I let you see them, what are you going to do for me?

W: I will show you my notes. That's fair enough, right?

M: That's like apples and oranges.

W: Well then, how about if I buy you lunch?

M: That sounds good. After you buy me lunch, I will show you my notes.

Q. What can be inferred from the conversation?

(a) The woman will show the notes to the man.
(b) The woman will have lunch with the man.
(c) The man will not give his notes to the woman.
(d) The man and woman will buy some apples and oranges.

해석_ W: 학기말 시험을 위해 네 노트를 보여 줄 수 있니?
　　M: 내가 노트 보여 주면 넌 날 위해 뭘 해줄 건데?
　　W: 내 노트 보여 줄게. 그게 공평하잖아, 맞지?
　　M: 그건 비교가 될 수 없어.
　　W: 그럼 내가 점심 사 주면 어때?
　　M: 그거 좋네. 네가 점심을 사 주고 나면, 내 노트를 보여 줄게.

　　Q. 대화를 통해 추론할 수 있는 것은?

　　(a) 여자는 남자에게 노트를 보여 줄 것이다.
　　(b) 여자는 남자와 함께 점심을 먹을 것이다.
　　(c) 남자는 여자에게 그의 노트를 주지 않을 것이다.
　　(d) 남자와 여자는 사과와 오렌지를 살 것이다.

해설_ 노트를 보여 주는 대가로 여자가 점심을 사기로 했으므로 (b)가
　　정답임을 알 수 있다. 대화 중에 나오는 apples and oranges는
　　비교가 될 수 없는 서로 완전히 다른 사람이나 사물을 가르킬 때
　　사용하는 표현이다.

어휘_ the end of semester 학기말

정답_ (b)

Part 4

46.

Lisa was in the stands in 2003 and watched her sister Jasmine help lead Copiague to a state championship. It was Lisa's turn last night, and she delivered. Lisa, who is the South Carolina point guard scored 28 points, nine rebounds, seven assists and four steals for Copiague in a 74-58 point win. Gabrielle ended with 28 points and sophomore Chelsea finished with 11 points.

Q. Which of the following best summarizes the report?

(a) Copiague mainly won because of Lisa's performance last night.
(b) Copiague has never lost a game since 2003.
(c) Lisa is the South Carolina point guard.
(d) Lisa's sister won the game last night.

해석_ 2003년에 리사는 관중석에서 그녀의 동생 자스민이 코피아그
　　를 주 챔피언 결승전으로 이끄는 것을 지켜보았습니다. 지난밤
　　에는 리사가 우승을 이끈 날이었고, 그녀가 해냈습니다. 사우스
　　캐롤라이나 주 팀의 포인트 가드인 리사는 74-58점으로 이긴
　　게임에서 코피아그를 위해 28득점, 9 리바운드, 7 어시스트, 그
　　리고 4번의 스틸을 기록했습니다. 가브리엘은 28득점을 하고, 2
　　학년생인 첼시는 11득점을 하였습니다.

　　Q. 기사를 가장 잘 요약한 것은?

　　(a) 지난밤 리사의 선전으로 코피아그가 이겼다.
　　(b) 코피아그는 2003년 이래로 경기에 패한 적이 없다.
　　(c) 리사는 사우스캐롤라이나 주 팀의 포인트 가드다.
　　(d) 리사의 동생은 지난밤 경기에서 이겼다.

해설_ 리사가 선전한 덕분으로 우승을 했다는 이야기를 전하고 있으므
　　로 정답은 (a)가 된다.

어휘_ stands 관중석　steal 스틸(상대 공격수로부터 볼을 빼앗는 플레
　　이)　point guard 포인트 가드

정답_ (a)

47.

A lot of cities have experienced this particular phenomenon. Sometimes it's fleeting and sometimes it seems to be ingrained in the very cultural makeup of the community. I like to call it alpha amateurs. This refers to when the college sports teams in an area are better than the professional offerings. Think North Carolina basketball versus the Bobcats, or Michigan football versus Detroit. Our state is going through an alpha amateur phase right now. The entertainment value from the local college programs is a product of such alpha amateurs.

Q. What is an alpha amateur?

(a) A phenomenon of college sports team playing better than the proffessional team

(b) Temporarily occuring cultural phenomenon

(c) Local college entertainment programs

(d) An element that forms culture

해석_ 많은 도시들이 이 특유의 현상을 경험했습니다. 가끔씩 생겼다 없어지기도 하고 가끔씩 공동 사회의 문화 구성 자체에 깊이 배어든 것처럼 보이기도 합니다. 저는 그 현상을 알파 아마추어라고 부르고 싶습니다. 이것은 프로팀보다 어느 한 지역의 대학 스포츠팀이 더 잘할 때를 가르킵니다. 노스캐롤라이나 대 밥캐츠의 농구 경기나, 미시간 대 디트로이트의 풋볼 경기를 생각해 보세요. 현재 우리 주도 알파 아마추어 단계를 겪고 있습니다. 지역 대학 프로그램이 주는 오락적 가치는 그러한 알파 아마추어의 산물입니다.

Q. 알파 아마추어가 무엇인가?

(a) 프로팀보다 대학 스포츠팀이 더 잘하는 현상

(b) 일시적으로 나타나는 문화 현상

(c) 지역 대학의 오락 프로그램

(d) 문화를 구성하는 한 요소

해설_ 네 번째 문장을 통해 정답이 (a)임을 알 수 있다.

어휘_ fleeting 잠깐 동안의, 나는 듯이 지나가는   ingrained in ~에 깊이 배어든   makeup 구성, 구조, 짜임새   go through ~을 겪다   a product of ~의 산물, 성과

정답_ (a)

48.

Anyone who has ever worked knows that there's a lot more to job satisfaction than a paycheck. A workplace's physical and psychological environments are two main points of focus which are essential for a happy employment situation. This is especially true for those who may experience discrimination, such as women, older workers, and workers with disabilities. Before accepting a job, it is important to be at least reasonably certain that you will be treated fairly and with respect.

Q. What is the main point the speaker is trying to make?

(a) Workplace where no discrimination exists must be selected.

(b) You don't need to consider the paycheck.

(c) Selecting the right job is important.

(d) It's difficult for the handicapped to get a job.

해석_ 일을 해본 사람이라면 누구나 직업에 관한 만족이 월급보다 훨씬 더 중요하다는 것을 압니다. 직장의 물리적, 심리적 환경은 직장 내에서의 만족스런 상황을 위해 필수적인 두 가지 주된 요건입니다. 이는 여성, 나이 많은 근로자, 그리고, 장애가 있는 근로자와 같이 차별을 경험할지도 모를 사람들에게 특히 해당되는 것입니다. 일자리를 받아들이기 전에 적어도 여러분이 공정한 대우와 존중을 받을 것이라는 점을 웬만큼 확신할 수 있는 것이 중요합니다.

Q. 화자가 이야기하려고 하는 요점은 무엇인가?

(a) 차별 없는 직장을 선택해야 한다.

(b) 월급은 고려할 필요가 없다.

(c) 올바른 직장을 선택하는 것이 중요하다.

(d) 장애가 있는 근로자들은 직장 구하기가 힘들다.

해설_ 월급보다는 직업에 관한 만족도나 환경적 요소가 훨씬 중요하며, 공정한 대우와 존중을 받을 수 있는 직장을 선택하는 것 또한 중요하다는 내용이므로 (c)가 정답임을 알 수 있다.

어휘_ paycheck 월급   disability (신체 등의) 장애   reasonably 상당히, 꽤, 무리 없이   fairly 공정히, 정당하게

정답_ (c)

49.

Something remodelers should consider is using paints and other finishes that are low in volatile organic compounds (VOC), an expert said. VOCs are toxic chemicals that are found in most household paints on the market. There are a lot of poisons involved in building and remodeling a home. You can usually look on the product label to tell whether a product has low VOC standards. An expert also suggested using water-based finishing products.

Q. Which is correct according to the report?

(a) VOC is a household paint.

(b) VOC is toxic but is not harmful to a human body.

(c) Lower the VOC standards, better the quality of a paint.

(d) Paints containing VOC must not be used.

Q. 기사에 따르면 맞는 것은 어느 것인가?

(a) VOC는 가정용 페인트다.

(b) VOC는 유독성이긴 하지만 인체에 해롭진 않다.

(c) VOC 기준치가 낮을수록 좋은 페인트다.

(d) VOC가 들어간 페인트는 사용해선 안 된다.

50.

The Chicago High School varsity dance team won three national titles, including the National Sweepstakes Award, during competition last weekend at the H&T Convention Center. The Sweepstakes Award was presented to the team for achieving the highest average score of any team in the competition. In addition, senior Alexandra came in fourth for her solo.

Q. What is the main focus of the report?

(a) The Chicago dance team won a total of times.

(b) The Chicago High School varsity dance team came off as the victor.

(c) Dance competition was held at H&T Convention center.

(d) The Chicago High School varsity dance team participated in the contest.

Q. 기사의 주된 내용은 무엇인가?

(a) 시카고 댄스팀은 전승을 거두었다.

(b) 시카고 고등학교 댄스 대표팀이 우승을 했다.

(c) 댄스 대회가 H&T 컨벤션 센터에서 열렸다.

(d) 시카고 고등학교 댄스 대표팀이 콘테스트에 참가했다.

51.

Tobacco users face a double hit as a 1 percent state sales-tax increase and the single largest federal tobacco tax hike both take effect Wednesday. Tobacco companies are trying to turn the situation to their advantage. The major cigarette makers unashamedly raised prices a couple of weeks ago, partly to offset any drop in profits once the per-pack federal tax climbs from 39 cents to $1.01.

Q. What is the main purpose of the report?

(a) To tell smokers where the non-smoking areas are

(b) To provide tobacco companies with statistical data

(c) To hold a non-smoking campaign for the smokers

(d) To announce the raise in the price of tabacco to the smokers

니다.

Q. 기사의 주된 목적은 무엇인가?

(a) 흡연자에게 금연 장소를 알려주기 위해

(b) 담배 회사들에게 통계자료를 제공하기 위해

(c) 흡연자들을 위한 금연 운동을 하기 위해

(d) 흡연자들에게 담배 가격 인상을 알리기 위해

해설_ 담배 값 인상에 관한 내용을 전하고 있으므로 정답은 (d)가 된다.

어휘_ state sales tax 주정부 판매세　hike (가격 등의) 인상　take effect 효력을 나타내다, 시행되다　unashamedly 뻔뻔스럽게, 주제넘게　offset 상쇄하다, 차감 계산하다　statistical 통계적인

정답_ (d)

52.

How will you celebrate? International Women's Day is right around the corner and it, officially honored as a national holiday on March 8, is a day to bring awareness about women's rights, as well as spreading awareness about the struggles of women all around the world. In Russia, International Women's Day is a day in which the men rise early in the morning to fetch flowers for not only their wives, but the mothers and daughters of the family as well.

Q. Which is correct about the International Women's Day?

(a) Every year on March 18th, variety of events for women are held.
(b) In Russia, men give flowers to women in his family.
(c) It is not a special day in Russia.
(d) It is a day of criticizing superiority of men.

해석_ 어떻게 축하하실 겁니까? 세계 여성의 날이 바로 코앞으로 다가왔습니다. 공식적으로 3월 8일에 국경일로 채택된 이 날은 여성의 권리에 관한 인식을 가져다주고 전 세계 여성의 투쟁에 관한 인식을 널리 알리는 날입니다. 러시아에서 세계 여성의 날은 남자들이 아침 일찍 일어나 자신들의 아내뿐 아니라 어머니와 딸을 위해 꽃을 갖다 주는 날입니다.

Q. 세계 여성의 날에 대해 맞는 것은 어느 것인가?

(a) 매년 3월 18일로 여성들만을 위한 다양한 행사가 열린다.

(b) 러시아의 남자들은 그날 집안 여자들에게 꽃을 준다.

(c) 러시아에서는 특별한 날이 아니다.

(d) 남성 우월주의를 비판하는 날이다.

해설_ 글 마지막 부분에 러시아에서는 남자들이 부인, 딸, 어머니를 위해 꽃을 갖다 주는 날이라고 했으므로 정답은 (b)가 된다.

어휘_ fetch 가지고 오다

정답_ (b)

53.

These teachers, with real-life experience and often with deep knowledge of their subjects, are answering a call to service that is part of a strategy to dramatically boost the size and quality of the teaching work force. Career switchers make up about one-third of the ranks of new teachers, and that number has jumped in the past decade. Now, as the recession deepens, even more people are deciding to become teachers.

Q. What is the tone of the speaker?

(a) Pessimistic
(b) Critical
(c) Agitative
(d) Objective

해석_ 실제 경험과 종종 자신들의 과목에 깊은 이해를 지니고 있는 교사들은 교사 인력의 규모와 질을 획기적으로 끌어올리기 위한 전략 중 하나로서 전화에 응답하는 서비스를 하고 있습니다. 직업을 바꾸려는 사람들이 신입교사 대열에 낀 사람들 중 약 3분의 1을 구성하고 있으며, 그 수는 지난 10년간 크게 증가했습니다. 이제, 경기 침체가 심각해짐에 따라 더 많은 사람들이 교사가 되기로 결심하고 있습니다.

Q. 화자의 어조는 어떠한가?

(a) 비관적인

(b) 비판적인

(c) 선동적인

(d) 객관적인

해설_ 현재 교사가 되려고 하는 사람들이 늘고 있다는 사실에 관해서 이야기하고 있으므로 정답은 (d)가 된다.

어휘_ career switcher 직업을 바꾸려는 사람　deepen (사태 등이) 심화되다, 심각해지다　pessimistic 비관적인

agitative 선동적인

정답_ (d)

54.

The belief that that's what women want has long been held by many. But many women are choosing to embrace love without marriage. Bonnie Eslinger, 44, is one of those women. "There's no piece of paper that is necessary if you have it in your head and heart to spend the rest of your lives together. Marriage is not necessary for emotional or intelligent commitment." She says.

Q. What is the talk about?

(a) The reason why women refuse marriage
(b) Change in what women want
(c) Needless pledge of marriage
(d) Woman who are in love

해석_ 여자들이 원하는 것에 관한 믿음은 오랫동안 많은 사람들에 의해서 유지돼 왔습니다. 그러나 많은 여자들이 결혼 없는 사랑을 받아들이는 것을 선택하고 있습니다. 44세의 보니 에슬링거는 그런 여자들 중 한 명입니다. "만약 당신이 당신의 남은 인생을 함께 보내기 위해 당신의 머리와 마음속에 사랑을 가지고 있다면 어떠한 서약도 필요하지 않습니다. 결혼은 감정적인 혹은 이성적인 서약에 필요하지 않습니다." 라고 그녀는 말합니다.

Q. 무엇에 관한 담화인가?

(a) 여자들이 결혼을 거부하는 이유
(b) 여자들이 원하는 것에 대한 변화
(c) 불필요한 결혼 서약서
(d) 사랑에 빠진 여자들

해설_ 이제까지 생각되어져 왔던 것과는 달리 여자들이 결혼 없는 사랑을 택하고 있다고 했으므로 정답은 (b)가 된다.

어휘_ embrace 껴안다, 받아들이다 commitment 서약

정답_ (b)

55.

Welcome to Decision for an Engineering Manager at the Harbor Hotel. The Harbor Hotel is a newly renovated, 136 room hotel located in San Francisco. It is the leading hotel in the area. The Engineering Manager has supervisory responsibilities including interviewing, hiring, and training employees. You will also need to ensure that the hotel is a safe place for both guests and employees.

Q. What is the purpose of this presentation?

(a) To advertise newly renovated hotels
(b) To explain about the hotel and the job to the potential engineering managers
(c) To boost about the hotel's leading status
(d) To explain about the job to the new hotel employers

해석_ 하버 호텔의 기술 담당자 모집 설명회에 오신 걸 환영합니다. 하버 호텔은 샌프란시스코에 위치한 새로이 단장된, 136개의 방을 갖춘 호텔입니다. 그 지역의 일류 호텔이죠. 기술 담당자는 직원 인터뷰, 고용, 그리고 훈련을 포함한 관리 책임을 맡습니다. 또한 호텔 고객과 직원들에게 이 호텔이 안전한 곳임을 확신시키도록 해야 합니다.

Q. 이 설명회의 목적은 무엇인가?

(a) 새로이 단장된 호텔을 홍보하기 위해
(b) 잠재적인 기술 담당자들에게 호텔 및 직무에 대해 설명하기 위해
(c) 일류 호텔임을 자랑하기 위해
(d) 새 호텔 직원들에게 직무에 대해 설명하기 위해

해설_ 호텔의 기술 담당자 모집 설명회이므로 (b)가 정답임을 알 수 있다.

어휘_ supervisory 감독(상)의, 관리(상)의

정답_ (b)

56.

Diabetes is a disease which millions of people live with every day. There's no cure. There's only life support in the form of insulin. Three-year-old Andrew was diagnosed in July. He is learning that finger sticks and needles will be a part of his life for a long time. Even if he manages it perfectly there are still no guarantees.

Q. Which of the following is true according to

the report?

(a) Diabetes is the most deadly disease.
(b) Andrew will receive psychical therapy.
(c) Andrew labors under his disease.
(d) There is a cure but it's too expensive.

해석 당뇨병은 매일 수백만 명의 사람들이 앓고 있는 병입니다. 치료 약은 없습니다. 인슐린을 맞는 것만이 유일한 생명 유지 장치입니다. 3살인 앤드류는 7월에 진단을 받았습니다. 그는 손가락 채혈 검사기와 주사 바늘이 오랫동안 그의 삶의 일부가 될 것임을 알고 있습니다. 비록 그가 완벽하게 병을 관리하더라도 여전히 나을 보장은 없습니다.

Q. 기사에 따르면 사실인 것은 어느 것인가?

(a) 당뇨병은 가장 치명적인 병이다.
(b) 앤드류는 심리 치료를 받을 것이다.
(c) 앤드류는 병마에 시달리고 있다.
(d) 치료약은 있지만 너무 비싸다.

해설 당뇨병을 진단받았다고 했으므로 (c)가 정답이다. (a)는 당뇨병이 심각한 병인 것은 사실이지만 가장 치명적인 병이라는 것은 언급돼 있지 않으므로 정답이 될 수 없다.

어휘 cure 치료제, 치료법 life support 생명 유지 장치 labor under one's disease 병마에 시달리다

정답 (c)

57.

Roommates are an important part of the residence hall experience. Most roommate relationships evolve successfully over time, especially when roommates demonstrate mutual respect and maturity in working out differences and communicate directly and honestly. While it's normal to have some anxiety about living together in new circumstances, it's important to keep in mind that roommate relationships can be very rewarding and are a great opportunity for learning about oneself and others.

Q. What is important in maintaining a good relationship with a roommate?

(a) Adapting to new circumstances quickly
(b) Keeping good company
(c) Keeping good memories with your roommate
(d) Understanding each other and having an honest conversation

해석 룸메이트는 기숙사 경험의 중요한 일부입니다. 대부분의 룸메이트 관계는 시간이 지나면서 성공적으로 서서히 발전하며, 특히, 룸메이트들이 서로 다른 점들을 이해하는 데 있어 상호 존중과 성숙함을 보여 주고, 솔직하고 정직하게 대화를 나눌 때 그렇습니다. 새로운 환경에서 함께 사는 것에 대해 불안한 마음을 갖는 것이 보통이지만, 룸메이트와의 관계는 큰 보람을 줄 수 있고, 자기 자신과 다른 사람들에 대해 배울 수 있는 아주 좋은 기회가 될 수 있다는 점을 명심하는 것이 중요합니다.

Q. 룸메이트와 좋은 관계를 유지하는 데 중요한 것은 무엇인가?

(a) 새로운 환경에 빠르게 적응하는 것
(b) 좋은 친구를 사귀는 것
(c) 룸메이트와 좋은 추억을 간직하는 것
(d) 서로 이해하고 솔직한 대화를 나누는 것

해설 특히 서로의 차이를 이해하고 마음을 터놓고 얘기할 때 좋은 관계로 발전한다고 했으므로 정답은 (d)가 된다.

어휘 residence hall 기숙사 evolve 서서히 발전하다 maturity 성숙(함) work out 이해하다 rewarding ～할 만한 가치가 있는, ～할 보람이 있는 keep good company 좋은 친구를 사귀다

정답 (d)

58.

In recent years, merchants have been pushing forward sales and expanded hours that were typically reserved for that day. This year, in a desperate bid to pull in shoppers, stores were even more aggressive, offering discounts of up to 70 percent in the days leading to the weekend, and widening those price cuts for a broader array of merchandise for the early morning deals.

Q. What can be inferred from the report?

(a) Shopping prices have risen compared with last year.
(b) The stores will open earlier in the morning.

(c) The merchants will not benefit due to the big discounts.

(d) People can save more money when shopping.

해석_ 최근 몇 년간, 상인들은 할인 판매를 추진해 오고 있으며, 원래 정해져 있던 영업 시간을 연장하고 있습니다. 올해는 더 많은 쇼핑객들을 끌어들일 필사적인 목적으로, 상점들은 일주일 내내 70퍼센트까지 할인을 제공하고, 이른 아침에 파는 더 많은 상품에도 70퍼센트 가격 인하를 확대하면서 더욱더 적극적이 되었습니다.

Q. 기사를 통해 추론할 수 있는 것은?

(a) 쇼핑 가격이 작년보다 올랐다.

(b) 상점들은 아침에 더 일찍 문을 열 것이다.

(c) 상인들은 대폭 할인 판매로 인해 이득을 보지 못할 것이다.

(d) 사람들은 쇼핑할 때 더 많은 돈을 아낄 수 있다.

해설_ 일주일 내내 70퍼센트까지 할인 판매를 하고 있다고 했으므로 (d)가 정답임을 알 수 있다. (a)는 내용과 상반되며, (b)와 (c)는 명확히 알 수 있는 사항이 아니므로 정답이 될 수 없다.

어휘_ push forward 추진하다 in a bid to ~할 목적으로

정답_ (d)

59.

The symposium will provide a unique opportunity for brain aneurysm survivors and their families to meet with other survivors, caregivers and health care professionals. The symposium will offer formal presentations and informational displays. Topics will include diagnosis, surgical treatments of brain aneurysms, conquering headaches and maintaining a positive attitude.

Q. What can be inferred about the symposium?

(a) The symposium will be held at the hospital.

(b) The symposium will be a great help to the brain aneurysm patients.

(c) The symposium will offer every information about brain disease.

(d) Many people will attend the symposium.

해석_ 이 토론회는 뇌동맥류 생존자들과 그들의 가족들이 다른 생존자들, 간병인들, 그리고 의료 전문가들과 만날 수 있는 특별한 기회를 제공해 줄 것입니다. 이 토론회에서는 공식 발표와 자료 화면을 제공해 줄 것입니다. 주제로는 진단법, 뇌동맥류 수술, 두통을 없애고 긍정적인 태도 유지하기가 포함될 것입니다.

Q. 토론회에 관해 추론할 수 있는 것은?

(a) 토론회는 병원에서 열릴 것이다.

(b) 토론회는 뇌동맥류 환자들에게 큰 도움이 될 것이다.

(c) 토론회는 뇌질환에 관한 모든 정보를 제공해 줄 것이다.

(d) 토론회에는 많은 사람들이 참석할 것이다.

해설_ 토론회를 통해 다른 생존자들과 간병인, 또 의료 전문가들과 만날 수 있고, 뇌동맥류 질환과 관련하여 여러 가지 정보를 얻을 수 있다고 했으므로 (b)가 정답임을 알 수 있다. (a)는 가능성 있는 내용이긴 하지만 글을 통해 명확히 알 수 있는 사항이 아니므로 정답이 될 수 없다. (d) 역시 알 수 없으며, (c)는 글 내용과 다르다.

어휘_ symposium 토론회   brain aneurysm 뇌동맥류   caregiver (병자·어린이 등을) 돌보는 사람

정답_ (b)

60.

A cold front will cross the region from the west tonight. Windy conditions will affect the higher ridge tops across the North Carolina mountains ahead of the front this evening. As the cold front sweeps through overnight, additional thunderstorms may develop. Brief damaging wind gusts will be the main threat. The greatest risk of severe storms will be across Northeast Georgia on Tuesday.

Q. What can be inferred from the weather forecast?

(a) A cold front will not go across North Carolina mountains.

(b) Tonight's weather conditions will be nasty.

(c) North Carolina mountains will be very cold because of the wind.

(d) The worst storm will hit the West during the night.

해석_ 한랭전선이 오늘 밤 서쪽 지역을 지나갈 것입니다. 바람 부는 날

씨는 오늘 저녁 전선이 아직 지나가지 않은 노스캐롤라이나 산맥을 가로질러 더 높은 산등성이 꼭대기 지역에 영향을 미칠 것입니다. 한랭전선이 밤새 휩쓸고 지나가면서 뇌우가 함께 발생할 가능성도 있습니다. 잠깐 동안 피해를 일으킬 돌풍이 주된 위협이 될 것입니다. 가장 큰 위험이 될 강력한 폭풍우는 화요일에 노스이스트 조지아를 거쳐갈 것입니다.

Q. 일기예보를 통해 추론할 수 있는 것은?

(a) 노스캐롤라이나 산맥에는 한랭전선이 통과하지 않을 것이다.

(b) 오늘 밤 날씨는 험악할 것이다.

(c) 노스캐롤라이나 산악지대는 바람으로 인해 몹시 추울 것이다.

(d) 밤사이 가장 심한 폭풍우가 서쪽 지역에 불어닥칠 것이다.

해설_ 한랭전선이 밤새 지나면서 뇌우가 발생할 수도 있으며 돌풍이 불 것이라고 했으므로 (b)가 정답임을 알 수 있다. (a)와 (c)는 명확히 알 수 없으며, (d)는 내용과 다르므로 정답이 될 수 없다.

어휘_ cold front 한랭전선 ahead of the front 전선이 아직 지나가지 않은 ridge 산등성이 sweep through ~을 휩쓸고 지나가다 thunderstorm 뇌우 gust 돌풍 nasty (날씨 등이) 험악한

정답_ (b)

Final Test 2

Part 1

1.

M: Life can get so stressful at times. I just want to hang it up and start over fresh.

W: ________________________________

(a) I have ants in my pants.

(b) I was struck dumb.

(c) Please cheer up! You've got me.

(d) You're grinning from ear to ear.

해석_ M: 사는 게 가끔 너무 힘들어. 다 때려치우고 새로 시작하고 싶다.

W: ________________________

(a) 나 불안해.

(b) 난 말문이 막혔어.

(c) 힘내! 너한텐 내가 있잖아.

(d) 아주 입이 귀에 걸려 있구나.

해설_ 다 관두고 새로 시작하고 싶다는 남자에게 힘내라고 격려해 주는 (c)가 가장 적절하다.

어휘_ hang it up 그만두다, 체념하다 have ants in one's pants 안절부절못하다, 불안해하다 be struck dumb 말문이 막히다 grin from ear to ear 입이 째지게 웃다

정답_ (c)

2.

W: Have you thought about what kind of college would be good for your son?

M: ________________________________

(a) He never pays any attention to me.

(b) Yes, but we don't see eye to eye on it.

(c) Good for you.

(d) He earned his way through college.

해석_ W: 어떤 대학이 아드님께 좋을지 생각해 보셨어요?

M: ________________________

(a) 그는 내 말을 귀담아듣지 않아요.

(b) 네, 하지만 우리는 의견이 맞질 않아요.

(c) 잘됐네요.

(d) 그는 고학으로 대학을 나왔어요.

해설_ 아들에게 적합한 대학을 생각해 봤는지 묻고 있으므로 이에 관해 언급한 (b)가 정답이다.

어휘_ see eye to eye 의견이 같다   earn one's way through college 고학으로 대학을 나오다

정답_ (b)

3.

M: If you don't sit down, I'm going to really blow my top!

W: ____

(a) I apologize. It won't happen again.
(b) When I tell you to stop, stop.
(c) The assignment is over our heads.
(d) You should do it, or you'll bomb this course.

해석_ M: 자리에 안 앉으면 정말 화낼 거야!

W: ________________________________

(a) 죄송해요, 다신 그러지 않을게요.
(b) 내가 그만하라고 할 때, 그만해.
(c) 그 숙제는 우리한테 너무 어려워요.
(d) 그걸 해야 해, 그렇지 않으면 넌 이 과목 낙제할 거야.

해설_ 자리에 앉지 않으면 화낼 거라고 했으므로 다신 그러지 않겠다고 말하는 (a)가 이어지는 것이 적절하다. blow one's top은 '화내다'란 뜻인데, 직역하자면 '머리 꼭대기를 날려버리다'로, 우리말의 '뚜껑이 열리다'와 아주 비슷한 표현이다.

어휘_ over one's head 이해하기 어려운, ~에게 이해되지 않는   bomb 실패하다

정답_ (a)

4.

M: This drug makes me drowsy and blurs my vision.

W: ____

(a) I think I need to take an antacid.
(b) Maybe you're not taking it right.
(c) There are instructions on the label.
(d) Let me feel your forehead.

해석_ M: 이 약 때문에 어지럽고 눈앞이 흐릿해 보여요.

W: ________________________________

(a) 제산제를 먹어야 할 것 같아요.
(b) 올바르게 복용하고 계신 게 아닐 수도 있어요.

(c) 라벨에 복용 방법이 있어요.
(d) 이마 좀 짚어 볼게요.

해설_ 약 때문에 문제가 있다고 말하고 있으므로 약을 잘못 복용해서 그럴지도 모른다는 (b)가 가장 적절하다.

어휘_ drowsy 졸음이 오는   blur (시야 등이) 흐릿해지다   vision 시력, 시야   antacid 제산제

정답_ (b)

5.

W: The most common way we spread germs and bacteria is through our hands.

M: ____

(a) You can say that again.
(b) He's seeing a shrink.
(c) I've got a lump.
(d) I threw my back out.

해석_ W: 우리가 세균과 박테리아를 퍼뜨리는 가장 흔한 방법은 우리의 손을 통해서야.

M: ________________________________

(a) 맞는 말이야.
(b) 그는 정신과 치료를 받고 있어.
(c) 혹이 났어.
(d) 허리를 삐었어.

해설_ 세균과 박테리아가 손을 통해 퍼진다고 했으므로 이에 동의를 표하는 (a)가 적절하다.

어휘_ germ 세균   bacteria 세균, 박테리아   lump 혹   shrink 〈속어〉 정신과 의사   throw one's back out 허리를 삐다

정답_ (a)

6.

M: What are you doing to your face?

W: ____

(a) Beauty is but skin deep.
(b) I want to make it shaggy.
(c) I'm giving myself a facial.
(d) I want it thinned out.

해석_ M: 얼굴에 뭘 하고 있는 거야?

W: ________________________________

(a) 미모는 가죽 한 꺼풀일 뿐이야.
(b) 샤기컷으로 잘라 주세요.

(c) 팩하고 있어.

(d) 머리숱 좀 쳐주세요.

해설_ 얼굴에 뭘 하고 있는지 묻고 있으므로 팩하고 있다고 응답한 (c)
가 정답이다. (a)는 '미모는 가죽 한 꺼풀'이라는 속담으로, 외모
가 전부가 아님을 나타내는 표현이다.

어휘_ shaggy 얽히고 설킨 facial 팩   thin out 숱다

정답_ (c)

7.

M: What seems to be the cause of the rift?

W: ___________________________________

(a) It all comes down to parking.
(b) He is a spitting image of his father.
(c) I wouldn't do that kind of work for peanuts.
(d) Have a heart.

해석_ M: 사이가 안 좋은 이유가 뭐야?

W: ___________________________

(a) 그건 모두 주차 때문이야.

(b) 그는 그의 아버지와 꼭 닮았어.

(c) 푼돈 받고 그런 일을 하진 않겠어.

(d) 사정 좀 봐줘라.

해설_ 사이가 안 좋은 이유를 묻고 있으므로 이에 관해 언급한 (a)가
정답이다. (d)는 '사정 좀 봐줘라', '인정을 베풀어라'의 뜻으로,
인정이나 선처를 베풀거나 사정을 봐달라고 간청하는 경우에 쓸
수 있는 표현이다.

어휘_ rift 불화   come down to ~로 귀착되다   spitting
image 빼닮음, 빼닮은 것 peanuts 아주 적은 액수, 푼돈

정답_ (a)

8.

M: Are you into the zodiac and reading the
stars to predict your fortune?

W: ___________________________________

(a) Would you get a grip?
(b) I read the little blurbs that are in most
newspapers, but not much more than that.
(c) Now, let's talk turkey.
(d) I'm going to have to eat humble pie tonight.

해석_ M: 12궁도에 푹 빠져서 별자리 운세를 읽고 있니?

W: ___________________________

(a) 좀 진정하지 그래?

(b) 대부분 신문에 나와 있는 걸 보긴 하지만 단지 그뿐이야.

(c) 이제 솔직하게 말해 보자.

(d) 내키진 않지만 오늘 밤은 내 잘못을 인정할게.

해설_ 별자리 운세를 보고 있냐는 질문에 이어질 응답으로, 신문에 나
와 있는 걸 보는 것뿐이라고 말한 (b)가 적절하다. (c)는 그 유래
를 살펴보면, 백인과 인디언이 함께 칠면조 사냥을 나가서 여러
마리의 칠면조를 잡았는데, 다 모으고 보니 까마귀 몇 마리가 끼
어 있었다. 백인은 칠면조를 혼자 다 가져갈 속셈으로 인디언에
게 까마귀 고기가 좋으니 다 가져가라고 했다. 그러나 인디언은
백인에게 까마귀 얘기는 관두라며 "Now, let's talk turkey."라
고 했는데, 여기서 유래하여 '솔직하게 말해 보자', '문제 해결을
위한 근본에 대해 얘기하자'란 뜻으로 쓰이게 되었다고 한다.
(d)의 eat humble pie는 '굴욕을 참다', '잘못을 마지못해 시인
하다'란 뜻으로, 16세기 영국에서 귀족들이 사냥을 해오면 하인
들이 그 고기의 내장(umbles)을 먹은 데서 유래된 표현으로, 원
래는 umbles였는데 후에 humble로 와전된 것이라고 한다.

어휘_ be into ~에 푹 빠져 있다 zodiac 12궁도 get a grip 진
정하다 blurb 광고

정답_ (b)

9.

W: How do you keep abreast of world affairs?

M: ___________________________________

(a) He always keeps me in stitches.
(b) But it was nip and tuck this time.
(c) It's a hand-me-down from my big brother.
(d) I learn all I need to know right from the
Internet.

해석_ W: 넌 세상일을 어떻게 그리 잘 아니?

M: ___________________________

(a) 그는 항상 날 배꼽 잡고 웃게 만들어.

(b) 하지만 이번엔 막상막하였어.

(c) 그건 우리 큰형한테 물려받은 옷이야.

(d) 난 인터넷에서 직접 내가 알아야 할 모든 걸 배워.

해설_ 세상일을 어떻게 잘 알고 있는지 묻고 있으므로 인터넷을 통해
배운다고 응답한 (d)가 적절하다.

어휘_ keep abreast of ~에 뒤지지 않다 keep ... in
stitches ~를 배꼽 잡고 웃게 하다 nip and tuck 막상막
하의 hand-me-down 물려받은 옷

정답_ (d)

10.

M: Saving is paramount! How much money do you have socked away in the vault?

W: _______________________________

(a) I stayed at home and vegged out.

(b) I'm ticked off at her.

(c) I feel like I am in a rut.

(d) If I spilled the beans, you would be surprised.

해석_ M: 저축이 최고야! 넌 금고에 돈을 얼마나 많이 모아 뒀니?

　　 W: _______________________________

　　 (a) 아무 일도 않고 죽 집에 있었어.

　　 (b) 그녀 때문에 화났어.

　　 (c) 다람쥐 쳇바퀴 돌듯이 무료함을 느껴.

　　 (d) 내가 비밀을 털어놓으면 넌 깜짝 놀랄 거야.

해설_ 돈을 얼마나 모았는지 묻는 질문에, 말하면 깜짝 놀랄 거라고 응답한 (d)가 적절하다. (a)의 veg out은 '움직임 없는 야채나 식물처럼 지내다', 즉 '아무것도 하지 않고 느긋하게 쉬다'란 의미로, 여기서 veg은 vegetable(야채)에서 파생된 말이다.

어휘_ paramount 최고의　sock away 돈을 모아 두다　vault 금고　tick off 화나게 하다　in a rut 틀에 박힌, 단조로운　spill the beans 비밀을 털어놓다

정답_ (d)

11.

W: What sort of vittles do you have in the morning?

M: _______________________________

(a) I think we can squeeze you in at 2:00.

(b) A little of this and a little of that. Just the basics really.

(c) I'm tickled pink.

(d) If I were to kick the bucket right now, I bet you'll miss me.

해석_ W: 아침에 무슨 음식을 먹니?

　　 M: _______________________________

　　 (a) 2시에 잠깐 시간을 낼 수 있을 것 같아.

　　 (b) 이것저것. 그냥 기본적인 것들만 먹어.

　　 (c) 좋아 죽겠어.

　　 (d) 내가 지금 당장 죽는다면, 넌 날 틀림없이 그리워할 거야.

해설_ 아침에 뭘 먹는지 묻고 있으므로 이에 답한 (b)가 정답이다. (d)의 kick the bucket은 '죽다'란 뜻으로, 양동이 위에 올라가 밧줄로 목을 맨 다음 양동이를 걷어차 버림으로써 자살을 하는 모습에서 유래된 속어 표현이다.

어휘_ vittles(= victuals) 음식물　squeeze ... in (바쁜 일정 중에) ~를 만나다, ~에게 시간을 내주다　be tickled pink 크게 기뻐하다

정답_ (b)

12.

M: Congratulations! When did Jake pop the question?

W: _______________________________

(a) You know, he likes hip-hop very much.

(b) He questioned it a long time ago.

(c) He didn't. I asked him to marry me.

(d) He didn't ask about the pop-up ads.

해석_ M: 축하해! 제이크가 언제 청혼했어?

　　 W: _______________________________

　　 (a) 알잖아, 그는 힙합을 매우 좋아해.

　　 (b) 그는 오래 전에 그걸 의심했어.

　　 (c) 그가 안 했어. 내가 그에게 청혼한 거야.

　　 (d) 그는 팝업 광고에 대해 묻지 않았어.

해설_ 제이크가 언제 청혼했는지 묻는 질문에 이어질 응답으로, 그가 한 게 아니라 자신이 청혼했다고 말한 (c)가 적절하다.

어휘_ pop the question 청혼하다　pop-up ads 팝업 광고

정답_ (c)

13.

M: I was stuck on the Olympic highway for an hour.

W: _______________________________

(a) Really? I want to take that road.

(b) Traffic is nuts on Friday evenings.

(c) What did you do in Olympic stadium?

(d) How did you get to the highway?

해석_ M: 1시간 동안 올림픽 고속도로에 갇혀 있었어요.

　　 W: _______________________________

　　 (a) 정말요? 그 도로를 타고 싶네요.

　　 (b) 금요일 저녁엔 교통이 장난이 아니죠.

(c) 올림픽 경기장에서 뭐했어요?

(d) 고속도로까지 어떻게 갔어요?

해설_ 1시간 동안 고속도로에서 꼼짝달싹 못했다고 했으므로 금요일 저녁엔 교통 체증이 심하다고 언급한 (b)가 가장 적절하다.

어휘_ be stuck on ~에 매여 꼼짝달싹 못하다 nuts 골칫거리

정답_ (b)

14.

M: Your cell phone has a GPS tracking function, doesn't it ?

W: ____

(a) Yes. It's tracking my every move.

(b) I want to have a multifunctional cell phone.

(c) No, I like call forwarding.

(d) No. M&T is my mobile phone service provider.

해석_ M: 네 휴대폰에 위치추적 기능이 있지 않니?

W: ____________________________________

(a) 응. 나의 모든 움직임을 추적하고 있어.

(b) 다기능 휴대폰을 갖고 싶어.

(c) 아니, 난 착신 전환 서비스를 좋아해.

(d) 아니. M&T가 내 휴대폰 서비스 업체야.

해설_ 위치추적 기능이 있는지 묻고 있으므로 이에 답한 (a)가 적절하다.

어휘_ GPS tracking function 위치추적 기능 multifunctional 다기능의 call forwarding 착신 전환 서비스 mobile phone service provider 휴대폰 서비스 업체

정답_ (a)

15.

M: I have the runs. Where's the john?

W: ____

(a) He is in City Hall.

(b) It's just around the corner.

(c) You should take some medicine.

(d) You have to run fast.

해석_ M: 설사했어. 남자 화장실이 어딨지?

W: ____________________________________

(a) 그는 시청에 있어.

(b) 모퉁이 지나면 바로 있어.

(c) 넌 약을 먹어야 해.

(d) 넌 빨리 달려야 해.

해설_ 남자 화장실이 어딨는지 묻고 있으므로 위치를 알려주는 (b)가 정답이다.

어휘_ have the runs 설사하다 john 남자 화장실

정답_ (b)

15.

W: Have you ever slept rough?

M: ____

(a) Yes, I slept very well.

(b) No, it was very difficult.

(c) I don't want to sleep right now.

(d) No, I haven't. Have you?

해석_ W: 너 야외에서 자본 적 있어?

M: ____________________________________

(a) 응, 아주 잘 잤어.

(b) 아니, 그건 너무 어려웠어.

(c) 지금 당장 자고 싶지 않아.

(d) 아니. 넌?

해설_ 야외에서 자본 적이 있는지 묻고 있으므로 이에 답한 (d)가 정답이다.

어휘_ sleep rough 아무 데서나[야외에서] 자다

정답_ (d)

Part 2

16.

M: We are running late for the movie. Let's hurry up!

W: I know, but he is still sleeping.

M: What? I was told that Jane was waking him up.

W: ____

(a) Jane is my best friend.

(b) She's trying to, but he's such a heavy sleeper.

(c) The movie was really nice.

(d) Yes, I did.

해석_ M: 영화 시간에 늦겠어. 서두르자!

W: 나도 알아, 근데 그가 아직 자고 있어.

M: 뭐라고? 제인이 깨우고 있었다고 들었는데.

W: _______________________

(a) 제인은 나의 가장 절친한 친구야.

(b) 그녀가 깨워 보려고 했는데, 그가 워낙 잠귀가 어두운 사람
이라서 말이야.

(c) 그 영화 정말 멋졌어.

(d) 응, 했어.

해설_ 깨우는 중이었다고 들었는데 아직도 자고 있냐고 했으므로 깨우
지 못한 이유가 언급된 (b)가 적절하다.

어휘_ be running late for ~에 늦다   heavy sleeper 잠귀가
어두운 사람

정답_ (b)

17.

W: I cannot stand the sexual harassment any
longer.

M: It's a very serious offense.

W: Even though I could get fired, I'm going to
have to tell my boss about it.

M: _______________________

(a) You are very sexual.

(b) I will help you.

(c) You'll get fired.

(d) I don't like him either.

해석_ W: 더 이상 성희롱을 못 참겠어.

M: 그건 아주 심각한 범죄야.

W: 해고당하게 되더라도, 그것에 대해 사장한테 말해야겠어.

M: _______________________

(a) 넌 아주 섹시해.

(b) 내가 도와줄게.

(c) 넌 해고될 거야.

(d) 나도 사장이 싫어.

해설_ 잘릴지도 모르지만 사장에게 말하겠다고 했으므로 도와주겠다
는 (b)가 가장 적절하다.

어휘_ sexual harassment 성희롱   offense 범죄, 위법 행위

정답_ (b)

18.

M: Have you ever been in a dangerous

situation?

W: When I was a high school student, I had a
car accident with my father.

M: Oh yeah! Your father told me about it. He
said that you are lucky to be alive.

W: _______________________

(a) It was a close call.

(b) My father told me, too.

(c) It was a long time ago.

(d) How was it?

해석_ M: 위험한 상황을 겪어 본 적 있니?

W: 고등학생이었을 때 아버지와 함께 교통사고를 당했어.

M: 아, 맞다! 니네 아버지가 말씀해 주셨어. 네가 살아서 다행이
라고 그러시더라.

W: _______________________

(a) 구사일생이었지.

(b) 우리 아버지도 내게 말씀하셨어.

(c) 오래 전 일이야.

(d) 그건 어땠어?

해설_ 살아서 다행이라는 말을 들었다고 했으므로 구사일생이었다고
응답한 (a)가 적절하다.

어휘_ close call 위기일발, 구사일생

정답_ (a)

19.

W: What's wrong?

M: Something is amiss with the engine.

W: Really? We're supposed to be there pretty
soon. Can you fix it?

M: _______________________

(a) The engine is the most important part of the
car.

(b) No, give me 20 minutes.

(c) Yes, but it'll take too long.

(d) I think they'll miss us.

해석_ W: 무슨 일이야?

M: 엔진에 뭔가 문제가 있어.

W: 정말? 그곳에 곧 도착해야 하는데. 고칠 수 있어?

M: _______________________

(a) 엔진은 차의 가장 중요한 부분이지.

(b) 아니, 20분만 시간을 줘.

(c) 응, 하지만 시간이 무척 오래 걸릴 거야.

(d) 그들이 우리를 그리워할 것 같아.

해설_ 고칠 수 있는지 묻고 있으므로 이에 답한 (c)가 정답이다.

어휘_ amiss 고장 난, 잘못된

정답_ (c)

20.

M: Why do you think that I'm the armed robber?

W: I saw you in the store with a gun.

M: Don't lie. I was at home. Besides, there's no way that you can attest to it.

W: ________________________________

(a) Is there a test for me?

(b) There is another witness.

(c) No, I don't have a gun.

(d) Yes, I saw a thief.

해석_ M: 왜 나를 무장 강도라고 생각해요?

W: 그 가게에서 총을 들고 있는 당신을 봤어요.

M: 거짓말 마요. 난 집에 있었어요. 게다가 당신은 그걸 입증할 방법이 없잖아요.

W: ________________________________

(a) 내가 받아야 할 테스트가 있어요?

(b) 다른 목격자가 있어요.

(c) 아뇨, 난 총을 가지고 있지 않아요.

(d) 네, 도둑을 봤어요.

해설_ 입증할 방법이 없지 않냐고 말했으므로 다른 목격자가 있다고 응답한 (b)가 가장 적절하다.

어휘_ armed robber 무장 강도   attest to ~을 입증하다 witness 목격자

정답_ (b)

21.

M: Do you have any idea about why she is giving the boot to so many workers?

W: I bet it's because of money.

M: But she should be fair.

W: ________________________________

(a) These boots are so expensive.

(b) Right, you should think about money.

(c) I don't think it is because of money.

(d) I agree with you.

해석_ M: 넌 왜 그녀가 그렇게 많은 직원들을 해고하려는지 아니?

W: 돈 때문인 게 확실해.

M: 하지만 그녀는 공정해야 해.

W: ________________________________

(a) 이 부츠는 너무 비싸.

(b) 맞아, 넌 돈에 대해 생각해야 해.

(c) 난 돈 때문이라고 생각하지 않아.

(d) 나도 같은 생각이야.

해설_ 공정해야 한다는 말에 동의하는 (d)가 이어지는 것이 적절하다.

어휘_ give the boot 해고하다

정답_ (d)

22.

W: How did you get this book? Someone told me that it's pretty expensive.

M: I paid 500 dollars to get this.

W: Was it worth it?

M: ________________________________

(a) Yes, it is useless.

(b) No, I paid much more than 500 dollars.

(c) Sure it was. I would pay handsomely for such a well written novel.

(d) Sure. One dollar is enough.

해석_ W: 이 책 어떻게 구했니? 누가 그 책 무지 비싸다고 그러던데.

M: 이거 사는 데 500달러 들었어.

W: 그게 그만한 가치가 있었어?

M: ________________________________

(a) 응, 쓸모없어.

(b) 아니, 난 500달러보다 훨씬 더 많이 냈어.

(c) 물론이지. 그렇게 잘 쓰여진 소설을 위해서라면 돈을 아끼지 않을 거야.

(d) 물론. 1달러면 충분해.

해설_ 그만한 가치가 있었냐는 말에 워낙 훌륭한 책이라 돈이 아깝지 않다고 응답한 (c)가 적절하다.

어휘_ pay handsomely 상당히 많은 돈을 지불하다

정답_ (c)

23.

M: Have you heard about our new teacher?

W: No, I haven't. Why?

M: Everybody is saying that he used to be a gangster.

W: ____

(a) Believe me.

(b) No, I like our new teacher.

(c) It's probably just hot air.

(d) I think so, too.

해석_ M: 새로 오신 우리 선생님에 대해서 들은 적 있어?

W: 아니, 없어. 왜?

M: 모두가 그러는데 그 선생님 예전에 깡패였대.

W: _________________________________

(a) 날 믿어.

(b) 아니, 난 새로 오신 우리 선생님이 좋아.

(c) 아마 그냥 헛소문일 거야.

(d) 나도 그렇게 생각해.

해설_ 새로 오신 선생님이 깡패였다는 말에, 헛소문일 거라고 응답한 (c)가 적절하다.

어휘_ hot air 거짓말, 허황된 말[이야기]

정답_ (c)

24.

M: Did you fail last Friday's test?

W: Who spilled my guts?

M: Mr. Jake. He is telling everyone. Do you want to know where he is?

W: ____

(a) Yes. It was a difficult test.

(b) No. I didn't fail the test.

(c) Yes. I'm going to kick his ass.

(d) That's right. He spilled water on me.

해석_ M: 지난 금요일 시험에 떨어졌니?

W: 누가 내 비밀을 누설했어?

M: 제이크 씨. 그가 모두에게 말하고 있어. 그가 어디 있는지 알고 싶니?

W: _________________________________

(a) 응. 어려운 시험이었어.

(b) 아니. 시험에 떨어지지 않았어.

(c) 그래. 내가 혼내 줄 거야.

(d) 맞아. 그가 나한테 물을 쏟았어.

해설_ 시험에 떨어진 사실을 얘기하고 다닌다는 말을 들었으므로 혼내 주겠다는 (c)가 적절하다.

어휘_ spill one's guts (아는 것을) 모조리 털어놓다, ~의 비밀을 누설하다 kick one's ass ~를 혼내 주다

정답_ (c)

25.

W: Why do you detest my son? He didn't do anything to you.

M: He told everyone in my class that I am a fool.

W: Really? I can't believe that. Are you sure?

M: ____

(a) That's the way I said it.

(b) Yes, I'm sure. He said it right in front of me.

(c) No. I just like him casually.

(d) Yes, he had a test.

해석_ W: 넌 내 아들을 왜 그렇게 싫어하니? 걔가 너한테 아무 짓도 하지 않았는데.

M: 걔가 우리 반 아이들 모두에게 내가 바보라고 말했어요.

W: 정말? 믿을 수가 없구나. 확실하니?

M: _________________________________

(a) 제가 그렇게 말했어요.

(b) 네, 확실해요. 바로 제 앞에서 그렇게 말했어요.

(c) 아뇨. 전 그저 아무 생각 없이 그를 좋아해요.

(d) 네, 그는 시험을 봤어요.

해설_ 바보라고 말한 게 확실한지 묻고 있으므로 이에 답한 (b)가 정답이다.

어휘_ detest 몹시 싫어하다, 혐오하다 casually 아무 생각 없이, 무심코

정답_ (b)

26.

W: Why are you distorting your face like that? Do you have a problem?

M: Yes, I've got a huge one. My girlfriend wants to break up with me.

W: Why would she want to do that? She is the one who wanted to go out with you in the first place.

M: _______________________________

(a) Yes, I did.
(b) Sure, it was wrong.
(c) No, she did.
(d) Yes, she was.

해석_ W: 왜 그렇게 얼굴을 찌푸리고 있는 거야? 문제 있니?
　　　M: 응, 아주 큰 문제가 있어. 여자 친구가 나와 헤어지길 원해.
　　　W: 그녀는 왜 그렇게 하길 원하는데? 그녀가 먼저 너랑 사귀고
　　　　 싶어 했잖아.
　　　M: _______________________________
　　　(a) 그래, 내가 그랬지.
　　　(b) 물론, 그건 틀렸어.
　　　(c) 아니, 그녀가 그랬어.
　　　(d) 그래, 그녀가 그랬지.
해설_ 먼저 사귀길 원했던 사람은 그녀였다는 말에 수긍하는 (d)가 정
　　　답이다.
어휘_ distort (얼굴 등을) 찌푸리다 go out with ~와 사귀다
정답_ (d)

27.
M: I'm going to take my car for a drive. Would
　 you like to join me?
W: Did you buy a car? You don't have a
　 driver's license, do you?
M: Don't worry, I will drive slowly. Don't muse
　 about it too deeply.
W: _______________________________

(a) I want to join a club.
(b) Yes, I will drive.
(c) My car is so expensive.
(d) But you really need to get a driver's license.

해석_ M: 내 차 가지고 드라이브 갈 거야. 너도 갈래?
　　　W: 너 차 샀어? 운전면허증 없지 않아?
　　　M: 걱정 마, 천천히 운전할게. 너무 깊이 생각하지 마.
　　　W: _______________________________
　　　(a) 클럽에 가입하고 싶어.
　　　(b) 응, 내가 운전할 거야.
　　　(c) 내 차는 매우 비싸.
　　　(d) 하지만 넌 운전면허증을 따야 해.
해설_ 운전면허증도 없이 운전을 하려는 남자에게 충고를 해주는 (d)

　　　가 이어지는 것이 적절하다.
어휘_ muse 깊이 생각하다
정답_ (d)

28.
M: How much did you pay for your brother to
　 help you out?
W: He wanted to get over 300 dollars, so that's
　 how much I gave him.
M: There's no free lunch in this world.
W: _______________________________

(a) You can say that again.
(b) No, he will pay for me.
(c) Lunch is too expensive here.
(d) My brother is a good guy.

해석_ M: 널 돕는 대가로 동생에게 얼마 줬어?
　　　W: 걔가 300달러 넘게 원해서 그렇게 줬지.
　　　M: 세상에 공짜는 없다니까.
　　　W: _______________________________
　　　(a) 내 말이 그 말이야.
　　　(b) 아니, 그는 내게 돈을 지불할 거야.
　　　(c) 여긴 점심이 너무 비싸.
　　　(d) 내 동생은 좋은 녀석이야.
해설_ 세상에 공짜는 없다는 말에 동감하는 (a)가 정답이다.
어휘_ There's no free lunch in this world. 세상에 공짜는 없
　　　다
정답_ (a)

29.
M: How's it going with your husband?
W: Not very good. He cheated on me last
　 month.
M: Really? Is he sorry?
W: _______________________________

(a) He is too polite towards people.
(b) He is walking on egg shells around me.
(c) He cheated on the test.
(d) He will go to jail.

해석_ M: 요즘 남편하고는 어때?
　　　W: 썩 좋지 않아. 그가 지난달에 날 속이고 바람을 피웠거든.

M: 정말? 그가 미안해하고 있니?

W: ___________________________

(a) 그는 사람들에게 너무 공손해.

(b) 내 눈치를 보고 있지.

(c) 그는 시험에서 커닝을 했어.

(d) 그는 감옥에 갈 거야.

해설_ 남편이 미안해하는지 묻고 있으므로 눈치만 살피고 있다는 (b)
가 적절하다.

어휘_ cheat on ~를 속이고 바람을 피우다, (시험에서) 부정 행위를
하다   walk on egg shells 조심스럽게 행동하다

정답_ (b)

30.

W: Driving is a kind of easy thing for me.

M: Don't let your guard down.

W: I'm fine. I could even drive with my feet if I
wanted to.

M: ___________________________________

(a) Me neither.

(b) Could you give me a ride?

(c) Your feet look so good.

(d) You should be careful.

해설_ W: 운전이 내겐 쉬운 것 같아.

M: 방심하지 마.

W: 괜찮아. 내가 원하면 발로도 운전할 수 있어.

M: ___________________________

(a) 나도 안 그래.

(b) 나 좀 태워 줄 수 있니?

(c) 네 발은 정말 좋아 보인다.

(d) 조심해야 해.

해설_ 발로도 운전할 수 있다고 했으므로 조심하라는 (d)가 가장 적절
하다.

어휘_ let one's guard down 경계를 늦추다, 방심하다

정답_ (d)

Part 3

31.

W: Have you heard about the new writer in our
section?

M: Yes. I heard he is very competent.

W: But he didn't meet our deadlines and he
just gave me the runaround.

M: So, why don't you fire him?

W: It's not easy to find someone who is as
good a writer as he is.

M: Then tell him to keep the deadlines.

Q. What are the speakers mainly talking
about?

(a) A new writer's talent in writing

(b) A new writer

(c) Due date

(d) Hiring a new writer

해설_ W: 너 우리 부서에 새로 온 작가에 대해서 들었니?

M: 응. 그 사람 매우 능력 있다고 들었어.

W: 하지만 그는 마감 기한도 안 지키고 핑계만 댔어.

M: 그럼 그를 해고하지 그래?

W: 그처럼 글을 잘 쓰는 사람을 찾기가 쉽지 않아.

M: 그럼 마감 기한을 지키라고 말해.

Q. 화자들은 주로 무엇에 관해 이야기하고 있는가?

(a) 작가의 뛰어난 글솜씨

(b) 새 작가

(c) 마감 기한

(d) 새 작가 구하기

해설_ 부서에 새로 온 작가에 관한 얘기를 나누고 있으므로 정답은 (b)
가 된다.

어휘_ competent 유능한   meet the deadline 마감 기한을 맞
추다   give ... the runaround ~에게 핑계를 대다

정답_ (b)

32.

W: Have you seen the Korean movie,
Marathon?

M: Yes. I felt a lump in my throat and cried
through the entire movie.

W: What's the plot of the movie?

M: A mother had her autistic son do a
marathon in order for him to get over his
illness.

W: Sounds sad. Which theater is it showing at?

M: It's playing at Central Theater until tomorrow.

W: Thanks for the tip.

Q. What is the conversation about?

(a) The movie
(b) The lump in the man's throat
(c) A mother and her autistic son
(d) Going to the movies

해석_ W: 한국 영화, 〈마라톤〉 봤니?

M: 응. 목이 메어서 영화 보는 내내 울었어.

W: 영화 내용이 뭔데?

M: 한 어머니가 그녀의 자폐증 아들에게 자신의 병을 극복할 수
있도록 하기 위해서 마라톤을 시켰어.

W: 슬프다. 어느 극장에서 상영 중이니?

M: 센트럴 극장에서 내일까지 상영해.

W: 정보 고마워.

Q. 무엇에 관한 대화인가?

(a) 영화

(b) 남자의 목에 있는 혹

(c) 한 어머니와 그녀의 자폐증 아들

(d) 영화 보러 가기

해설_ 영화 〈마라톤〉에 관한 이야기를 나누고 있으므로 정답은 (a)가
된다.

어휘_ feel a lump in one's throat (감동하여) 목이 메다, 가슴이
벅차다 autistic 자폐증의

정답_ (a)

33.

M: I need to tell you something.
W: Oh, is it anything serious?
M: Yes. My boss can't afford to keep me on.
W: What if you can't get a new job in this
recession?
M: Don't worry. I'll cross that bridge when I
reach it.
W: Okay. Cheer up.

Q. What is the main focus of the conversation?

(a) Man's lay-off
(b) Getting a new job
(c) Crossing the bridge
(d) Boss being in financial difficulty

해석_ M: 할 말이 있어.

W: 아, 심각한 거야?

M: 응. 사장이 날 계속 고용할 여력이 안 돼.

W: 이 불경기에 새 직장을 못 구하면 어떡해?

M: 걱정 마. 그건 그때 가서 생각하지 뭐.

W: 알았어. 힘내.

Q. 대화의 주된 내용은 무엇인가?

(a) 남자의 정리 해고

(b) 새 직장 구하기

(c) 다리 건너기

(d) 재정적 어려움에 처한 사장

해설_ 남자가 여자에게 정리 해고당했다는 사실을 얘기하고 있으므로
정답은 (a)가 된다.

어휘_ keep on 계속 고용해 두다 cross the bridge when a
person reaches it (문제를) 그때 가서 생각하다, 지레 걱정
하지 않다

정답_ (a)

34.

M: Look out!
W: You startled me! Do you want me to cause
an accident?
M: You nearly side-swiped that van.
W: I saw him out of the corner of my eye.
M: When you change lanes, you should
shoulder-check!
W: Please, stop being such a backseat driver.

Q. What are the speakers mainly talking
about?

(a) A man at the corner
(b) Something that happened during the drive
(c) Changing the lane
(d) A driver at the backseat

해석_ M: 조심해!

W: 깜짝 놀랐잖아! 내가 사고 내길 바래?

M: 저 소형 트럭을 옆에서 칠 뻔했다구.

W: 곁눈질로 그 사람 봤어.

M: 차선을 바꿀 땐 고개를 돌려서 뒷차를 확인해야 해!

W: 제발 뒤에서 잔소리 좀 그만해라.

Q. 화자들은 주로 무엇에 관해 이야기하고 있는가?

(a) 모퉁이에 있는 남자
(b) 운전 중 발생한 어떤 일
(c) 차선 변경
(d) 뒷좌석의 운전자

해설_ 운전 중에 여자가 소형 트럭을 칠 뻔한 것 때문에 벌어지는 대화이므로 정답은 (b)가 된다.

어휘_ startle 깜짝 놀라게 하다   side-swipe 스치듯 충돌하다   van 소형 트럭   out of the corner of one's eye 곁눈질로   backseat driver 자동차 뒷좌석에서 운전에 대해 잔소리하는 사람, 참견 잘하는 사람

정답_ (b)

35.

W: I'm happy I caught you before you headed out.
M: What's up?
W: I heard you broke up with your girlfriend.
M: So what?
W: I want to set you up with my friend.
M: Well, I'm not going to date for the time being.
W: Look. Here. I've got a picture of her.
M: Yeah? Let's see... Oh. Well, I'm not really sure.
W: Oh, she is much better looking in person.

Q. What is the main purpose of the conversation?

(a) To set the man up with the woman's friend
(b) To show the man a picture of the woman
(c) To cheer the man up who just broke up with his girlfriend
(d) To give an advice before the man leaves

해석_ W: 너 나가기 전에 만나서 다행이다.
M: 무슨 일인데?
W: 네가 여자 친구랑 헤어졌다고 들었어.
M: 그래서 뭐?
W: 너한테 내 친구 소개시켜 주고 싶어서.
M: 글쎄, 당분간은 데이트 안 하려고 하는데.
W: 봐봐, 여기. 내 친구 사진이야.
M: 그래? 어디 보자… 글쎄, 뭐 잘 모르겠다.

W: 아, 걘 실물이 훨씬 나아.

Q. 대화의 주된 목적은 무엇인가?

(a) 남자에게 여자의 친구를 소개시켜 주기 위해서
(b) 남자에게 여자의 사진을 보여 주기 위해서
(c) 여자 친구와 헤어진 남자를 위로하기 위해서
(d) 남자가 떠나기 전에 조언을 해주기 위해서

해설_ 여자 친구와 헤어진 남자에게 소개팅을 제안하고 있으므로 정답은 (a)가 된다.

어휘_ head out 출발하다, 떠나다   set A up with B A에게 B를 소개시켜 주다

정답_ (a)

36.

M: Help me please.
W: Hold on. Let me catch my breath.
M: I need to get this balance sheet done.
W: I think you can do it yourself.
M: Please. I've been pulling my hair out over this.
W: Okay. Just leave it up to me.
M: Thanks. You're a lifesaver!

Q. Which is correct according to the conversation?

(a) The woman saved the man's life.
(b) The woman was out of breath.
(c) The man has lots of stress due to his hair.
(d) The man needs the woman's help.

해석_ M: 도와줘, 제발.
W: 잠깐만. 숨 좀 돌리자.
M: 이 대차 대조표를 끝내야 해.
W: 너 혼자서도 할 수 있을 것 같은데.
M: 제발. 나 이거 땜에 스트레스가 이만저만이 아니야.
W: 알았어. 나한테 맡겨.
M: 고마워. 넌 생명의 은인이야!

Q. 대화에 따르면 맞는 것은 어느 것인가?

(a) 여자가 남자의 목숨을 구해 주었다.
(b) 여자는 숨이 찼다.
(c) 남자는 그의 머리 때문에 스트레스가 심하다.
(d) 남자는 여자의 도움이 필요하다.

해설_ 여자에게 대차 대조표 끝내는 걸 도와 달라고 부탁하고 있으므

로 (d)가 정답임을 알 수 있다.

어휘_ catch one's breath 숨을 돌리다 balance sheet 대차대조표 pull one's hair out 스트레스를 많이 받다 leave it up to ~에게 맡기다 lifesaver 생명의 은인 be out of breath 숨이 차다

정답_ (d)

37.

W: Do you still smoke?
M: Yeah. What's the big deal?
W: Nothing. But you said you had quit smoking.
M: Yeah. But I started to smoke again because of stress.
W: What made you do it?
M: My mom passed away 2 weeks ago.
W: I'm so sorry. That's too bad.
M: I'm okay now and I'll quit smoking again soon.
W: I hope you quit cold turkey.

Q. Which is correct about the man?

(a) He stopped smoking 2 weeks ago.
(b) He had cold turkey.
(c) He went through a hard time after his mother's death.
(d) He wants to smoke again.

해석_ W: 아직도 담배 피우니?
M: 응. 뭐 문제 있어?
W: 아무것도 아냐. 하지만 네가 담배 끊었다고 했잖아.
M: 그래. 근데 스트레스 땜에 다시 피우기 시작했어.
W: 뭣 때문에 그러는데?
M: 엄마가 2주 전에 돌아가셨어.
W: 정말 미안해. 그거 너무 안 됐구나.
M: 지금은 괜찮아. 그리고 곧 다시 금연할 거야.
W: 단칼에 끊길 바랄게.

Q. 남자에 관해 맞는 것은 어느 것인가?

(a) 그는 2주 전에 담배를 끊었다.
(b) 그는 차가운 칠면조를 먹었다.
(c) 그는 어머니의 죽음으로 많이 힘들었다.
(d) 그는 담배를 다시 피우고 싶어 한다.

해설_ 2주 전에 돌아가신 엄마 때문에 힘들어서 담배를 다시 피우게 됐

다고 했으므로 (c)가 정답임을 알 수 있다. cold turkey는 '(담배 등을) 단번에 끊다'란 뜻으로, 금단 현상으로 인해 피부가 창백해지고 닭살이 돋는 모습이 마치 칠면조와 비슷하다고 해서 유래된 표현이라고 한다.

어휘_ pass away 돌아가시다

정답_ (c)

38.

W: I hear you recently opened a gas station.
M: Yea, 3 weeks ago.
W: Is it lucrative?
M: I only just break even.
W: You must serve customers in a friendly manner.
M: You are right. And also, I would have to make a plan to attract customers.

Q. Which is correct according to the conversation?

(a) The man is running a gas station.
(b) The woman thinks that the man is not polite to customers.
(c) The woman visited the man's gas station.
(d) The man is about to go into bankruptcy.

해석_ W: 최근에 주유소를 개업했다고 들었어요.
M: 네, 3주 전에요.
W: 장사는 잘 되나요?
M: 겨우 본전만 건져요.
W: 고객에게 친절하게 대해야 해요.
M: 맞아요. 그리고 고객을 끌어들일 방안을 강구해야겠어요.

Q. 대화에 따르면 맞는 것은 어느 것인가?

(a) 남자는 주유소를 운영하고 있다.
(b) 여자는 남자가 손님들에게 불친절하다고 생각한다.
(c) 여자는 남자의 주유소를 방문했다.
(d) 남자는 파산 직전에 있다.

해설_ 3주 전에 주유소를 개업했다고 했으므로 (a)가 정답임을 알 수 있다.

어휘_ lucrative 돈이 벌리는 break even 수입과 지출이 같다, 득실이 없다 go into bankruptcy 파산하다

정답_ (a)

39.

W: Why are you out of breath?

M: There's a huge traffic jam, so I didn't want to take a bus.

W: So you ran three blocks from your office to get here on time?

M: Yes! And you know what shape I'm in after pulling an all nighter yesterday at work.

W: I feel terrible that I made you run.

M: No problem.

Q. Why was the man out of breath?

(a) Because he pulled an all nighter

(b) Because he was stuck in a traffic jam

(c) Because he was in a bad condition

(d) Because he ran all the way to the place of appointment

해석_ W: 왜 숨을 헐떡이는 거야?

M: 길이 너무 막혀서 버스를 타고 싶지 않았어.

W: 그래서 여기 시간 맞춰 오려고 사무실에서 세 블록을 뛰어왔단 말이야?

M: 그래! 그리고 어제 회사에서 밤새 일해서 지금 내 컨디션이 어떤지 알 거야.

W: 여기까지 뛰어오게 만들어서 너무 미안하다.

M: 괜찮아.

Q. 남자는 왜 숨을 헐떡였는가?

(a) 밤새 일했기 때문에

(b) 교통 체증에 걸렸기 때문에

(c) 몸 컨디션이 안 좋았기 때문에

(d) 약속 장소까지 뛰어오느라고

해설_ 길이 너무 막혀서 사무실에서부터 뛰어왔다고 했으므로 (d)가 정답임을 알 수 있다.

어휘_ pull an all nighter 밤새 일하다[공부하다]

정답_ (d)

40.

W: So, what are you up to this weekend?

M: I'm going to see that movie with my brother.

W: Why are you thinking about watching that movie?

M: Well, the actress in that movie is pretty easy on the eyes.

W: Don't waste your money. It's boring.

M: Oh, yeah? Well, thanks for giving me the "heads-up."

Q. Why is the man going to watch the movie?

(a) Because he made a promise with his brother

(b) Because it's a relaxing movie to watch

(c) Because there was nothing else to do on the weekend

(d) Because there is an attractive actress in it

해석_ W: 그래서, 이번 주말에 뭐 하니?

M: 우리 형이랑 그 영화 보러 갈 거야.

W: 왜 그 영화를 보려는 건데?

M: 음, 그 영화에 나오는 여배우가 아주 매력적이야.

W: 돈 낭비하지 마. 지루해.

M: 어, 그래? 음, 주의 줘서 고마워.

Q. 남자는 왜 그 영화를 보려고 하는가?

(a) 그의 형과 약속했기 때문에

(b) 마음 편하게 볼 수 있는 영화라서

(c) 주말에 다른 할 일이 없어서

(d) 영화에 매력적인 여배우가 나와서

해설_ 남자의 두 번째 대사를 통해 (d)가 정답임을 알 수 있다.

어휘_ easy on the eyes 매력적인, 예쁜   give a heads-up 주의를 주다, 미리 알려주다

정답_ (d)

41.

W: Did you miss me?

M: Oh, yeah. Did you have a good run?

W: No. I got leg cramps halfway through, so I couldn't set a record.

M: Well, better luck next time.

W: Say. Do you want to work out with me before dinner?

M: No thanks. I prefer to just lounge around the house in my pajamas on weekends.

Q. Which is correct according to the conversation?

(a) The man wishes to go to the hotel lobby near his house.

(b) The woman hurt her legs while she was running.

(c) The woman will exercise after dinner.

(d) The man does not like going outside on weekends.

해석_ W: 나 보고 싶었니?

　　　M: 어, 그래. 잘 뛰었어?

　　　W: 아니. 뛰는 도중에 다리에 쥐가 나서 기록을 세우지 못했어.

　　　M: 음, 다음 번엔 잘될 거야.

　　　W: 저 말이야. 나랑 저녁 먹기 전에 운동할래?

　　　M: 사양할래. 주말엔 잠옷 차림으로 집에서 빈둥거리며 노는 게 더 좋아.

　　　Q. 대화에 따르면 맞는 것은 어느 것인가?

　　　(a) 남자는 집 근처에 있는 호텔 로비에 가고 싶어 한다.

　　　(b) 그녀는 달리는 도중 다리를 다쳤다.

　　　(c) 그녀는 저녁을 먹은 후 운동을 할 것이다.

　　　(d) 남자는 주말에 외출하는 것을 좋아하지 않는다.

해설_ 남자의 마지막 대사에서 집에서 빈둥거리며 노는 게 좋다고 했으므로 (d)가 정답임을 알 수 있다.

어휘_ get leg cramps 쥐가 나다　halfway through 도중에　set a record 기록을 세우다　lounge 빈둥거리다

정답_ (d)

42.

M: Hi. How are things in the general affairs section?

W: Actually, I have come by to let you know I'm leaving soon.

M: Oh, I see. But why?

W: I'm going to work at an entry-level position in a bigger company.

M: Well, it's a foot in the door, right?

W: Yes. I think I have a chance for promotion there.

M: Well, then, that's a good move for you.

Q. Which is correct about the woman?

(a) She will quit her job soon.

(b) She will move to a new house.

(c) She came to say goodbye to the man.

(d) She does not like companies that are small in scale.

해석_ M: 안녕. 총무부에서는 잘 지내?

　　　W: 실은, 나 곧 회사 그만둔다고 말하려고 들렀어.

　　　M: 아, 그렇구나. 근데 왜?

　　　W: 더 큰 회사에서 신입사원으로 일하게 될 거야.

　　　M: 음, 첫걸음을 내딛는 거구나, 그렇지?

　　　W: 그래. 거기서는 승진할 기회가 있다고 생각해.

　　　M: 음, 그럼 너한텐 잘된 거네.

　　　Q. 여자에 관해 맞는 것은 어느 것인가?

　　　(a) 그녀는 곧 직장을 그만둘 것이다.

　　　(b) 그녀는 새집으로 이사갈 것이다.

　　　(c) 그녀는 남자에게 작별 인사를 하러 왔다.

　　　(d) 그녀는 규모가 작은 회사를 싫어한다.

해설_ 남자에게 곧 떠날 거라고 했고, 더 큰 회사에서 일하게 되었다고 했으므로 (a)가 정답임을 알 수 있다. (d)는 현재 다니고 있는 회사보다 좀 더 큰 회사로 가게 되었다는 것이지 규모가 작은 회사를 싫어하는지는 알 수 없으므로 정답이 아니다. 남자의 세 번째 대사에 나오는 a foot in the door는 외판원이 물건을 팔기 위해 집집마다 방문할 때 문을 못 닫게 하기 위해 발을 문에 대는 것에서 유래된 표현으로, 성공적으로 첫걸음을 내딛거나 들어가기 힘든 직장 등에 들어간 경우에 쓸 수 있는 표현이다.

어휘_ the general affairs section 총무부　entry-level 초보적인

정답_ (a)

43.

W: We need creative minds, so we recruit new members.

M: What are you getting at, exactly?

W: Well, we know you've done great work for us.

M: So what? You don't need to beat around the bush.

W: There are younger people full of creativity who are anxious to get your position.

M: That's why you're being forced to let me go, right?

Q. What can be inferred from the conversation?

(a) The woman wants the man to quit the job.

(b) The man is too old to work.

(c) The woman has worked hard for the company.

(d) The man did not follow what the woman said.

해석_ W: 우리는 창의적인 생각이 필요해요. 그래서 새 인재를 뽑을 거예요.

M: 정확히 무슨 말씀을 하시려는 건가요?

W: 음, 우리 회사를 위해 열심히 일한 거 알아요.

M: 그래서 뭡니까? 빙빙 돌리지 말고 요점만 말씀하세요.

W: 당신 자리를 얻고 싶어 하는 창의력 가득한 젊은이들이 많아요.

M: 그게 저를 해고시키려는 이유군요, 그렇죠?

Q. 대화를 통해 추론할 수 있는 것은?

(a) 여자는 남자가 회사를 그만두길 원한다.

(b) 남자는 일하기에 나이가 너무 많다.

(c) 여자는 회사를 위해 열심히 일해 왔다.

(d) 남자는 여자가 한 말을 이해하지 못했다.

해설_ 창의력 있는 새 인재를 뽑을 예정이고, 남자의 직책을 원하는 젊은이들이 많다고 한 것으로 보아 (a)가 정답임을 알 수 있다. 남자의 첫 번째 대사에 나온 get at은 '~에 도달하다', '~에 가다'란 뜻으로, What are you getting at? 하면 '대체 어디로 가는 거냐?', 즉 '대체 무슨 얘기를 하려는 거냐?'의 뜻이 된다.

어휘_ beat around the bush 빙빙 돌려 말하다   be anxious to ~을 원하다

정답_ (a)

44.

M: Where do you think you're going?

W: Home. It's time to head out.

M: Aren't you forgetting something?

W: Well, I don't think so.

M: Does "Harmer Presentation" ring any bells?

W: Oh, right! It totally slipped my mind.

M: If we don't get this wrapped up today, we'll be up the creek!

Q. What can be inferred from the conversation?

(a) The woman will go home.

(b) The man and woman have things left to do.

(c) The woman forgot to ring the bell.

(d) The man and woman need to finish wrapping gifts today.

해석_ M: 어디 가려는 거야?

W: 집에. 나갈 시간이야.

M: 뭐 잊은 거 없어?

W: 글쎄. 없는 것 같은데.

M : "하머 발표" 하면 뭐 떠오르는 거 없어?

W: 아, 맞다! 까맣게 잊고 있었어.

M: 오늘 발표 준비를 끝내지 못하면 우린 궁지에 빠질 거야!

Q. 대화를 통해 추론할 수 있는 것은?

(a) 여자는 집에 갈 것이다.

(b) 남자와 여자는 해야 할 일이 남아 있다.

(c) 여자는 벨 울리는 것을 깜박 잊었다.

(d) 남자와 여자는 오늘 선물 포장을 끝내야 한다.

해설_ 발표 준비를 끝내야 한다고 했으므로 (b)가 정답임을 알 수 있다.

어휘_ ring a bell 생각나게 하다   wrap up 마무리하다, 끝마치다   be up the creek 궁지에 빠지다

정답_ (b)

45.

W: Slow down please.

M: I'm not even going 100 yet.

W: The maximum speed on this road is 80. Slow down!

M: Why are you so tense and stressed out?

W: I don't want you to cause an accident.

M: But if we miss the train, we can kiss our vacation good bye.

Q. What can be inferred from the conversation?

(a) The man will slow down the car.

(b) The woman almost got in an accident.

(c) The man and woman will miss the train.

(d) The man and woman are heading somewhere for a vacation.

해석_ W: 제발 속도 좀 줄여.

해석_ W: 제발 속도 좀 줄여.

　　　M: 아직 100도 안 되는데.

　　　W: 이 도로의 최고 속도는 80이야. 속도 줄여!

　　　M: 왜 그렇게 긴장하면서 스트레스를 받는 거니?

　　　W: 네가 사고를 일으키는 것을 원치 않아.

　　　M: 하지만 기차를 놓치면 휴가를 못 가게 될 거야.

　　　Q. 대화를 통해 추론할 수 있는 것은?

　　　(a) 남자는 주행 속도를 줄일 것이다.

　　　(b) 여자는 사고를 낼 뻔했다.

　　　(c) 남자와 여자는 기차를 놓칠 것이다.

　　　(d) 남자와 여자는 휴가를 위해 어디론가 가는 중이다.

해설_ 기차를 놓치면 휴가를 못 가게 될 거라고 한 것으로 보아 (d)가
　　　정답임을 알 수 있다. (a)와 (c)는 명확히 알 수 있는 사항이 아니
　　　므로 정답이 될 수 없다.

어휘_ kiss ... good bye ~에게 이별의 키스를 하다

정답_ (d)

Part 4

46.

Eating beans is so healthy. In addition to protein, beans are often rich in calcium, fiber and iron. They're inexpensive canned and downright cheap dried. Fill a pot with water and add lentils, garbanzo, navy or butter beans. Let them soak overnight and they're ready to go by morning. Beans are a nutritional powerhouse. There are 7 grams of protein per half cup serving. Adding beans to chicken or beef is a healthy way to stretch a dish.

Q. What is the main purpose of the talk?

(a) To introduce a recipe for cooking beans
(b) To explain what benefit beans give to health
(c) To introduce way to keep healthy
(d) To suggest eating low calorie food

해석_ 콩을 먹는 것은 건강에 참 좋습니다. 단백질뿐만 아니라, 콩은 칼
　　　슘, 섬유질, 그리고 철분이 풍부합니다. 저렴한 가격의 통조림으
　　　로 만들어지기도 하고, 아주 싼 말린 콩으로도 만들어집니다. 용
　　　기에 물을 채우고, 렌즈콩, 병아리콩, 흰 콩, 또는 버터 콩을 넣으
　　　세요. 밤새 담가 두면 아침에 바로 먹을 수 있습니다. 콩은 영양

의 발전소입니다. 반 컵 분량에 7그램의 단백질이 들어 있습니
다. 닭고기나 쇠고기에 콩을 추가하는 것은 음식의 양을 늘리는
건강한 방법입니다.

　　　Q. 담화의 주된 목적은 무엇인가?

　　　(a) 콩 요리법을 알려주기 위해

　　　(b) 콩의 건강상 이점을 설명하기 위해

　　　(c) 건강을 지키는 방법을 알려주기 위해

　　　(d) 칼로리가 낮은 음식을 먹도록 제안하기 위해

해설_ 콩을 먹는 것은 건강에 좋으며, 칼슘, 섬유질 등 풍부한 영양소가
　　　들어 있다고 했으므로 정답은 (b)가 된다.

어휘_ calcium 칼슘　fiber 섬유질　iron 철분　canned 통조림
　　　된　downright 완전히　dried 건조시킨, 말린　lentils 렌
　　　즈콩　garbanzo 병아리콩　navy 흰 콩　soak 적시다, 담
　　　그다　be ready to go 준비가 다 되다　powerhouse 발
　　　전소　stretch (술·음식 등을) 다른 것과 섞어서 양을 늘리다

정답_ (b)

47.

Buying a sport utility vehicle seemed like a good idea at the time. It was big, and with all that room, you could take long trips and carry just about anything. But with gas hovering around $4 per gallon, you want to get out of the SUV and buy something smaller and more economical. The problem is that the value of your SUV has fallen. The laws of supply and demand have taken over, and SUV owners can't get as much for their vehicles as they could six months ago.

Q. What is the main idea of the talk?

(a) It is convenient to go by SUV because it's spacious.
(b) People these days prefer small and cheap cars.
(c) SUV's value is lower than it used to be.
(d) If sold right away, you can receive SUV's original price.

해석_ 당시에는 SUV를 구입하는 것이 좋은 생각인 것처럼 보였습니
　　　다. 크고 넓어서, 당신은 긴 여행을 가거나 어떤 것이든 실을 수
　　　있었습니다. 하지만 갤런 당 약 4달러 나가는 기름 값 때문에 당

신은 SUV를 버리고 더 작고 보다 경제적인 차량을 사길 원합니다. 문제는 당신의 SUV의 값어치가 떨어졌다는 것입니다. 수요 공급의 법칙이 적용되면서, SUV 소유주들은 그들의 차량에 대해 6개월 전에 받을 수 있었던 만큼의 값을 받을 수 없습니다.

Q. 담화의 요지는 무엇인가?

(a) SUV는 크고 넓어서 여행갈 때 편하다.

(b) 요즘 사람들은 작고 값이 싼 차를 선호한다.

(c) 예전과 달리 SUV의 값어치가 떨어졌다.

(d) SUV를 지금 당장 팔면 제값을 받을 수 있다.

해설 예전엔 SUV가 차량이 크고 넓어서 좋았지만 지금은 값어치가 떨어졌다는 것이 중심 내용이므로 정답은 (c)가 된다.

어휘 sport utility vehicle(= SUV) 스포츠 범용 차, 트럭 차대의 튼튼한 사륜 구동차　hover 빙빙 맴돌다, 주저하다　take over 인계받다, (대신해서) 우세해지다

정답 (c)

48.

People who pop a daily aspirin to ward off heart trouble might have another option. It's canned tomatoes. Growers of processed tomatoes, meeting this week, heard about a marketing effort that includes research into the cardiovascular benefits of the vegetable. For some people, it can be a daily discipline, just like taking an aspirin. It's easy to add tomato products to one's daily consumption.

Q. What is the report about?

(a) The relationship between tomatoes and heart disease

(b) Indispensable medicine for patients suffering heart disease

(c) Reason why tomatoes should be consumed regularly

(d) Recipes for making food with tomatoes

해석 심장병을 피하기 위해 매일 아스피린을 먹는 사람들은 또 다른 선택권을 가지고 있을지도 모릅니다. 그것은 토마토 통조림입니다. 이번주에 만날 가공 처리된 토마토 재배자들은 야채가 심장 혈관에 좋은 점에 관한 조사를 포함한 마케팅 노력에 대해서 들었습니다. 어떤 사람들에게 그것은 마치 아스피린을 복용하는 것처럼 매일의 규율이 될 수 있습니다. 토마토 제품을 매일 먹는

것은 쉽습니다.

Q. 무엇에 관한 이야기인가?

(a) 토마토와 심장 질환의 관계

(b) 심장 질환자에게 꼭 필요한 약

(c) 토마토를 꾸준히 먹어야 하는 이유

(d) 토마토를 사용하여 음식을 만드는 방법

해설 심장병 예방을 위해 아스피린을 복용하는 것처럼 매일 토마토를 먹으면 역시 심장병 예방에 좋다는 내용을 다루고 있으므로 정답은 (a)가 된다.

어휘 pop 〈속어〉 (알약을) 상용하다　ward off 피하다　grower 재배자　processed 가공 처리된　cardiovascular 심장 혈관의　discipline 규율, 훈련, 수양　indispensable 필수 불가결한

정답 (a)

49.

Japan began offering money for unemployed foreigners of Japanese ancestry to go home, mostly to Brazil and Peru, to stave off serious unemployment problems. Thousands of foreigners of Japanese ancestry, who had been hired on temporary or referral contracts, have lost their jobs recently, mostly at manufacturers such as Toyota Motor Corp. and its affiliates, which are struggling to cope with a global downturn.

Q. Which of the following best summarizes the report?

(a) Foreigners of Japanese ancestry are being laid off unreasonably.

(b) Toyota Motor Corp. has a plan to hire foreigners.

(c) Many Japanese have emigrated to Brazil or Peru recently.

(d) Japan is paying money for unemployed foreigners of Japanese ancestry.

해석 일본은 심각한 실업 문제를 막기 위해, 실직한 일본계 외국인들이 고향으로, 대부분 브라질과 페루로, 돌아가도록 돈을 제공하기 시작했습니다. 임시로 고용됐거나 추천을 받아 일해 왔던 수천 명의 일본계 외국인들은, 대부분 세계적인 경기 침체에 대처

하기 위해 분투하고 있는 도요타 자동차와 그 계열 회사들과 같은 제조업체에서 최근 그들의 일자리를 잃었습니다.

Q. 기사를 가장 잘 요약한 것은?

(a) 일본계 외국인들이 부당하게 해고되고 있다.

(b) 도요타 자동차는 외국인들을 고용할 계획을 가지고 있다.

(c) 많은 일본인들이 최근 브라질이나 페루로 이민을 갔다.

(d) 일본은 실직한 일본계 외국인들에게 돈을 주고 있다.

해설 기사 첫 문장이 주제문이다. 실직한 일본계 외국인들에게 돈을 제공하고 있다는 내용이므로 정답은 (d)가 된다.

어휘 ancestry 조상, 가계, 계보 stave off (위험·파멸 등을) 피하다, 저지하다 referral 소개, 추천, 위탁 affiliate 계열 회사 downturn 경기 침체 emigrate 이주하다

정답 (d)

50.

Seamus Heaney, the greatest living English-language poet, turned 70 this week. Ireland commemorated his birthday with an exhibit of art inspired by his work, with newly written string quartets and a symphony based on his poems, and with a nationally televised documentary on his life and writings. More than 400 invited guests listened to the poet deliver a birthday address, which was broadcast live over one of the national radio stations, and, afterward, there followed more than 12 continuous hours of Heaney in recorded readings of his collected poems.

Q. Which of the following is the best title for the report?

(a) Documentary Film on Seamus Heaney and His Works

(b) Broadcasting and Literature

(c) Various Works Inspired by Heaney's Poems

(d) National Celebration of the Greatest Poet

해설 영어로 글을 쓰는, 생존하는 가장 위대한 시인 시무스 히니가 이번주 70세가 되었다. 아일랜드는 그의 작품에 영감을 받은 예술 작품 전시와, 새로이 작곡된 현악 사중주 작품들과 그의 시를 기반으로 한 교향곡 작품, 그리고 그의 삶과 작품에 대해 전국적으로 방영된 다큐멘터리와 함께 그의 생일을 기념하였다. 400명

넘게 초대된 손님들이 시인의 생일 연설을 들었는데, 그 연설은 국립 라디오 방송 중 한 곳 이상에서 생중계되었다. 그리고 후에, 녹음된 히니의 시집 낭송이 12시간 이상 연속으로 이어져 방송되었다.

Q. 기사의 제목으로 가장 적절한 것은?

(a) 시무스 히니와 그의 작품에 대한 다큐멘터리 영화

(b) 방송과 문학

(c) 히니의 시에 영감을 받은 다양한 작품

(d) 가장 위대한 시인의 전국적인 생일 축하

해설 시무스 히니의 생일을 기념하여 그의 삶과 작품에 대한 다큐멘터리를 방영하고 그의 생일 연설을 생중계하는 등 전국적인 축하를 했다는 내용이므로 정답은 (d)가 된다.

어휘 commemorate 기념하다, 축하하다 string quartet 현악 4중주 symphony 교향곡 televise 텔레비전으로 방송하다 broadcast live 생방송하다 collected poems 시집

정답 (d)

51.

The "latte effect" of the go-go years had Americans spending $4 a day on coffee. Now the downturn is forcing them to rethink the wisdom of such habits. As inflation squeezes budgets, middle-class Americans are taking fresh stock of their spending in search of ways to save a nickel or a dime. As a result, people are giving up a variety of small financial vices.

Q. What is the report about?

(a) Change in attitude of Americans on spending

(b) Middle-class Americans trying to save even small sums of money

(c) A trend in the age of inflation

(d) A way to escape from the economic crisis

해설 경기가 좋았던 시절의 "라떼 효과"는 미국인들이 커피 값으로 하루에 4달러를 쓰도록 했다. 이제 경기 침체는 미국인들에게 그러한 습관이 현명한 것인지 재고해 보도록 강요하고 있다. 인플레이션으로 생활비에 압력이 가해지자 미국의 중산층은 5센트 내지는 10센트를 절약하기 위한 방법을 찾기 위해 자신들의 소비생활을 다시 들여다보고 있다. 그 결과, 미국인들은 작은 여러 가지 경제적으로 나쁜 습관을 버리고 있다.

Q. 무엇에 관한 기사인가?

(a) 미국인들의 달라진 소비습관

(b) 푼돈을 줄이려 애쓰는 미국의 중산층

(c) 인플레이션 시대의 추세

(d) 경제 위기에서 벗어나는 방법

해설_ 경기 침체로 인해 미국인들이 자신들의 소비생활에 대해 재검토하며 나쁜 소비습관을 버리고 있다는 내용이므로 정답은 (a)가 된다.

어휘_ go-go years 경기가 좋았던 시절   squeeze 압박하다   take fresh stock of ~을 새롭게 들여다보다   vice 나쁜 습관

정답_ (a)

52.

During his prime time news conference on March 24, the president pledged to send more money, technology and manpower to help Mexico fight the drug cartels. In a subsequent committee hearing, Lieberman and Graham safely predicted that more resources would be needed. However, all of them missed opportunities to emphasize the core problem.

Q. What was the president's promise?

(a) Supporting military force in need
(b) Providing money, technology, and manpower
(c) Fight against the drug cartels
(d) Providing more resources

해석_ 3월 24일, 황금 시간대에 그의 기자회견을 하는 동안 대통령은 멕시코가 마약 범죄 조직과 싸우는 것을 돕기 위해 더 많은 돈과 기술, 그리고 인력을 보낼 것을 약속했습니다. 뒤이은 의회 청문회에서 리버맨과 그라함은 더 많은 지원이 필요할 것이라고 조심스럽게 예측했습니다. 그러나 그들 모두 핵심 문제를 강조할 기회를 놓쳤습니다.

Q. 대통령은 무엇을 약속했는가?

(a) 필요한 병력 지원

(b) 돈과 기술, 그리고 인력의 제공

(c) 마약 범죄 조직과의 싸움

(d) 더 많은 자원의 제공

해설_ 마약 범죄 조직과 싸우도록 멕시코에 돈과 기술, 그리고 인력을

지원하겠다고 했으므로 정답은 (b)가 된다.

어휘_ prime time 황금 시간대, 시청률이 가장 높은 시간대   subsequent 그 후의, 뒤이은   committee hearing 의회 청문회

정답_ (b)

53.

The HuckleBerry Center presents an exciting seminar on Learning Styles and Motivation. Joy will speak about how to really listen to and watch your child to determine the learning style that fits best, and to use words. This is amazing, practical information that you can put to use instantly and achieve fantastic results. So mark it on your calendar and come to this free community event. Hope to see you there.

Q. What is the advertisement about?

(a) Practical information
(b) HuckleBerry Center
(c) Lecturer of the seminar
(d) An invitation to free seminar

해석_ 허클베리 센터에서는 학습 스타일과 동기 부여에 관한 흥미로운 세미나를 엽니다. 조이는 가장 적합한 학습 스타일을 결정하기 위해 어떻게 자녀의 말에 귀기울이고 그들을 관찰해야 하는지, 그리고 단어를 어떻게 사용해야 하는지에 대해 이야기할 것입니다. 이것은 즉시 활용하여 엄청난 결과를 얻을 수 있는 놀랄 만한 실용 정보입니다. 따라서 여러분의 달력에 세미나 날짜를 표시해 두시고 이 무료 지역 행사에 오십시오. 거기서 뵙기를 바랍니다.

Q. 무엇에 관한 광고인가?

(a) 실용 정보

(b) 허클베리 센터

(c) 세미나 강연자

(d) 무료 세미나로의 초대

해설_ 학습 스타일과 동기 부여에 관한 무료 세미나에 오라는 내용이므로 정답은 (d)가 된다.

어휘_ put to use 사용하다

정답_ (d)

54.

Prioritize, delegate, outsource. They're all good management concepts for keeping businesses running smoothly. But can they help get the laundry done and put dinner on the table? Absolutely, say life coaches. Heads of households should set goals, outsource tasks and review team performance at home just as business managers do.

Q. What kind of tips will you most likely find in this talk?

(a) Tips on how to set up realistic marketing goals
(b) Tips about business management
(c) Tips on becoming a CEO
(d) Tips on how to start a business

해석_ 우선 순위를 매기는 것, 파견하는 것, 외부에서 조달하는 것. 그것들이 모두 원활한 사업 운영을 유지하는 데 좋은 경영 콘셉트입니다. 그러나 그것들이 빨래도 해주고 저녁도 차려 줄 수 있습니까? "물론이죠."라고 인생 코치들은 말합니다. 집안의 가장은 사업 경영자가 하는 것처럼 가정에서도 목표를 정하고, 과제를 조달하고, 협동하는 것을 실천해야 합니다.

Q. 이 담화에서 어떤 종류의 정보를 찾을 수 있겠는가?

(a) 현실적인 마케팅 목표를 세우는 방법에 대한 정보
(b) 경영 관리에 대한 정보
(c) 최고 경영자가 되는 것에 대한 정보
(d) 사업을 시작하는 방법에 대한 정보

해설_ 사업 운영이나 가정 생활의 운영을 원활하게 하는 데 있어서 좋은 관리법에 대해 언급했으므로 정답은 (b)가 된다.

어휘_ prioritize 우선순위를 매기다   delegate 특파[파견]하다   outsource 외부에서 조달하다   head of household 세대주, 가장

정답_ (b)

55.

Alicia stood with her mouth open and smiling on Tuesday at the Employment Security Commission. That's because Heels.net showed up there to give away lady's shoes. Heels.net is a North Carolina-based online shoe retailer. Company representatives arrived just after 2:30 p.m. Tuesday, surprising those who were there looking for jobs or filing for unemployment. The idea was to give away a new pair of shoes to women so they could wear them to job interviews.

Q. Why was Alicia standing at the Employment Security Commission?

(a) Because Heels.net held a charity event
(b) Because Heels.net provided women with shoes at a discount price
(c) Because Heels.net was looking for new employees
(d) Because Heels.net gave women shoes for free

해석_ 앨리사는 화요일에 고용 안전 위원회에서 입을 벌리고 미소를 지으며 서 있었습니다. 그 이유는 Heels.net이 여성용 구두를 공짜로 나눠 주기 위해 그곳에 나타났기 때문입니다. Heels.net은 노스캐롤라이나에 기반을 둔 온라인 구두 소매점입니다. 회사 대표들은 그곳에서 일자리를 찾고 있거나 실직 신고를 하고 있던 사람들을 깜짝 놀라게 하면서 화요일 오후 2시 반 직후에 도착했습니다. 그 아이디어는 여성들에게 새 구두를 무료로 제공하여 그들이 그 구두를 신고 취업 면접을 할 수 있도록 하기 위한 것이었습니다.

Q. 앨리사는 왜 고용 안전 위원회에서 서 있었는가?

(a) Heels.net이 자선행사를 열었기 때문에
(b) Heels.net이 여성들에게 구두를 싼값에 제공했기 때문에
(c) Heels.net이 새 직원들을 구하고 있었기 때문에
(d) Heels.net이 여성들에게 무료로 구두를 주었기 때문에

해설_ Heels.net이 여성용 구두를 무료로 제공하기 위해 그곳에 왔다고 했으므로 정답은 (d)가 된다.

어휘_ show up 나오다, 나타나다   give away 거저 주다

정답_ (d)

56.

Thanksgiving is bringing turkey producers little to celebrate this year, while diners anticipating the most poultry-centric of holidays are grateful. Meat producers have been struggling this year with higher costs for key ingredients like corn, soybeans and oil, which is also part of why the cost of beef and chicken has risen so much. Some 4,000 turkeys will be eaten on Thanksgiving Day in New York, an increase of some 300 turkeys compared with the previous year.

Q. How many turkeys did people buy last year?

(a) 300 turkeys
(b) 3,700 turkeys
(c) 4,000 turkeys
(d) 4,300 turkeys

해석_ 올해 추수감사절은 칠면조 생산업자들에겐 그다지 기뻐할 일이 없겠지만, 휴일들 중 조류를 가장 즐기는 날을 기대하는 소비자들에겐 고마운 날이 될 것입니다. 육류 생산업자들은 옥수수, 콩, 오일과 같은 주재료의 가격 인상으로 인해 올해 분투해 오고 있습니다. 이는 또한 쇠고기와 닭고기 비용이 급격히 오른 이유 중 하나이기도 합니다. 전년에 비해 300마리가 증가된 4,000마리의 칠면조가 뉴욕에서 추수감사절에 소비될 것입니다.

Q. 작년에 얼마나 많은 칠면조가 소비됐는가?

(a) 300마리의 칠면조
(b) 3,700마리의 칠면조
(c) 4,000마리의 칠면조
(d) 4,300마리의 칠면조

해설_ 마지막 부분에 300마리가 늘어난 4,000마리의 칠면조가 올해 소비될 것이라고 했으므로 작년엔 300마리를 뺀 3,700마리의 칠면조가 소비되었음을 알 수 있다. 따라서 정답은 (b).

어휘_ diner 식사하는 사람 poultry 가금류 soybean 콩

정답_ (b)

57.

The Civil Department says that the death toll in Italy's earthquake has risen to 250. The department said Wednesday that 11 of the victims remained to be identified. The magnitude-6.3 quake hit L'Aquila and several towns in central Italy early Monday, leveling buildings and reducing entire blocks to a pile of rubble and dust. Strong aftershocks have caused further fear for residents, as rescue efforts continue.

Q. Which of the following is true according to the report?

(a) There was a magnitude-6.3 quake in Milano.
(b) Salvage work is almost coming to a close.
(c) When the quake stopped, strong aftershocks were followed.
(d) Buildings have given way due to the continuous aftershocks.

해석_ 민원부는 이탈리아의 지진으로 인한 사망자 수가 250명으로 늘어났다고 말했습니다. 민원부는 희생자 중 11명의 신원이 확인되었다고 말했습니다. 월요일 아침 규모 6.3의 지진이 라퀼라와 이탈리아 중부의 몇몇 도시를 강타하면서 건물들을 무너뜨리고 도시 전체를 파편 조각과 먼지 더미로 만들었습니다. 구조 노력이 계속되고 있는 가운데, 강한 여진은 지역 주민들에게 더 큰 공포를 야기시켰습니다.

Q. 기사에 따르면 사실인 것은 어느 것인가?

(a) 밀라노에서 규모 6.3의 지진이 있었다.
(b) 구조 작업이 거의 끝나가고 있다.
(c) 지진이 멈춘 후 강한 여진이 이어졌다.
(d) 건물들이 계속되는 여진 때문에 무너졌다.

해설_ 기사 마지막 부분에 강한 여진이 지역 주민들에게 공포를 주고 있다는 내용이 나오므로 정답은 (c)가 된다.

어휘_ magnitude 지진 규모 level (건물을) 무너뜨리다 rubble 파편 aftershock 여진 salvage work 구조 작업 come to a close 끝나다 give way 무너지다

정답_ (c)

58.

In February 1952, Ian Fleming began writing his first James Bond novel. At the time, Fleming was the foreign manager for Kemsley Newspapers, owners of The Daily Express in London. Upon accepting the job, Fleming asked for two months yearly vacation in his contracttime spent writing in Jamaica. Between 1953 and his death in 1964, Fleming published twelve novels and one short-story collection. Later, continuation novels were written by Kingsley Amis, John Gardner, Charlie Higson and Raymond Benson.

Q. Which is correct according to the talk?

(a) The very first James Bond novel was published in 1952.

(b) Fleming published 13 books in total from birth to death.

(c) Fleming wrote books only between 1953 and 1964.

(d) The sequels of the James Bond novel were written by 4 writers.

Q. 담화에 따르면 맞는 것은 어느 것인가?

(a) 첫 번째 제임스 본드 소설은 1952년에 출간됐다.

(b) 플레밍은 일생 동안 총 13권의 책을 출간했다.

(c) 플레밍은 1953년과 1964년 사이에만 책을 썼다.

(d) 제임스 본드 소설의 속편은 4명의 작가에 의해 쓰여졌다.

해설_ 글 마지막 부분을 통해 (d)가 정답임을 알 수 있다. (b)는 1953년과 1964년 사이에 출간한 것이 13권이므로 틀리다.

어휘_ continuation(= sequel) 속편

정답_ (d)

59.

American workers whose taxes pay for major government health programs are getting squeezed like no other group by private health-insurance premiums that are rising much faster than their wages. Although most retirees are covered, and nearly 90 percent of children have health insurance, workers are at much higher risk of being uninsured than in the 1990's. The problem is cost. Total premiums for employer plans have risen six to eight times faster than wages.

Q. What can be inferred from the report?

(a) Insurance bills are beyond worker's affordability.

(b) Health insurance policies have changed more and more.

(c) Almost everyone has bought insurance since 1990.

(d) Children under 10-years-old should have health insurance.

Q. 기사를 통해 추론할 수 있는 것은?

(a) 보험료는 근로자들이 감당하기에 벅차다.

(b) 건강 보험 정책은 점점 더 변화했다.

(c) 1990년 이래로 거의 모든 사람이 보험에 가입했다.

(d) 10세 이하의 어린이는 건강 보험에 들어야 한다.

해설_ 임금보다 훨씬 빠르게 오르는 보험료에 의해 근로자들이 압박받고 있다고 했으므로 (a)가 정답임을 알 수 있다.

어휘_ retiree 퇴직자 premium 보험료, 할증금

정답_ (a)

60.

The average American family of four spends about $107 a week on groceries. So, how do you stretch your dollars at the grocery store? It's a good idea to leave the kids at home, because it is often hard for kids to resist pricey sweets. If the children have to come along, provide a coloring book or handheld video game to occupy them. Quick and Simple also suggests skipping specialty items grouped together. Things like chips and dips together can result in impulse buying.

Q. What can be inferred from the talk?

(a) If parents bring along their children to the

store, it is hard to save money.
(b) Buying specialty items which are grouped together can cut down expenses.
(c) It's good to shop with the entire family.
(d) Children can concentrate better if given a coloring book.

해석_ 4인 구성의 일반 미국 가정에서는 식료품비로 일주일에 약 107달러를 소비합니다. 그렇다면, 여러분은 식료품점에서 어떻게 돈을 절약하십니까? 집에 아이들을 두고 오는 것이 좋은 아이디어입니다. 왜냐하면 아이들이 비싼 군것질거리의 유혹을 참아내기가 어려운 경우가 많기 때문이죠. 만약 아이들이 따라와야 한다면 색칠하기 그림책이나 아이들의 주의를 사로잡을 포켓용 비디오 게임기를 주세요. Quick and Simple에서는 또한 함께 묶어서 파는 행사 품목들을 사지 않을 것을 권장합니다. 묶음으로 파는 것들은 충동 구매로 이어질 수 있습니다.

Q. 담화를 통해 추론할 수 있는 것은?

(a) 부모가 자녀들을 가게에 데려간다면, 돈을 절약하기 힘들 것이다.

(b) 함께 묶어 파는 행사 품목을 사는 것은 비용을 줄일 수 있다.

(c) 가족 전부와 쇼핑하는 것이 좋다.

(d) 아이들은 색칠하기 그림책을 주면 집중을 더 잘할 수 있다.

해설_ 아이들과 함께 가게 되면 비싼 과자들을 사 달라고 하는 경우가 많다고 했으므로 (a)가 정답임을 알 수 있다.

어휘_ stretch (식량·돈 등을) 오래 지탱하게 하다 pricey 비싼, 돈이 드는 coloring book 색칠하기 그림책 handheld 손가락 크기의, 포켓용의 bring along 데려가다

정답_ (a)

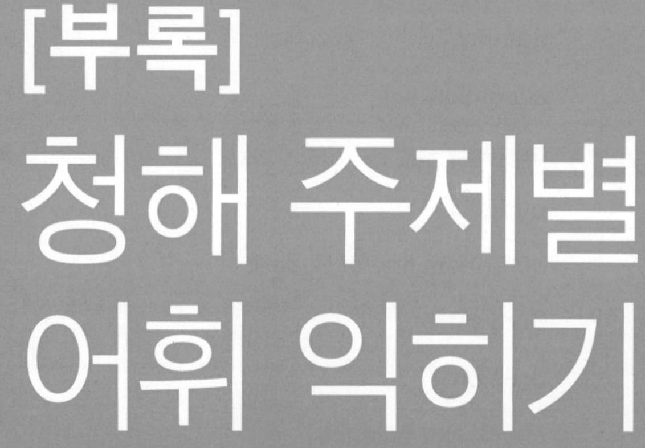

[부록]
청해 주제별
어휘 익히기

affiliate	계열회사, 지부
appraise	평가하다, 견적하다
appropriation	충당금
assess	평가하다, 액수를 정하다
a state of boom	호황
atone	보상하다
autarky	자급자족
avocation	취미, 도락, 부업
barter	물물 교환하다
budget	예산
cf. bottom line of budget	예산의 최대 절감
buoyant	(시세가) 오름세의
cession	할양, 양여
check and balance	견제와 균형
clearing house	물물 교환소
confiscation	압수
consign	위탁하다
covenant	계약
current price	시가
deflation	통화긴축
depreciation	가치하락
devaluation	평가절하
donation	기증, 증여
due	지불 기일이 된, 당연히 치러야 할
fiscal	국고의
fiscal year	회계연도(방향, 위치, 상황 등의) 변동, 오르내림
fund	자금, 기금
futility	무익 공급 과잉
gratuitous	무상의
gross national product	국민 총 생산

increment	증가분, 이윤
indemnity	손해배상
index	지표
interest	이자
inventory	재고
levy	징수하다, 징발하다
lucre	이익(부당한 수단에 의한 혹은 명예스럽지 못한)
mischief	장난, 해악, 해, 손해
monger	상인 cf. -monger 주로 복합어에서 결합적으로 쓰임
mortgage	저당, 저당 잡히다
national treasury	국고
offset	상쇄하다
outlay	소비
output	생산고
parvenu	벼락부자
pauper	극빈자
pawnshop	전당포
pecuniary	돈의
pension	연금
preferential	특혜를 주는
pry	엿보다, 동정을 살피다
pumping priming	경기 부양책
recession	퇴거, (경기) 후퇴, 불경기
relegation	좌천
remuneration	보수, 보상, 급료
revenue	세입, 세수
rush	급수요
rush	주문 쇄도
sampling	표본 추출
sequestrate	가압류하다

account	은행의 계좌
audit	회계 감사
bill	어음
bidding	입찰
black ink balance	흑자
blue chips	우량주
bond	채권
bust	파산시키다
debenture	채무 증서
deficit	적자, 결손
endorse	뒷면에 기재하다
fiat money	불환 화폐
incorporation	합병
inflation	통화 팽창
liquidate	청산하다, 갚다
cf. liquidation	청산, 상환, 변제, 정리
monetary system	통화 제도
monopoly and oligopoly	독과점
monopoly	독점, 전매
moratorium	지불 유예
paper note	지폐
passbook	은행통장
principal	원금
promissory note	약속어음
proprietary	독점의
reimbursement	재지급, 환급
stagflation	산업 성장이 없는 통화 팽창
stagnation	불경기
usury	고리대금업

addressee	수신인
airmail	항공우편
area code	지역번호
basic rate	기본요금
busy	전화가 통화 중인
cellular phone	휴대폰(= mobile phone)
collect call	수신인 요금 지불 통화
country code	국가번호
direct mail	광고 우편물, 약칭 DM
directory	(이름·주소 등을 알파벳 순서로 배열한) 주소 성명록, 인명록
extension number	내선 번호
hot line	긴급 직통 전화
junk mail	(광고물·선전 책자 등을 수취인의 명시도 없이 사서함 따위에 넣는) 광고 우편물
local call	시내전화
long-distance call	시외전화, 장거리전화
long-distance operator	장거리 전화 교환수
mail	우편(물) 우편으로 부치다, 우송하다
mobile communication	이동 통신
operator	전화 교환수; (기계, 기구 등을 조작하는) 기사
operator-assisted call	교환수를 통한 통화
overseas call	국제전화
parcel post	소포 우편
postage paid	우편요금 지불됨
postage stamp	우표
postscript	추신(=P.S.)
registered mail	등기 우편
router	데이터 전송 시 최적의 경로를 선택하는 장치
salutation	(편지의) 인사말
self-addressed	(회신용 봉투에) 수신인 주소 및 성명

adrift	(배가) 표류해서
alley	골목, 소로
armada	함대 [The Armada: 무적함대]
avenue	거리
blind alley	막다른 골목
boulevard	도시의 넓은 길
bypass	순환 도로
cargo	선하, 뱃짐
crosscut	지름길
crosswalk	횡단보도
depot	정거장, 역; 창고
derailment	탈선
detour	우회하다
devious	꾸불꾸불한
dinghy	작은 경주용 요트
dirigible	비행선, 기구
embargo	입출항 금지 명령, 수출 금지
embark	(배나, 비행기에) 태우다, 싣다, 착수하다, 시작하다
expressway	고속도로
flying saucer	비행접시
highway	간선도로
hulk	노후한 배
Jolly Roger	해적기
labyrinth	미로
lane	좁은 시골길
license plate	자동차 번호판
lift-off	(우주선 등의) 수직 이륙, 발사
liner	정기선
manned	사람을 실은, 유인의

acid rain	산성비
atmospheric pressure	기압
barometer	기압계
bleak	황량한, 쓸쓸한
cloudburst	소나기
congeal	얼리다, 얼다
damp	습기
dreary	음산한
glacier	빙하
haze	아지랑이
humidity	습도
icecap	만년설
mackintosh	비옷
meteorology	기상학
mizzle	이슬비
monsoon	계절풍
muggy	후덥지근한
overcast	구름으로 덮다, 흐리게 하다
precipitation	강수량
serene	고요한, 잠잠한
sleet	진눈깨비
sultry	찌는 듯이 더운
thermometer	온도계
thunderstorm	뇌우
torrid	매우 더운
trade wind	무역풍
tropical	열대의
weather	날씨, 풍화시키다
weather bureau	기상대
weather phenomenon	기상 현상

alluvial	충적의
archipelago	군도; 다도해
arctic	북극(의)
asteroid	소행성의
astrology	점성학, 점성술
astronomy	천문학
aurora	극광
brine	소금물, 해수, 바다
bulge	융기하다
canyon	협곡
comet	혜성
constellation	별자리, 성좌
corrosion	부식, 침식
crescent	초승달
delta	삼각주
earth's axis	지축
eccentricity	이심율
eclipse	일식, 월식
equinox	춘분, 추분
erosion	비바람에 의한 침식
excavation	굴착, 발굴
firmament	하늘, 창공
galactic nebula	은하성운
geyser	간헐온천
gorge	골짜기, 협곡
granite	화강암
graphite	흑연
gravel	자갈
heavenly body	천체
inlet	후미; (액체의) 주입구

interstellar matter	성간물질
Jupiter	목성
kaolin	고령토
lapidary	돌에 새긴
latitude	위도; (행동, 의사의) 자유
lava	용암
leap year	윤년
lightning rod	피뢰침
lime	석회
limestone	석회암
loam	양토
marble	대리석
Mars	화성
mason	석수
meander	굽이쳐 흐르다
Mercury	수성
mercury	수은
meteor	유성, 운석
molten	용해된
natural levee	자연제방
Neptune	해왕성
nova	신성
ooze	진흙
orbit	궤도, 행로
pebble	조약돌
planet	행성, 유성
Pluto	명왕성
polestar	북극성
Uranus	천왕성
Venus	금성

avalanche	눈사태
blast	돌풍
blizzard	눈보라
downfall	폭우
drought	가뭄, 한발
earthquake	지진
epicenter	진원지, 진앙, 중심
erupt	폭발하다, 분출하다
fallout	(핵폭발의) 낙진; 부산물, 여파
gale	강풍
hail	우박, 싸리눈
heat wave	열파
inundation	범람, 홍수
landslide	산사태
seismic intensity	진도
tempest	폭풍우
volcanic ashes	화산재
vortex	회오리 바람

administration	행정
agenda	의제, 의사일정
anarchy	무정부 상태
aristocracy	귀족정치
aristocrat	귀족
autocracy	독재권, 독재정치
ballot box	투표함
bicameral	양원제의
bourgeois	유산계급
bureaucracy	관료정치(주의, 제도), 관료
by-election	보궐선거
cabinet	내각
candidate	후보자, 지원자
canvass	표를 얻으러 돌아다니다
chauvinism	국수주의
communism	공산주의
defection	변절
delegate	대표자
demagogue	선동적인 정치가
deputy	대리인, 부관
egalitarian	평등주의
executive	행정부
Fabian	점진적 사회변혁을 추구하는 사람
filibuster	의사진행 방해자
gerrymander	선거구를 유리하게 고치다
hard-liner	강경파
hegemony	패권, 지배권
inaugurate	취임시키다
inauguration	취임, 개시
independent	무소속

intransigent	바꿀 수 없는, 비타협적인
matriarchy	모계사회
McCarthyism	정적 박해, 극단적인 반공 운동
militarism	군국주의
nepocracy	족벌정치
official	관료, 공무원
parliament	(영국) 국회
plebiscite	국민투표
plurality	과반수, 겸직
plutocracy	금권정치
proletariat	무산계급
protocol	의전, 의례, 의식
rapprochement	화해, 친선
referendum	국민투표
regent	섭정
regime	정권
reign	통치기간
riot	폭동
secession	탈당
solon	현명한 입법가
stopgap	미봉책
suffrage	참정권; 투표
theocracy	신권정치
totalitarianism	전체주의
treason	반역, 배신
turmoil	소란, 소동
viceroy	총독
wire-puller	막후의 인물

accord	협정
agreement	조약, 협약
air space	영공
behind-the-scene	이면의, 막후의
blue-ribbon committee	특별 위원회
brinkmanship	벼랑 끝 전술
cease fire	휴전
concession	양보, 인정
conflict	분쟁
consul	영사
crackdown	탄압, 강경 조치
delegate	대표, 파견의원
detent	(국가간의) 긴장 완화
diplomat	외교관
diplomatic immunity	외교적 면책 특권
donor	원조국
embargo	통상금지
envoy	특명 전권 공사, 특사, 외교사절
espionage	스파이 행위, 첩보활동
expulsion	추방, 퇴학, 제명, 배출
frontier	국경
hostage	인질
intervention	내정 간섭
nuclear disarmament	핵군축
ratify	비준하다
repatriation	강제 송환
representative	대표자, 대의원
snag	(예상치 못한) 난제, 장애
summit talk	수뇌[정상] 회담
territorial waters	영해

abduct	유괴하다
abuse	오용하다, 남용하다
accessory	부품, 액세서리; 종범; 보조[부속]적인; 종범의
act	법령, 조례
administration of justice	사법
alleged	(증거없이) 주장된
amnesty	사면하다
arbitration	조정
arson	방화범
atrocity	독재, 폭정, 잔인
attorney	변호사
bail	보석금, 보석금을 지불하다
barrister	법정 변호사
blackmail	협박하다
breach	위반, 불이행
bugging	도청
by-law	내규
civil law	민법
civil suit	민사소송
code	법규, 법전, 암호, 약호
complaint	불만, 고소
constitution	헌법
contingency	우발적 사건
conviction	유죄 판결; 확신
corollary	당연한 결과, 자연적 결과
criminal law	형법
cross-examine	반대신문하다
culprit	범죄자, 형사 피고인
custody	구속, 보호
defendant	피고, 피고인

delinquency	범죄(비행)
due process of law	적법절차
embezzle	횡령하다
ex-convict	전과자
felony	중범죄
fine	벌금
fraud	기만, 사기
guilt	유죄, 죄가 있음, 죄
holdup	노상강도
homicide	살인
illegal	불법의
implication	암시, 연류, 관련
imprisonment	투옥,구금,금고,자유형
indemnity	배상, (형벌의) 면책
indict	기소하다, 나무라다
innocence	무죄
iniquity	불이익, 불의
intimidate	위협하다
invalidity	무효
judicial	사법의
judiciary	사법부
jury	배심원
kidnap	유괴하다
kleptomania	도벽, 절도광
larceny	절도, 절도죄
law court	법정
lawsuit	소송
legislature	입법부
life imprisonment	무기징역
lose a case	패소하다

manipulate	교묘하게 다루다
mediation	중재
misdemeanor	경범죄, 비행
null	무효화하다
ouster	추방; 축출; 몰수
outlaw	법외자, 무법자
parole	가석방
patent infringement	특허권 침해
penal	형법의, 형사상의
penalty	형벌, 벌금
penitent	회개하는, 참회하는
perjury	위증 거짓맹세
phon(e)y	가짜의, 허위의
plaintiff	원고
plea	탄원
postmortem	검시
practitioner	개업의, 변호사
principal	주범
promulgate	선포하다, 공포하다
prosecution	기소
proviso	(법령·조약 등의) 단서(但書)
public prosecutor	검사
racketeering	부정한 돈벌이를 하는 사람
reconciliation	화해
search-warrant	수색 영장
shackle	속박하다, 굴레를 씌우다
smuggle	밀수하다
suit	구혼하다, 소송; 탄원
summons	소환장
surveillance	감시, 정찰

accusation	고소, 고발
assassin	암살자
blackmail	공갈, 협박
break-in	불법 침입
burglar	강도, 밤도둑
conspiracy	공모, 음모
cop	경찰관
crime rate	범죄 발생률
criminal	범죄의, 형사상의, 범인
custody	구금, 보호관리
detain	감금하다
embezzle	횡령하다, 착복하다
felon	중죄인
fine	벌금, 벌금을 부과하다
fraud	사기 (행위); 사기꾼
homicide	살인죄, 살인
hostage	인질
house breaker	가택 침입자
imprisonment	투옥, 구금
investigate	취조하다, 조사하다
kidnap	유괴하다, 납치하다
libel	명예훼손, 모욕
murder	살인, 살해하다
penalty	형벌, 처벌; 벌금
pickpocket	소매치기
ransom	몸값, 배상금
shoplift	슬쩍 훔치다

abortion	임신 중절
acute	급성의
aggravate	성나게하다, 악화시키다
alternative medicine	대체의학
amnesia	기억상실
anatomy	(동식물의) 해부
anemia	빈혈
anesthesia	마취
anesthetic	마취제
anorexia	거식증
antidote	해독제
antifebrile	해열제
aphasia	실어증
artery	동맥
arthritis	관절염
asthma	천식
astigmatism	난시
athlete's foot	무좀
barren	황폐한, 불임의
belly	배
bladder	방광
bone marrow	골수
bosom	가슴
bowel	장
brain-fag	신경쇠약
brain-storm	정신착란
breast	유방
breast cancer	유방암
bronchitis	기관지염 *cf.* bronchi 기관지
bruise	타박상

bump	혹
caesarian section	제왕 절개 수술
cardiac	심장의
cartilage	물렁뼈
cataract	백내장
cerebellum	소뇌
cerebral death	뇌사
cerebral	대뇌의
cerebrum	대뇌
checkup	(종합) 건강 진단
chest	가슴, 흉부
choke	질식시키다
chronic	만성의
clairvoyant	투시의, 천리안의
coagulation	(혈액의) 응고
coma	혼수 상태
constipation	변비
contagion	전염
contraceptive	피임약
corporal	육체의
cranium	두개골
cure-all	만병통치약
delivery	해방, 석방, 분만
dentist	치과의사
denture	틀니, 의치
depilatory	탈모제
dermatology	피부과
dextral	오른손의
diabetes	당뇨병
diagnose	병을 진단하다, 법을 진단하다, 사태를 분석하다

diarrhea	설사
dimple	보조개
dispensary	(병원, 학교 등의) 조제실, 약국
disinfect	소독하다
dose	(1회) 복용량
duodenum	십이지장
dyspepsia	소화불량
epidemic	유행병, 전염병
epidermis	표피, 외피
excrement	배설물
field medicine	응급처치
fit	발작
fracture	골절상
furrow	주름
gallstone	담석
gastric juice	위액
gastric ulcer	위궤양
genetic	유전의
germ	세균
gullet	식도
hangover	숙취, (약의) 부작용
heal	고치다
heart disease	심장혈관병 (= cardiac failure/cardiovascular disease)
hepatitis	간염
hiccup	딸꾹질
hoar	백발의
hooked nose	매부리코
hygiene	위생학
hypnosis	최면
hypochondria	히포콘드리증, 우울증

altruistic	이타주의의
awareness	자각
concept	개념
conscious	자각하고 있는
deduction	연역
demonstration	증명
dialectic	변증법적인, 논증을 잘하는
drive	동기, 동인
ego	자아
egocentrism	자기 중심(주의)
empiricism	경험론
epistemology	인식론
feedback	반응
hang-up	콤플렉스
humanism	인본주의
hypothesis	가설, 가정
idealism	이상주의
identity crisis	자기상실
identity	자아, 동질성
induction	유도, 유발, 서론
inference	추론
metaphysics	형이상학
motivation	동기 부여
nescience	무지
nihilism	허무주의
nonverbal communication	비언어적인 의사 소통
norm	표준, 규범
ontology	존재론
parallelism	유사성; 평행; 비교
philanthropy	박애, 자선

advent	다가옴, 출현, 도래, 그리스도의 강림
anathema	파문, 이단 배척
apocalyptic	묵시의, 예언적인
apparition	환영, 허깨비
archbishop	대주교, 대감독
atheism	무신론
baptism	세례
benediction	축복, 감사기도
blaspheme	불경스러운 말을 지껄이다, 모독하다
bode	~의 전조가 되다; 예언하다
cathedral	대성당
celestial	천상의, 천국같은
confucian	유교
contemplation	명상, 묵상
deification	신격화
demon	악마
divination	점, 예언
domestication	교화
doom	불길한 운명
Easter	부활절
eschatology	종말론
fabulous	전설적인
fairy	요정
heterodox	이단의
icon	성화
immolation	희생, 제물
inferno	지옥
infidel	무신론자
jihad	(회교도의) 성전
malediction	저주, 악담

martyrdom	순교
mission	사절단, 특명, 임무, 작전
mundane	현세의, 세속의, 평범한
Muslim	회교도
myth	신화
nirvana	열반, 해탈
omnipotent	전능한, 절대 권력을 가진
orthodox	정설의, 정통파의
persecution	박해
phantom	환영, 착각
pilgrim	순례자, 성지 참배자
pluralism	다원주의
protestant	신교도
puritan	청교도
resurrection	부활, 그리스도의 부활
Sabbath	안식일
sacrilege	신성모독
sacrosanct	신성불가침의
salvation	구원, 구제
sanctity	신성
sect	종파
spell	주문
theism	유신론
theology	신학
Trinity	삼위일체
worship	예배(하다)

amoral	도덕적 판단력이 없는
beneficiation	선행, 희사
bogus	가짜의, 모조의
candid	정직한, 솔직한
caprice	변덕, 주책없음
comity	예의, 우의
decency	품위, 예의바름
estrange	(사람을 친구, 가족 등에게서) 떼어놓다, 사이를 멀어지게 하다, 이간하다
feign	~을 가장하다, ~인 체하다
goodwill	선의
hocus	속이다
hocus-pocus	속임수
immoral	비도덕적인, 부도덕한
indifference	무관심, 냉담
naughty	장난이 심한, 나쁜
oath	맹세, 서약
precept	교훈
prevaricate	얼버무리다, 속이다
propriety	단정, 예의바름
quibble	핑계
rectitude	정직, 청렴
retribution	보복, 앙갚음
spite	악의, 원한
surreptitious	내밀의, 부정한
true-blue	지조가 굳은 (사람)
true lie	새빨간 거짓말
white lie	선의의 거짓말

abolition	폐지
accomplished fact	기정사실
alienation	소외
anomaly	변칙, 이례
anomie	무규제 상태, 사회적 무질서
anthropology	인류학
authorities	당국
autonomy	자치, 자치권
box office	흥행 성적
capitalism	자본주의
census	인구조사
charity	자선
civic movement	시민운동
collective behavior	집단행동
colony	식민지
commonwealth	국가, 연방
communism	공산주의
confederacy	연합, 동맹
consensus	합의
contrariety	모순점, 불일치
debunk	폭로하다
discrepancy	모순, 불일치
disperse	흩어지다, 흩뜨리다
donation	기부
equilibrium	균형, 평형
ethnic	인종의, 민족의
exploitation	착취
functionalism	기능주의
fund	자금, 기금
generalization	일반화

gregarious	군거하는, 군집의
imbalance	불균형의, 어울리지 않는
institution	제도, 단체, 조직
kinship	친척관계, 혈족관계
life expectancy	평균 수명
objectivity	객관성
panic	공포, 당황
paradigm	이론적 틀, 모범, 전형
peer group	동류집단, 또래집단
population density	인구밀도
practice	실행하다, 행동으로 옮기다
public utilities	공익시설
racialism	인종차별주의
realism	현실주의
realm	왕국, 영역
recruit	보충하다, 사원을 모집하다
social disorders	사회불안
social integration	사회통합
sociology	사회학
sovereignty	주권, 통치권, 독립국
subject peoples	피지배 민족
throng	군중, 사람 떼
totalitarianism	전체주의
underpopulated	인구가 희박한

abdication	(권력의) 포기, 기권
anachronism	시대착오
anecdote	일화
archaeology	고고학
armistice	휴전, 정전
artifact	전시물, 유물
barbarian	야만인, 미개인
bloodshed	살육
bohemian	전통에 얽매이지 않는 사람
Bronze Age	청동기시대
carnage	송장, 대학살, 살육
chivalry	기사도
class warfare	계급 투쟁
coronation	대관식
cromlech	고인돌
diggings	발굴물
emancipation	해방
enlightened wing	개화파
era	시대
excavation	굴착, 발굴
extinct	멸종된, 끊어진, 사라진
feudal age	봉건시대
feudalism	봉건제도
flourish	번영하다, 번창하다
flowering	번영
hierarchy	서열
hieroglyph	상형문자
hominoid	유인원
homo erectus	직립원인
Ice Age/glacial epoch	빙하기

infantuationhood	신생국
Invincible Armada	무적함대
Iron Age	철기시대
monument	기념비
mound	고분
peer	동등한 사람, (영)귀족
plebeian	평민, 보통의, 평범한, 속된, 천한
prehistory	선사시대사
prehistoric times	선사시대
primeval	원시의, 태고의
progenitor	(동식물의) 원종, 조상
Rag	(인도) 지배, 통치, 주권
Reformation	종교개혁
regal	제왕다운, 왕같은
regime	정권
relics	유물
ruins	유적
serf	농노
slavery	노예 신분, 노예 신세
specimen	표본
Stone Age	석기시대
stratigraphy	지층학
stratum	층, 사회적 계층
thrall	노예
turmoil	소란, 소동
unearth	발굴하다
uprising	(조직적인 반란의 전조로서 소규모의) 반란, 봉기
ups and downs	영고성쇠

abstract painting	추상화
accompaniment	반주
adagio	고요하게, 느리게
aesthete	유미주의자, 심미가
aesthetic	미의, 심미적인, 미적 감각이 있는
andante	느리게
andantino	조금 느리게
antique	옛날의
appreciation	(예술품의) 평가, 이해
apron	앞무대
arrange	정돈하다, 배열하다
avant-garde	전위적인
azure	하늘색
brushwork	화풍, 화법
bust	반신상
cacophony	불협화음
caricature	풍자화
cartoon	시사만화
chamber music	실내악
chiaroscuro	명암법
choir	합창단
chord	(악기의) 현, 줄
choreography	(발레의) 안무
chromatic	색채의
cinematography	영화 촬영법
composition	구성, 조립, 작문, 작곡
connoisseur	감정가, 감식가, 권위자
connotation	함축, 내포
contour line	윤곽미
contribution	공헌, 기부금액

copperplate print	동판화
co-star	공연하다
denotation	의미, 외연
destruction	파괴, 멸망
dissemination	유포, 보급
distribution	유통, 분배, 배포
diversity	다양성, 변화
emboss	(무늬 도안을) 양각으로 하다, 돋을무늬로 새기다
etching	부식 동판술, 에칭
execution	연주 솜씨
famine, starvation	기근, 기아
fiddle	바이올린
fine arts	미술, 조형예술
formative arts	조형미술
fresco	프레스코 화법
gallery	화랑
hue	색조
illustration	삽화
kitsch	저속한 작품
largo	매우 느리게
liberalization	자유화
limped	투명한
lithograph	석판화
lucent	빛나는, 반투명의
luminous	빛을 내는
lurid	창백한, (창백하게) 무서운
lustre	광택
manner	(미술, 문학) 형식, 양식
masque	가면극
metronome	박자 측정기

moderato	보통 빠르게
monochrome	단색화
motif	주제
motley	잡색의
mural/wall painting	벽화
musical notation	기보법
obscenity	외설적인 말이나 행동
obscure	어두컴컴한, 불명료한
opaque	불투명한
opus	음악 작품
orchestra	교향악단
overture	서곡
percussion	타악기
performance	공연
piece	작품
pigment	안료, 그림물감
pirate	표절하다, 표절한 자
pirouette	(무용에서) 발끝으로 돌기
plagiarism	표절
plaster cast	석고상
portrait	초상화
preservation	보호, 보전
profile	옆얼굴, 반면상
recital	독주회
refrain	후렴, 반복구
rendering	(극, 음악 따위의) 표현, 묘사; 연출
reproduction	재생, 복제, 복사
restoration	복원, 복구
retouch	손질하다
ritual	의식(儀式)

romantic	낭만적인
sculptor	조각가
star-studded	유명인이 다수 출석한
still life	정물
still picture	정물화
strings	현악기
tempera	템페라화(법)
threnody	만가
timbre	음색, 음질
tone-deaf	음치의
transparent	투명한
tune	곡조, 가락
undertone	저음
vandal	예술품 파괴자
virtuoso	미술품 애호가
washes	담채(화)
water-color	수채물감
wind instrument	관악기
wood carving	목각(술, 화)

affordable rate	구입 가능한 가격
bargain	매매, 거래, 흥정
brochure	(제품이나 회사에 대한 정보를 제공하는) 소책자, 팜플렛
browse	구경하다
bulk buying	대량 구매
change	잔돈, 거스름돈
commodity	상품, 일용품
convenience store	편의점
emporium	상업 중심지, 시장
extravagance	낭비
full-credit	상품 구매 후, 반환 · 환불 · 교환을 보장해 주는 것
giveaway	(손님을 끌기 위한) 무료 증정품, 염가품
haggle	실랑이하다
installment	할부금, 1회분어치 할부금
list price	정가(= regular price)
lump sum	총액 일시불
make a pickup	찾아오다
peddler	행상인
retail	소매, 소매상
retail outlet	소매점
sale on credit	외상판매
sky-rocket	물가가 치솟다
tab	계산서, 청구서, 명찰, 짐표
tag	꼬리표, 가격표, 꼬리표(정가표)를 달다
vending machine	자동판매기
vendor	노점상
voucher	보증서, 상품권
warrant	증명(서), 보장하다; 정당화하다
wholesale	도매

accommodation	숙박(설비); 편의, 도움
admission	입국(허가); 입장(허가), 입학(허가); 입장료
baggage claim area	수화물 찾는 곳
boarding pass	(비행기의) 탑승권
carry-on baggage	기내 휴대 수화물
change trains	열차를 갈아타다
checkout	(호텔에서) 계산하고 나오는 절차
complimentary service	기내 무료 서비스
customs clearance	통관
customs duties	관세
declaration	신고(서); 선언, 포고
duty-free shop	면세점
embarkation card	출국 기록 카드
entry permit	입국 허가
excess baggage charge	수화물 초과 요금
final destination	최종 목적지
flight attendant	기내 승무원
immigration	(공항·항구 등에서의) 입국 심사; (다른 나라로부터의) 이민, 이주
in-flight meals	기내식
itinerary	여행 계획, 일정표; 여행 안내서
jet lag	(비행기 여행의) 시차에 의한 피로
local time	현지시간
one-way ticket	편도표
overhead rack	(짐을 넣는) 선반
quarantine	검역
reservation	(호텔·교통편 등의) 예약
round-trip ticket	왕복표
seasick	배멀미
security checkpoint	검문소

sightseeing	(명승지) 관광
souvenir store	기념품 가게
stand-by passenger	탑승 대기 승객
suite	(거실과 침실이 있는 호화로운) 호텔 특별실
take a tour	패키지 여행을 하다
via	~을 경유하여; ~에 의하여
window seat	창가 좌석

allegory	우화
alliteration	두운법
anecdote	일화
annotation	주석
anthology	시선집, 전집
aphorism	경구, 격언
argot	암호말, 은어
babel	언어가 섞여 알아들을 수 없는 상태
bibliography	저서목록, 서지학
biography	전기
braille	(소경용) 점자
censorship	검열
cliche	진부한 표현
commentator	주석자
compendium	개략, 요약
copyright	판권, 저작권
crib	표절
denouement	대단원
dialect	방언, 지방 사투리
epic	서사시
epitome	전형
euphemism	미사여구
excerpt	발췌록, 인용구
fable	우화, 지어낸 이야기
flowery	미사여구를 쓴
genre	(특히 예술 작품의) 유형, 형식, 풍속화
hyperbole	과장법
inconsistency	불일치, 모순
innuendo	암시
jargon	특수 용어, 은어

laureate	계관 시인
lingo	알 수 없는 말, 외국어
literacy	읽고 쓰는 능력
literati	문학자
lyrical	서정적인
narrative	이야기, 소설
orthography	정자법, 철자법
piracy	불법 복제
platitude	평범한 말, 상투어, 단조로움
plot	줄거리, 음모
polyglot	여러 나라 말을 아는 사람
preamble	머리말, 서론
prose	산문
protagonist	주인공, 주역
pseudonym	익명, 필명, 가명
rhyme	각운
royalty	특허 사용료
saga	무용담
satire	풍자
scrabble	낙서
semantics	의미론
stenography	속기
synopsis	줄거리
syntax	구문론
tale	이야기, 실화
verse	운문, 시가
version	(특히 성경의 여러 개로 되어 있는) 번역

all rights reserved	저작권 소유
announce	방송하다
article	(신문·잡지의) 기사; (계약의) 조항; 품목
bring (come) to life	폭로하다(되다)
broadcast	방송하다, 방송
bulletin board	게시판
canned program	녹화된 프로그램
cartoon	시사 풍자 만화
classified ad	해당 항목별 광고
commentator	방송 해설자, 시사문제 해설자
copyright	판권, 저작권
correspondent	특파원
edit	편집하다
editor-in-chief	편집장
feature	특집기사, ~을 크게 다루다
from the horse's mouth	믿을 만한 소식통으로부터
front-page	제 1면에 실을 만큼 중요한
gazette	관보
head count	여론조사
headline	표제; 중요 뉴스
hit the headlines	중대 뉴스가 되다, 유명해지다
Hooper rating	시청률, 청취율
impression	(지난번 것과 내용의 변경 없이 그대로 인쇄되는) 쇄
in-depth	심층의, 철저한
journal	신문; 잡지, 정기 간행물
live	생방송의
looker-in	텔레비전 시청자
newsstand	신문·잡지 가판대
off the record	비공식의, 발표하지 않는
out of print	절판되어

periodical	정기간행물
poll	투표, 투표소, 여론조사
press conference	기자회견
press release	보도자료
proclaim from the housetops	널리 알리다
release the news	뉴스를 발표하다
revise	개정하다, 개편하다
scoop	〈특종 기사를〉 내다
soap opera	연속극, 드라마
soft news	중요하지 않은 뉴스
subscribe	정기 구독하다
take the air	방송을 시작하다
up-to-the-minute	최신 정보의

academic advisor	지도 교수
academic standing	학업 성적
alma mater	모교, 출신교
alumnus	졸업생, 동창생
application form	입학원서
assignment	과제
bachelor	학사
coeducational	남녀 공학의
commencement	졸업식
commute	통근하다, 통학하다
crux	난문; 요점, 급소
cultural subject	교양 과목
curriculum	교육 과정
curve	상대 평가
dean	학장
diploma	졸업장, 졸업증서, 학위 수여증
disciple	문하생, 제자
doctor	박사
drop-out	중퇴(자), 낙제
edification	지덕 함양
education for gifted children	영재 교육
enrollment	등록, 입학
erudite	박학한
faculty	교직원
flunk	낙제하다
G.P.A.	Grade Point Average의 약어, 학점의 평점
Gordian knot	어려운 문제
graduate school	대학원
higher education	고등 교육
illiteracy	문맹, 무식

informal education	비정규 교육
instructor	강사
I.Q.	Intelligence Quotient의 약어, 지능지수
lifelong education	평생 교육
major subject	전공 과목
make-up course	보충 강좌
master	석사
matriculate	입학을 허가하다
monograph	모노그래프, 특수 연구서, 전공 논문
optional subject	선택 과목
pedagogue	교육자, 교사, 현학자
pedagogy	교육학
phonetics	음성학
polemics	논증법
postgraduate	대학원의
prerequisite	선수 과목; 필수적인
primary education	초등 교육
rector	총장
repeater	유급생
required subject	필수 과목
roll	명부
scholarship	장학금
secondary education	중등 교육
straight scale	절대 평가
student council president	학생 회장
student services	학생처
student union building	학생 회관
syllabus	강의 요지
thesis	논제, 제목
transcript	사본

tuition	학비
tutor	가정교사
undergraduate	대학생